The Ethic of
Democratic Capitalism

ROBERT BENNE

The Ethic of
Democratic Capitalism

A *Moral Reassessment*

FORTRESS PRESS   PHILADELPHIA

Library of Congress Cataloging in Publication Data

Benne, Robert
  The ethic of democratic capitalism.

  Bibliography: p.
  1. Capitalism—Moral and religious aspects.
  2. United States—Economic conditions. I. Title.
  II. Title: Democratic capitalism.
  HB501.B42   174   80-2385
  ISBN 0-8006-1445-3   AACR2

8575B81   Printed in the United States of America   1-1445

Contents

Preface   vii

1. The Great Refusal and My Discontent   1

PART I   PERSPECTIVES ON THE JUST SOCIETY   21

Introduction to Part I   23

2. Human Nature and Its Predicament   27

3. Love and Human Moral Striving   39

4. Rawls on Justice   49

5. Implications for Social Philosophy   69
    Efficiency and Growth   69
    Subsidiarity—Protecting and Using the
      "Equilibrium of Power"   72
    Role of the State   76
    Critical Reflections   82

PART II   THE CASE FOR DEMOCRATIC CAPITALISM   89

6. Is There Such a Thing as Democratic Capitalism?   91
    Important Definitions   91

CONTENTS

Is it Real?   96
Brief Reflections on Economic Theory   119

7. The Virtues of Democratic Capitalism   125
   Efficiency and Growth   126
   The Decentralization of Power—Subsidiarity   136
   The Intentional Role of the State   155

PART III   THE CHALLENGES AND POSSIBILITIES OF
           DEMOCRATIC CAPITALISM   177

Introduction to Part III   179

8. The Challenges Surrounding Efficiency and Growth   181
   The Future of Market Economies   208

9. The Challenges of Justice   215
   Liberty   215
      The "Worth" of Liberty   216
      Industrial Democracy   217
   Equality   224
      Income Distribution   224
      The Severely Disadvantaged and the
         Difference Principle   230
      Fair Equality of Opportunity   239

10. The Challenges of Meaning and Value—
    The Sociocultural Substratum   247
    The Significance of the Substratum   248
    Threats to the Guidance System   250
       Market Hedonism   250
       Adversary Culture   252
       Government Entitlements   255
    A Call to Response   257

Bibliography   263

Preface

Those who want to transform American society radically cannot afford the sense of proportion warranted by the brawling mixture of highs and lows that is America. For those desiring booming prophetic peals against that society and stirring calls for radical change, the following pages will be disappointing, for I do not intend to assume the heavy mantle of the prophet, or even to be "prophetic." My intention, rather, is to offer a viewpoint that provides a sense of proportion about the strengths and weaknesses of American democratic capitalism. Perhaps this more modest task is appropriate for an ethicist, which I purport to be.

Positively stated, my thesis argues that the combination of democracy and market economy peculiar to the United States is a *thesis* *paragraph* morally defensible arrangement. Further, it has a good deal of promise in dealing with its many challenges if it proceeds in accordance with gifts and possibilities inherent in democratic capitalism. It can abort this promise if it allows democracy—in the form of political intervention—to fetter and finally swallow up the positive features of the private sector, or, conversely if it allows private economic power to obstruct the interventions for justice of its polity. A good deal of the promise of democratic capitalism depends upon the extent and mode of public intervention.

Negatively stated, my thesis argues that all moral authenticity is not on the side of the sharp critics of democratic capitalism, especially the second part of the combination. It *is* possible to prize justice and at the same time support market arrangements, particularly if these arrangements are qualified by democratic polity. But liberally educated persons are all too facile in their rejections of competitive market systems, "capitalism," if you will. "Capitalism," along with companion words such as "bourgeois," "profit," or "competition," are code words for moral callousness that can perfunctorily end good discussion among educated persons without further arguments. My contention is that there is much to say from a moral point of view for capitalism, along with those other targeted aspects of liberal society. Therefore, the following is a polemic against easy dismissals.

It is particularly directed at those who seem to have so little sense of proportion in their judgments of American society. Some of these are my compatriots in the church, who all too often make statements like the recent one made by American theologians at the Bangalore meeting of the World Council of Churches' Faith and Order Commission. In that pronouncement American society is characterized as "an overall system which causes loss of dignity for all," having "destructive implications," and being marked by "oppressed minorities" and "powerlessness for the many."[1] Usually at the heart of these criticisms is a deep antipathy for market systems as a means of economic choice. It is this antipathy that needs challenging.

I have attempted to write the following from a Christian perspective and, more specifically, from a Niebuhrian perspective. Reinhold Niebuhr has provided the formative notions of my theological and ethical position, though I am sure that he would not agree with all the conclusions I have reached. The same can be said about the philosophical concepts of John Rawls. Rawls has provided important philosophical supplements to my basically Niebuhrian viewpoint, but again, his views have been subjected to my own interpretations and conclusions.

Further, I write from the viewpoint of a generalist in the economic and social sciences. In interpreting American social reality, I aim at a comprehensive view that I hope is shaped by a good deal of sound judgment. In doing so, I pass by many of the technical debates going on in economics, particularly concerning economic theory. There has been a surprising amount of ethical reflections going on in recent theoretical discussion, as the unquestioned hegemony of utilitarian economic philosophy has been challenged from many directions. But such discussion is extremely technical and peripheral to my concern here, which is a more general assessment of the realities and possibilities of American democratic capitalism. Thus, the criteria of judgment do not come from within economic theory but rather from the political philosophy of Niebuhr and Rawls.

Naturally, interpretations of social reality are conditioned by the social history of the author. My history has been shaped by relative success within the American system, but I do not believe such experience is exceptional. Rather, I believe "relative success" is normative, which accounts for the persisting legitimacy of American democratic capitalism. But my positive experience has been qualified by long residence in the inner city of Chicago and by extensive exposure to social criticism leveled at American society by academics and activists. Thus, I do not consider my defense of democratic capitalism to be oblivious to its flaws, though I would be the first to admit that more depressing experiences of those flaws might lead to more radical criticism.

The contours of my own experience and reflection lead me to a "mixed" political perspective. If liberalism in its classical sense means a limited state, pluralism, and a reliance on checks and balances, then the perspective developed herein is liberal. If liberalism in its American sense means public intervention in economic life to ensure those checks and balances and, even more important, to redress imbalances that make for unjust relations among persons and groups, then this is liberal in that sense also. If conservative means that, given a certain level of economic well-being, the most important things in life are not political and cannot be reached by political means, then this book is deeply conservative. If radical means going to the root of challenges that beset us, perhaps there is even a whiff of radicalism in this book, particularly in the last chapter on the culture of democratic capitalism. Such a maverick mix in my own temperament may represent something in the broader American outlook, something that is both the bane and blessing of our national character.

Throughout the book the phrase "democratic capitalism" is used to refer to the American political economy. Other phrases such as "liberal capitalism," "reform capitalism," or "social market capitalism" would also work. But "democratic capitalism"—first used, I believe, by Michael Novak—has become the most commonly used designation for the American system, especially by those who want to affirm the practical and moral possibilities of that system.

My attention in the following pages is directed toward American society, but many of the insights here can be applied to other nations with a democratic capitalist bent. These pages were written during a year's stay in Great Britain, at a time when the already high level of self-consciousness about economic life was heightened by a national election. Such an atmosphere, plus the many conversations with British academics of diverse perspectives, furnished a stimulating context for reflection.

There has been a two-year time lag between the times of writing and publication, caused in part by the very workings of the market system that I defend in the book. The basic manuscript was finished before the election of Ronald Reagan and the many debates surrounding his policies. Were I finishing the manuscript today I would address those policies directly since I find them deficient in their concern for justice. They do, however, try to address the issues of efficiency and decentralization. It is one of the major thrusts of this book that policy thinking and making in the eighties will have to combine that triumvirate of values in fresh and imaginative ways. I still await that persuasive combination.

Finally, I wish to thank my school, the Lutheran School of Theology at Chicago, and the Aid Association for Lutherans, for providing the time and support necessary to pursue this project. Both organizations are examples of the benefits of an extensive and free private nonprofit sector. They have generously supported an independence of spirit and viewpoint that I hope this project exhibits.

ROBERT BENNE

Cambridge, England
July 1979
Chicago, Illinois
May 1981

NOTE

1. As cited by Wolfhart Pannenberg in "Faith and Disorder in Bangalore," *Worldview* 22, no. 3 (March 1979): 39.

The Ethic of
Democratic Capitalism

1

The Great Refusal and My Discontent

Socialism is the only possible economic system from the Christian point of view.

                              Paul Tillich[1]

It is often the case that creative reflection emerges from anguishing situations. I can point confidently to many anguishing situations in recent years related to the ethical assessment of capitalism at home and in the world. Although much reflection has been generated out of these situations, I can with less confidence call the situations themselves creative. One such situation occurred recently in Dublin, Ireland, where I was attending an international consultation on human rights. I chose to attend a working group on human rights and the economic order because I thought there might be an enlightening discussion on the complexities of national and international economic problems.

I had—perhaps naively—little expectation of what was in store. The group was made up of Catholic missionary teachers from Third World countries and Protestant and Catholic officials of various international church agencies. Rounding things out were a highly articulate Hungarian Marxist and myself, the lone American. The full-blown theory of dependent capitalism came out quickly and unanimously—the Western industrial-capitalist nations were wealthy primarily because of exploitation of the Third World; the United States through its CIA kept all oppres-

1

sive governments in power; the world was neatly divided into oppressors and oppressed; democratic governments were simply the tools of the ruling capitalist classes and therefore shams (the choices offered in democratic elections were between Tweedledum and Tweedledee); arms sales by capitalist countries were the primary source of war and the threat of war; and so on. Every last bit of cant and hypocrisy on the part of the West was sniffed out and "unmasked." Participatory socialism was the answer, and on the other side of the revolution workers and peasants would manage their destinies with productivity, peace, and justice.

I put up some resistance at first. I knew enough of development studies to believe that poor countries faced tough economic problems common to them whether they were socialist or capitalist, and I knew there were competing, credible theories of what was happening in the emerging international economic order. But my arguments got nowhere. I decided to sit back and take my lumps as an American and see if I could learn any new twists in the theory of dependent capitalism. I didn't learn any and endured that part of the consultation under conditions of acute distress.

It would not always have been that way. Earlier in my teaching career, when I was more susceptible to "liberal guilt," I would have eagerly and gratefully assimilated this "prophetic" perspective into my teaching agenda. It would have fit neatly with the clear and coherent synthesis I have constructed out of the theology of Reinhold Niebuhr and the economic interpretations of John Kenneth Galbraith. The two thinkers made a nice fit; I knew as a trained theologian that Niebuhr wrote theology and ethics credibly, and I assumed that Galbraith's theories were all I needed to know about economic analysis. Wasn't he *the* economic beacon for the liberal intelligentsia? Such a Niebuhr-Galbraith synthesis gave me a persuasive position from which to criticize a decadent and dying capitalism—oligopoly, private affluence and public squalor, stagnation, consumerism—and to pursue the expected coming of democratic socialism. The Dublin conference would have simply given me macrocosmic data for an interpretation that had been worked out on the domestic level.

2

But, alas, the tidy, coherent, "prophetic" synthesis was shattered. I began eating from the tree of economic knowledge, and the unified world I had constructed came down in shambles. I had gotten acquainted with faculty members of the University of Chicago Business School and Economics Department, and each one of my pet Galbraithian notions was cut to shreds by sharp, and empirically documented, rejoinders to the conventional wisdom I floated out. At the root of their perspective was a radically different assessment of the realities and values of democratic capitalism. And they could make intellectually respectable what I had always viewed as the barely concealed ideology of the business world. This newfound challenge was hard to assimilate, so I began reading economic texts and delving into the mountains of economic literature dealing with the American economy. As the interpretations of mainstream American economists began to be taken more seriously, I began to doubt both the Galbraithian analysis of the American economic world and the assessment of democratic capitalism as a sociopolitical system. Perhaps our economy was workably competitive; perhaps profits had a useful economic function; perhaps free markets were the most efficient way of allocating economic resources; perhaps there was a connection between economic freedom and civil and political liberties; perhaps capitalism fostered a separation of economic and political power and enhanced social pluralism; perhaps the private sector, if used imaginatively, could handle more of our social problems better than an ever-enlarging public sector; and perhaps the poor were faring better under capitalism than under socialism. Indeed, I began to believe that the particular combination of democratic polity and capitalist economy found in many Western lands was defensible not only on economic grounds but also on ethical grounds. Not—heaven knows!—that these systems are perfect, or even near perfect, but they have enough going for them to legitimate them and to warrant pressing for reforms to make them more just. Now this was really too much—a Christian ethicist seeing enough reformable virtue in democratic capitalism to assess it as "ambiguously positive." A voice was crying in

3

the wilderness, and it was not a voice announcing the Messiah but a voice that was willing to say some good things about capitalism.

Further, it was not as if the world of theological ethics had stood still while I had moved out of my synthesis to a new appreciation of democratic capitalism. Indeed, the Galbraithian view now seems to constitute the right wing of most theological ethicists who write about political and economic matters. The center has moved decidedly leftwards. Those who carry forward the legacy of Niebuhr and Tillich—the Shaulls, Bennetts, and Browns—carry forward a vision of democratic socialism supplanting a decadent capitalism. Even so mild and balanced a commentator as Philip Wogaman in his *The Great Economic Debate* opts for socialism as the embodiment of Christian ethical hope.

To the left, the field is dominated by the various strands of liberation theology. Bonino, Segundo, Assmann, Gutiérrez, and others take as their prime target the capitalism represented by American multinational corporations. They have swallowed the Marxist analysis of dependent capitalism and hope for a revisionist socialism in Latin America. Indeed, as Dom Helder Camara has succinctly put it: "The Church must do with Marx today what Thomas did with Aristotle in medieval times." The social ethics of both the World Council and the National Council of Churches are hostile toward Western capitalism and partisan toward the socialist movements of the developing world. Marxist thought has become the major tool of economic analysis and prescription for Christian liberation theology and ethics.

This completes the description of the polarities of my schizophrenic world. The mainstream of American economic thought leads toward an appreciation of market economies on both economic and ethical grounds. The mainstream of Christian social ethics leads toward outright condemnation of democratic capitalism and a passionate hope for an ideal democratic socialism. It is difficult to get these two streams to flow together. One either has to choose minority economists to fit with majority ethicists or minority ethicists to fit with majority economists. (The minority

4

of ethicists who are willing to dissent publicly are gathered under the umbrella of *Worldview* magazine. They are quickly written off by the majority as the religious part of the "neoconservative reaction" led in the secular world by figures such as Irving Kristol, Daniel Bell, and Edward Banfield. Other prominent figures in theological ethics—Ramsey and Gustafson, inter alios—are involved on other fronts and write little on political economy.)[2]

This unhappy situation creates a good deal of pain in my life. I share enough basic theological and ethical convictions with the Christian ethics fellowship to want to be critical of all systems but especially our own democratic capitalism. But I share enough of the viewpoint of the mainstream of the American economics establishment to arrive at quite a different interpretation of the American economy than that of the ethics establishment. I find that many of the judgments of the ethics establishment are imposed simplistically upon ambiguous and complex economic phenomena and their "prophetic insights" are often misguided.

All this might possibly be interesting as an example of a painful personal odyssey or as a colorful internecine fight among a small group of Christian ethicists—possibly, but not probably. But this little story takes on added gravity, I believe, when one views it as a small reflection of a much broader public rift.

The bias against democratic capitalism is not simply the province of a small fellowship of Christian social ethicists at war with American society. It rests in a much broader spectrum of society that has increasing power to delegitimate the social order that I have been calling democratic capitalism. It attacks at both a theoretical and a practical level the shared values and assumptions that have undergirded our social system. It has enough power and influence to provoke in time a crisis of legitimation.

This sector of society has emerged from broad changes in the social structure of postindustrial society. Daniel Bell has provided the most important profile of this new society.[3] As industrial societies mature into postindustrial societies, there is a shift from manufacturing to services, an attendant emphasis on the "knowledge" component within those services, and an elevation of a new elite that deals with the codification of theoretical knowledge

5

for directing innovation and the formulation of policy.[4] This "New Class" embraces a large number of occupations, ranging from intellectuals to technicians.

> Like previous classes, the New Class is stratified within itself; in this hierarchy, no doubt, those deemed to be the cultural elite occupy a high position. Institutionally, prestige universities and other centers of knowledge production (such as think tanks) are centers of New Class Power, while publishing houses, periodicals, and foundations serve as distributing agencies.... Below these elite institutions, however, there is a much larger complex of New Class population in the lower reaches of the educational system.... Then, of course, there is the powerful center of national communications media which is allied with the cultural elite through a network of inter-locking occupations that provide services through the administra-tion of symbols, most though not all in the public sector of employment—people who staff the welfare and regulatory agen-cies on all levels of government, the planning and propaganda arms of these agencies, and the miscellaneous therapeutic, guidance, and counselling institutions.[5]

The phenomenon of the New Class is characteristic not only of American society, since Raymond Aron and Helmut Schelsky have sketched portraits of it in Western Europe, but it is more advanced and numerous in the United States because the tran-sition to postindustrial society is further along here. The minions of the New Class are in competition with the old business elite, which is losing the battle for the legitimation of democratic capitalism. The business elite has few intellectuals within it or supporters within academe in general who make a credible case for the present order. A good share of intellectuals—particularly those of a humanist bent—are aligned with the left-liberal or socialist propensities of the New Class. And although they are less important to the broader society than they believe, they do occupy positions in which they define reality for a large number of people.

What holds the New Class together ideologically is so well stated by Peter Berger that it is worthwhile to quote him at some length:

> The New Class is marked by a strong hostility to the capitalist system and to the business community. This animus ranges from the

6

left–liberal orientation of the majority to more pronounced socialist view of a vocal minority.... The greater part of the New Class derives its livelihood from public-sector employment; it has the most tangible interest in expanding this type of employment. Thus the vested interest in this group in replacing market forces with government intervention is, at the very least, as important in explaining the statist inclinations of the New Class as more idealistic aspirations.... Because government interventions have to be legitimated in terms of social ills, the New Class has a vested interest in portraying American society as a whole, and specific aspects of that society, in negative terms. Bad news about America is *ipso facto* good news for New Class aspirations. This ideological function serves to explain the consistently "critical" orientation of New Class interpretations (such as the facts of income distribution, poverty, the state of civil rights, or the changes in the racial situation). The same ideological function helps to account for the consistent sympathy of New Class individuals for foreign movements and regimes, *provided* these can plausibly be pictured as some sort of antithesis to American society.[6]

This broadly sketched picture is no doubt too simplistic, but it does have persuasive commonsense appeal. We shall later have occasion to look more closely at the characteristics of and reasons for the alienation of the New Class from the social system of democratic capitalism. Be that as it may, the New Class is in considerable tension with the older business elite, the "heartland" population of farmers and small-town people, middle-class suburbanites, and a considerable portion of blue-collar workers. These segments have very few articulate spokespersons who can provide a more positive rationale for the evolving democratic capitalism of our time.

This very large public rift is duplicated in many of the institutional structures of our society, among them the church. The laity and local clergy—especially after they have been socialized for some years in parish life—tend to side with the "unenlightened," old "producer" segments of the population, whereas the thinkers of the church—particularly those who are the most distant from the currents of local life—tend to side with the New Class. This is not to say that these "cosmopolites" have no useful prophetic function, but their bread is buttered by

7

coming up with enough critical interpretations to keep them in the business of being "change agents" in the church and society. They also have an "interest." They tend not to understand or be sympathetic with the struggles of the producer elements of society but rather are concerned with the distribution of what is produced. This makes them indifferent or hostile to the productive possibilities of democratic capitalism and friendly toward the interventionist tendencies of left–liberalism or democratic socialism. Meanwhile, the patient but somewhat befuddled producer elements continue to pay the bill for the delegitimating activities of their own intellectual elite. Great patience have they who are willing to finance the destruction of their own cherished beliefs and practices.

It is not that this visible rift in the body politic is about to break American society apart. The reality-defining role of the New Class cannot muster enough power at the present time to overturn the deeply entrenched practice, and commonsense legitimation, of democratic capitalism in America. But there are long-term hazards and short-term liabilities. In the long run, fewer justifying rationales will be elaborated to undergird the theory and practice of many of the values that democratic, pluralist societies hold dear. The negative acids of the New Class will erode what pale legitimations are left. And when dramatic challenges come to our society, which they are bound to do, there will be a vacuum of justifying frameworks to maintain valuable parts of the American legacy. Doctrines new and strange will insert themselves into such a vacuum and capture the idealism of the young. I am not at all sanguine about the direction of such alternatives—witness the early 1970s in the United States. The stronger *reaction* to such alternatives is even more disturbing, however. It would be safe to assume that on American soil such reactions would not be dominated by socialist ideals and practice, but more likely by an authoritarian populism based on the anger and frustration of the old producer classes.[7]

If delegitimation is the long-run danger of the negative interpretations of the New Class, the short-run problems have to do with its positive prescriptions. These prescriptions move toward gathering more and more functions under the state at all its levels as well as consolidating the power needed to perform, or attempt to perform, those functions. A state apparatus is being constructed that may well fall to someone else besides the New Class in the event of crisis.

The reality definers of the burgeoning knowledge industries, allied with an older intellectual elite, share many of the negative interpretations of democratic capitalism with the Christian ethics establishment. Later we shall pay detailed attention to the nature of these interpretations. Right now it is important to offer some brief reflections on why such a large majority of the American intelligentsia, at least that section of the intelligentsia that deals publicly with economic and political matters, harbors such antipathy toward democratic capitalism.

The first possibility is that they may be right. And this possibility accounts for some of the anguish in my own reflective life. Certainly the socialist passion for social justice is admirable. Perhaps the sociopolitical system we have known as democratic capitalism is in principle inefficient, unjust, and destructive of higher human values. It is obsolete, so we should move on to the next stage of social evolution—democratic socialism. Hasn't this been the consensus of the great Christian theologians of the twentieth century? Certainly Barth, Tillich, and the early Reinhold Niebuhr were socialists of a sort. There seems to be a religious consensus on the prima facie appeal of socialism. Indeed, Tillich's *Religious Socialism* has just been translated and will find a good deal of renewed attention among Christian social ethicists.[8] How can one fight such a consensus? One reality that keeps disturbing my faith in such a consensus is the fact that socialism is no longer simply a vision. It has been incarnated in many nations, both developed and underdeveloped; socialism now has a historical track record. And that record is certainly not obviously superior to that of Western democratic capitalism in key categories—liberty, democracy, equality, quality of life, productivity, peaceful intentions and actions, cultural creativity, and others. The most dramatic symbol that sums up the limitations of the vast majority of mature socialist lands is that of the fence.

Generally, the citizens of these lands are forcibly kept within their boundaries. If free emigration were allowed, the population would decline drastically as people made their way to better opportunities. But few seem to be fleeing the horrors of democratic capitalism. Even those who "know" how bad it is remain. The harshest critics seem to have little aversion to reaping the benefits from sales of their books. And, irony of ironies, some of those who are cast out of socialist lands spend most of their efforts attacking the systems that harbor them.

Why are there so few measured defenses of democratic capitalism and so many attacks on it in the wider intellectual world? Joseph Schumpeter, whose classic *Capitalism, Socialism and Democracy* remains a continuing source of penetrating insight, gives a compelling answer to this very question. "Unlike any other type of society capitalism inevitably and by virtue of the very logic of its civilization creates, educates and subsidizes a vested interest in social unrest."[9] Then follows what he calls an "excursion into the Sociology of the Intellectual." This is a much earlier interpretation of the New Class phenomenon proposed later by Bell and Berger.

First, Schumpeter notes that two of the characteristics that distinguish intellectuals from other people who wield the power of the spoken and written word are the absence of direct responsibility for practical affairs and of the firsthand knowledge of them that only actual experience can give. "The critical attitude, arising no less from the intellectual's situation as an onlooker—in most cases also as an outsider—than from the fact that his main chance of asserting himself lies in his actual or potential nuisance value, should add a third touch."[10]

This critical attitude, necessary for calling attention to one's thoughts and thus surviving professionally, is supported by the collective patron, the bourgeois public. The intellectual can find financial sustenance from a plethora of private institutions and from a wide-ranging reading public, which are both created by bourgeois society, the former by its commitment to the voluntary principle in associational life and the latter by technical achievements making possible cheap communication through books, newspapers, journals, radio, and television.

10

As the criticism mounts, efforts are made to bring the intellectuals to heel. But all efforts at that fail because any attack on intellectuals must run up against the very principles that define the society. The freedom that the bourgeoisie disapproves in the intellectuals is also the freedom that it approves for itself. The bourgeoisie defends itself and its scheme of life and in doing so protects the intellectuals.

> Only a government of non-bourgeois nature and non-bourgeois creed—under modern circumstances only a socialist or fascist one—is strong enough to discipline them. In order to do that it would have to change typically bourgeois institutions and drastically reduce the individual freedom of *all* strata of the nation.[11]

As capitalist society develops, there is a vigorous expansion of the education apparatus. This provides more ground upon which intellectuals may operate. The expanded educational apparatus produces a growing number of trainees who increasingly occupy the administrative and bureaucratic niches of the society. There they have a vested interest not only in expanding the competency of the state but also in denigrating the capacity of the private sector to handle the social challenges that emerge. Thus, Schumpeter asserts, hostility toward the capitalist order increases instead of diminishes with every achievement of capitalist evolution.[12]

Although Schumpeter accounts for a good number of the reasons why the New Class, and particularly its intellectuals, are aligned as adversaries of "bourgeois society," he does not delve very deeply into the reasons why those intellectuals have, and historically have had, an affinity for socialism as the alternative to democratic capitalism. One obvious reason is that the rhetoric of socialism contains many close parallels to deeply embedded values in Judeo-Christian tradition. Moral rhetoric is very close to the surface in the *theory* of socialism whereas the moral values of democratic capitalism are much less visible, at least in its theoretical foundations. The convergence of value systems in the traditions of socialism and Judeo-Christian humanism is readily grasped; the case for democratic capitalism is much more subtle and complex. Indeed, the fact that the concrete embodiment of

11

values in its practice is more convincing than its present theoretical justifications dictates that its case can never be made simple.

But the appeal of democratic socialism is simple and coherent. Justice, cooperation, democracy, peace, community, equality, and ecological sanity are all a part of the promise. What is more convincing, the very poor shall be lifted up, the rich sent away empty-handed, and the oppressed set free. Further, we will live according to ennobling values and be liberated from repression. This vision is in direct continuity with the escatological hope of the great religious traditions of the West; Marxism and socialism are clearly secular offshoots of Western religion.

It is easy to see why economists who keep these values visibly active in their analyses and prescriptions are appealing to humanist intellectual readers. From the Galbraith–Lekachman pole leftwards toward the more Marxist-oriented Union of Radical Economists, such value visibility is evident. This approach is very appealing to sociologists, political scientists, historians, philosophers, and theologians who read these authors. Moreover, most of these liberally trained readers are not known for their economic sophistication. Many have avoided the "dismal science" for much of their academic careers and are therefore unable and unwilling to go after their economic analysis firsthand. They gravitate toward writers on economic affairs who write for lay audiences and whose value orientations are close to their own and readily visible. Thus, they tend to accept too quickly the economic analyses that go with the value orientations they admire. By a neat methodological leap, highly dubious economic analysis is accepted primarily because writers exhibit pursuasive and coherent value systems. Humanist readers swallow Marxist and socialist economic interpretations for their moral appeal, not for their empirical validity. And then, as is the case with the theory of dependent capitalism, morality tales with all their righteous indignation and revolutionary flourish are substituted for the hard intellectual grappling that gets at a highly variegated and complex reality.

Another variation of this interpretation of intellectuals' affinity for socialism is put forward by Peter Berger. He believes that the

12

crucial reason for this affinity lies in the specific characteristics of what he calls the "socialist myth." By "myth," of course, he means not something false or imaginary but rather a paradigmatic drama which interprets and organizes experience, judges the present, and provides a prescriptive model for the future.

> *The socialist myth derives much of its power from its unique capacity to synthesize modernizing and countermodernizing themes.* Modernization—its ideas, values, aspirations—continues to be the dominant theme of our time, and it is fully integrated into all the various versions of socialism. The socialist program is based on all the standard cognitive assumptions of modernity—history as progress (an idea which must be understood as a secularization of biblical eschatology), the perfectibility of man, scientific reason as the great liberator from illusion, and man's ability to overcome all or nearly all of his afflictions by taking rational control of his destiny.[13]

Socialism thus takes up the trends of modernity within its myth, as does its cousin of the Enlightenment, liberalism. But socialism has also incorporated into its myth some of the powerful protests against modernity, that is, themes dealing with renewed community. Liberalism, in contrast, has not been able to bring off such an incorporation.

Berger believes that modernity has been brought about only at great cost. The forces of industrialization—with attendant urbanization and secularization—have eroded the small social settings marked by intense solidarity and moral consensus that have constituted normative human habitation for most of human history. With these organic social settings went the comforts of shared, stable systems of meaning and identity. These settings were often stifling, stagnant, and oppressive, but they never suffered from *anomie*. The community was real and all-embracing, for better or worse.

Modernity, on the other hand, means the movement away from *Gemeinschaft*—organic, "given" community—to *Gesellschaft*—voluntary association built upon individual choice. The individual participates in many associations of limited ends. Market economies eat away at traditional ways of doing things. Technical rationalism erodes the metaphysical verities. We live in an increasingly "disenchanted" world. Shared meanings are replaced by a great marketplace of competing worldviews. It is not surprising in this situation of modernity that countermovements arise. Indeed, we see such a countermovement in the present resurgence of conservative Islam. It longs for restoration of community, for overcoming the fragmentation of modernity.

> In its political manifestations, countermodernization is usually perceived as backward looking, as "reactionary." This perception is often adequate, but it is important to see that it can also be forward looking, "progressive"—whenever the longed-for community is located in the future rather than the past. There are religious prototypes (Jewish as well as Christian) for either type of anti-modern sentiment. Socialism is the secular prototype *par excellence* of projecting the redemptive community into the future. The genius of socialism, though, is that its secularized eschatology incorporates in addition the central aspirations of modernity—a new rational order, abolition of material want and social inequality, and complete liberation of the individual. Socialism, in other words, promises all the blessings of modernity and the liquidation of its costs, including, most importantly, the cost of alienation. To grasp this essentially simple fact about the socialist myth and to recall at the same time that modern secularism has greatly weakened the plausibility of competing religious eschatologies is to remove the mystery of the magnetic appeal of socialism. Indeed, if any mystery remains, it is that socialism has not yet triumphed completely.[14]

In our society those most alienated from traditional "competing religious eschatologies" are the intellectuals. Religious commitment tends to be part of the "bourgeois" background that is sloughed off as persons make their way toward intellectual respectability. But a vacuum of religious and moral meanings can be tolerated by only a very few; the socialist myth provides a persuasive alternative for the many.

Even religious intellectuals are prey to the synthesizing qualities of the socialist myth. Protestants flee from the otherworldly tendencies of pietism and evangelicalism by historicizing their own Christian eschatologies. Christian theological ethics becomes "relevant" again by clothing its social ethics in the socialist myth. The heavenly hope is brought down to earth. Particularly for those Protestants who accept historical guilt for unleashing

14

unguided technical rationalism on the world through a secularized Protestant ethic, the appeal of renewed human and ecological community inherent in the socialist myth is persuasive.
Protestantism tends to patch up its social-ethical deficiencies by
appropriating the relevant aspects of the socialist myth.

Roman Catholics do not need to participate in such strategies
of compensation. Their traditional social theories have often been
unitive. The Christian revelation, with its hierarchy of values, is to
be synthesized with one political and social philosophy. Medieval
civilization at its apex was such a synthesis: one God, one pope,
one king, one realm, and one system of shared values and
meanings that order politics, economics, and culture. Catholicism
fought a long rearguard action against the forces of modernity
that were intruding themselves into the synthesis. The old synthesis holds sway in very few places, although the legacy of the
old synthesis continues in the travail of many "Catholic" lands—a
legacy of semifeudalism, authoritarian government, and a conservative church. Curiously, the anguish of these lands is all too
simply blamed on the dominating economic power of the democratic capitalist world.

Now the assumptions of modernity are making their way into
the post-Vatican II church. The old synthesis is being jettisoned.
Modernity is being embraced. But the old dreams of synthesis do
not disappear. They only search for new partners in the wedding.
And what will pull together the assumptions of modernity with a
hope of Christian community in society? Why, socialism, of
course. The socialist myth combines modernity with the yearning
for "Catholic substance." It is a potent combination.

Meanwhile, mainstream economists bury the moral appeal of
democratic capitalism under the baffling equations of welfare
economics. They pursue their specialties without addressing
directly either the values they hold or the direction in which they
think society should move. Their concern for the poor is covered
over by technical argument, which is rarely appealing to social
idealism. Is there any doubt why the socialist myth holds such
appeal for intellectuals—religious and secular alike? Socialism, as
Michael Novak quips, has become the thinking person's eco-

nomics. More than that, it has become the thinking person's religious myth.

The purpose of the following reflections, however, is not to attack socialism. Rather, the purpose is to achieve a fairer assessment of democratic capitalism. We must reassess the Great Refusal. Reassessment should not mean uncritical ideological defense. I intend to establish an ethical perspective—in this case one derived from Christian theological ethics—that transcends democratic capitalism and provides a ground for criticism. Such a perspective must be supplemented by philosophical elaborations that refine and specify the more general notions that are a part of the Christian tradition. Further, these reflections will then move toward a critique of democratic captitalism as it has been practiced in the last quarter of the twentieth century. Finally, I will attempt to give some prescriptions following from the normative perspective developed early on that may offer options other than benign neglect or creeping statism.

The execution of these tasks is, first of all, a personal effort at intellectual integrity. I want to be true to the transcendent norms of Christian faith and life; at the same time I want to be responsible to respected economic opinion. I aim to relate the two in a way that is both realistic and critical, without lapsing into morality tales or defensive ideology. In a small way this grappling may also contribute to overcoming the serious public rift that I described earlier. In the long run, democratic capitalist practice without legitimate *affirmation* will become a hollow shell (and lose its gifts); democratic capitalist practice without legitimate *criticism* will become an unguided monster. Careless withdrawal of both kinds of legitimation by the intellectual community accentuates and accelerates both tendencies.

In conclusion, a more detailed agenda must be spelled out. In Part I I will develop a normative moral position based primarily upon the theological and ethical insights of Reinhold Niebuhr. I will have to assume, rather than demonstrate, that a number of facets of Niebuhr's thoughts are of enduring value and can be used profitably in reflections of this kind. His analysis of human nature with its penetrating insights into human freedom, sin, and moral capacity remains an enduring legacy. The economic and political implications of his anthropological insights are taken as pivotal. The human capacity for egocentricity makes a separation and balancing of powers necessary; but the human capacity for justice makes a *fair* balancing and redressing of power possible. Niebuhr, however, never developed in great detail the concepts of liberty and equality—the content of justice. The content emerged in concrete and topical analysis as he attended with great imaginative power to the stuff of history. Therefore, the Niebuhrian approach must be supplemented by the specifications offered by philosophical reflection on the meaning of justice. For that supplementation we will look to the theory of justice presented in contemporary form by John Rawls. We will not be uncritical in our appropriation of Rawls, however, since there are significant points of tension between his and our Niebuhrian perspectives. Moreover, it is obvious that the Niebuhr–Rawls synthesis itself is open to criticism for its location in a specific intellectual tradition. That problem will be grappled with, at least to some extent.

Part II will put forward the case for democratic capitalism as it is practiced in the United States. The strengths of the "system" will be indicated. A good portion of the chapter will be devoted to primarily economic considerations. How is the system operating as an *economy*? Is it productive? After all, a crucial requirement of economy is that it economize on its allocation and use of scarce resources for chosen ends, thereby accumulating wealth for the possibility of civilization. This extremely important requirement is not discussed often or well even by commentators such as Niebuhr and Rawls. They are both interested in the *distribution* of what is produced, and not in the sources of productivity themselves. However, considerations about the sources and mode of production do have moral dimensions. What are the unintended effects, both positive and negative, of the kind of productivity achieved by capitalism?

A defense of democratic capitalism must rest finally on criteria of justice. Later in Part II, then, we shall continue the argument by pointing out the ways in which the democratic capitalist society of the United States approximates the criteria of justice we have elaborated in Part I. Where is American society achieving a defensible modicum of justice? Where is our practice promising enough to legitimate the system?

Part III will deal with the challenges of democratic capitalism. The criteria of justice developed in Part I will be used as critical norms by which to judge our practice. Here, also, the basic criticisms brought by theorists will be described and assessed. Certainly it would be foolish to write off the mountains of critical material as self-interested machinations of the New Class or as dogmatic Marxism. Thus, we will try to take seriously basic criticisms and to integrate them into our own critique of democratic capitalism. Alongside these challenges, we will be constructing a set of prescriptions based on the interaction of the normative principles and the challenges of democratic capitalism. The prescriptions will aim at strategies for significant improvement that both respect the achievements of the system and take seriously its deficiencies.

In short, the following chapters aim at a critical assessment of democratic capitalism that is more sensitive to its gifts than the left-liberal and socialist camp and yet more value-visible and value-critical than mainstream economic thought in its discussions of the moral challenges facing it. Following from this, an effort will be made to move toward constructive suggestions that do not ignore the gifts of democratic capitalism nor short-circuit our moral concern. Democratic capitalism can be legitimated as a relatively just form of society now, with the prospect of significant improvement in the future.

NOTES

1. Quoted in Philip Wogaman, *The Great Economic Debate* (Philadelphia: Westminster Press, 1977), p. 133.

2. An interesting exception to the above categories is Paul Heyne, one of the few Christian commentators who is professionally trained in both theological ethics and economics. His work is definitely provocative and worth examining. He has written a text in introductory economics as well

18

as two books on economic life from an ethical perspective, *Private Keepers of the Public Interest* (New York: McGraw-Hill, 1968), and *The World of Economics* (St. Louis: Concordia Publishing House, 1965).

3. Daniel Bell, *The Coming of Post-Industrial Society* (New York: Basic Books, 1973).

4. Ibid., p. 487.

5. Peter Berger, "Ethics and the Present Class Struggle," *Worldview* 21, no. 4 (April 1978): 7.

6. Ibid., p. 10.

7. See the fascinating article on this subject by Dale Vree in *Worldview* 20, no. 11 (November 1977): 14-23.

8. Paul Tillich, *Religious Socialism*, trans. Franklin Sherman (New York: Harper & Row, 1978).

9. Joseph Schumpeter, *Capitalism, Socialism and Democracy* (New York: Harper & Row, 1940; 1975), p. 146.

10. Ibid., p. 147.

11. Ibid., p. 150.

12. Ibid., p. 153.

13. Peter Berger, *Facing Up to Modernity* (New York: Basic Books, 1977), pp. 59-60.

14. Ibid., pp. 61-62.

PART I

PERSPECTIVES ON
THE JUST SOCIETY

Introduction to Part I

Reinhold Niebuhr made at least three enduring contributions to the field of theological social ethics that will be of great use to us as we develop our moral perspective. First, his writings on human nature and its predicament continue to be insightful and accurate. Their assessment of many varieties of modern anthropology still carry the sting of truth. Although his work on redemption is less original, it includes the transcendent ethical norm of agape love which is crucial to other contributions.

Second, Niebuhr's struggle to relate the norm of love to both the principles and achievement of justice is of perennial value. He was able to keep love in a creative relationship to justice which avoided both complacency about any achievement of justice and sentimentalism about the ease by which love can deepen and widen the structures of justice. The problem of relating the radical love ethic of Jesus to the compromises and ambiguities of social reality has challenged Christian ethicists for centuries. Niebuhr's attempt at relating the two is one of the most sophisticated in a theoretical sense and useful in a practical sense.

Third, the implications for the economic, social, and political orders that follow from these first two contributions remain an important legacy for theological ethicists as well as secular theorists and practitioners. The impact of Niebuhr on people such as Hans Morgenthau, George Kennan, and Kenneth Thompson bears witness to Niebuhr's wisdom in all three areas. Indeed, it can be safely said that Niebuhr, more than any theologian in recent times, penetrated the world of secular social and political thought in America. His judgments and prescriptions were and are important to the broader world because his prophetic realism *in fact* achieved what more recent theologians of *praxis* only call for *in theory*.

In elaborating a moral perspective for the assessment of democratic capitalism, then, we will make use of these three contributions of Niebuhr. In order to build a sufficient base for the relevant critical principles, a measure of expository material must be included.

There is one important deficiency in our Niebuhrian perspective, however, which must be compensated for by drawing upon the contributions of moral philosophy. Although Niebuhr knew what *he* meant by justice and could demonstrate it by exposing injustice and proposing reforms to correct that injustice in concrete situations, he did little in spelling out carefully what the content of justice is. He was clear enough that it meant the distribution of liberty and equality. But, as seems endemic to theological ethics, Niebuhr did not attempt a precise and systematic specification of the meaning of liberty and equality. Moral philosophers seem to be the ones who pursue such a task. In recent philosophical ethics, no one has pursued it with more significance than John Rawls in his *Theory of Justice*.

Rawls's *Theory of Justice* will be used to flesh out the meaning of justice found in skeletal form in Niebuhr. Thus, as I see it, the Niebuhrian perspective provides us with a base anchored in a biblical and theological tradition that transcends both Western society and the philosophical reflections that emerge from it. This perspective constitutes a plausible vision of human nature and destiny. It grounds love and justice in that vision. And although the basic contours of the meaning of both love and justice are established in this perspective, the specific content must be defined and redefined in relation to our particular historical situation. Rawls has come up with a theory of justice that is just such a redefinition. Its significance is attested to not only by its monumental and comprehensive nature, but also by the impact it has had on the ongoing discussion of the meaning of social justice. There is a burgeoning literature on Rawls's formulations, and, although Rawls himself tries to establish his principles in a manner that demonstrates their universality and necessity, it is also clear that those principles are in continuity with the best traditions of Western society. So, the "synthesis" I intend to make aims at pulling together the undergirding religious notions that shape, but yet transcend, Western culture with the best philosophical reflections that emerge from it.

It would be intellectually naive to think that such a partnership would be without friction internally or be accepted free of external criticism. After working through what such a synthesis would mean in terms of establishing principles of social philosophy, therefore, we will conclude Part I with critical reflection on the very selection of these partners themselves.

2

Human Nature
and Its Predicament

Humans are an inextricable mixture of nature and spirit.[1] These polarities of nature and spirit can be broken into two further polarities: vitality and form. First, there is the nature pole, which humans share with all animate beings. This is the creaturely dimension of our existence. It is characterized by cyclical shape—growth, maturation, death; need, satisfaction, and need again. We as natural beings participate in certain *forms*. We are *Homo sapiens*; either male or female; white, black, yellow, or brown. The species form is extremely important, the others less so though not negligible. Further, as natural creatures we participate in the *vitalities* characterizing animate life in general and our own form in particular. The common drives of survival, hunger, sex, and pleasure pulsate through us. No matter how much we seem to transcend the vitalities and form of creaturely existence through exercise of our reason and freedom, we remain natural beings. The vitalities and form of our natural character impinge upon and condition our reason and freedom. And, further, from a Christian and biblical point of view, that is good. We are affirmed in our naturalness, in our creaturely vitality and form. Our biological nature is a good gift of God.

Then there is the spirit pole of human existence, which distinguishes us from the animal world. Again this pole can be broken into form and vitality. Form on the spirit side refers to rational capacity. We are able to grasp through reason the patterns of

27

causation in the world about us, which gives us a certain transcendence over it. We can stand outside, understand, shape, and control the world. Our rational capacities for consistent and coherent thinking enable us to plan, organize, and build up a civilization as a superstructure above the natural world, even though we always remain dependent on it. Reason is not only technical but also serves as a guide in moral, aesthetic, and philosophical concern. Its capability for grasping fairness and proportionality, and its drive for comprehensiveness undergird these perennial human concerns. Reason as spiritual form gives us transcendence over natural life.

Beyond this is spirit as vitality. This is spirit as freedom, as indeterminate self-transcendence, and it is the essence of human nature. It is the "soul" or "spirit" breathed into us by God according to the biblical account. In our self-transcending freedom we can stand outside ourselves and assess the meaning and quality of our lives. We can use language like "I am disappointed in myself." We can become an object of our own subjective consciousness. But freedom does not stop there. It is indeterminate. In our self-transcendence, we can stand outside our communities, our nation, our world, and indeed our universe and ask questions of origin and end, meaning and fulfillment. This all-surpassing transcendence is the source of an essential human homelessness. It cannot be satisfied with anything that it can go beyond. Therefore, as free spirit we seek a principle of comprehension that lies beyond what we can grasp. Anything short of God is unsatisfying to the demands of spirit. As St. Augustine said, "Our hearts are restless until they rest in Thee." Indeterminate freedom accounts for the heights and depths of human existence. All interpretations that neglect this freedom miss the grandeur and tragedy of our lives.

It is important to remember that the spirit–nature poles cannot be separated in our concrete lives. Every natural human vitality is affected by spirit; the natural drive of hunger can be transposed by spirit into inordinate greed, with rational faculties creating the know-how to realize the greed. On the other hand, soaring exercises of the spirit's freedom are limited and conditioned by our natural forms and vitalities. Creative efforts in music or art can be shot through with sexual energy and drive, as Freud pointed out so well. The history of philosophy is replete with mistaken assessments of human nature, with one school absolutizing the forming dimension of spirit, as in idealism, and another absolutizing the forms and vitalities of nature, as in naturalism. Only a few perspectives on human nature have grasped the essential freedom of human beings and have seen this freedom in all its intricate relations to natural vitality and form, on the one hand, and to reason, on the other. Niebuhr believes that only the biblical view of humankind approximates the truth about human nature and destiny.

Any and all human willing is therefore a complex combination of nature and spirit. Human willing, as it was intended by the Creator, would be ensconsed in harmonious relations with God, with itself, and with the world in its natural and human components. The essential structures of existence are governed by the law of love. Our lives as nature and spirit can be fulfilled only in loving mutuality with God, ourselves, and others. This is the essential ground in which our lives take place. If we trusted in God—who is the transcendent reality that alone can encompass the self-transcending freedom we possess—we could accept with equanimity the mortality of our creaturely selves, a mortality we are painfully aware of through our capacity for self-consciousness. If we could accept ourselves, we could use our creativity in ways that expressed our unique gifts. We could accept ourselves as our freedom rested in God and thereby accept our neighbor, living in harmony with other persons and groups. This is a picture of harmonious life according to the intentions of the Creator.

But this is our state only under the conditions of "dreaming innocence," before the Fall. The Fall is not a historical event, just as Paradise is not a historical time. Paradise refers to the essence of our lives before our freedom is realized in willing and acting. The Fall refers to the tragedy of our willing and acting as we exercise our freedom. Both are symbols that attempt to interpret the tragic facts of our existence. The Fall particularly is an effort to hold together both the inevitability of our fate and our responsibility for it.

The dynamics of sin are characterized in the following way. As we stand outside of ourselves in our self-transcendence, we become aware that we are small, mortal, even insignificant in the great scheme of things. But we are also aware of the unique circumstances and gifts of our being and the need to use them under conditions of scarcity in time and energy. This exercise in self-reflection gives rise to our ontological anxiety. We are anxious about our limits and our possibilities. This deep anxiety is the occasion for both our creativity and our sin. It is the occasion for creativity because it impels us to use our possibilities while there is yet time and opportunity. Without ontological anxiety, we would be flat and limp.

But anxiety is also the occasion, not the cause, of our sin. Instead of fastening to God in trust and obedience in the face of our uneasiness, we fasten on something less than God: self, family, class, race, nation, or culture. It is our bias toward idolatry—our tendency to fasten on partial values and incomplete realities—that constitutes the fate of original sin. But we act out that bias in freedom. In assertive pride of self, nation, and so on, we enflesh our tendency toward idolatry. This, of course, destroys our harmony with God, the ground and destiny of our being. We attach our indeterminate freedom to lesser things that are finally unable to satisfy our freedom, but our inchoate awareness of their mortality, a product of the irrepressibility of freedom itself, makes us redouble our efforts in support of our gods—which leads us further from the true Source of All. Because we do not accept God, we also fall out of harmony with ourselves. We cannot accept our mortality and we are bothered deeply by our idolatry. And the deep inner tuggings of our being toward harmony will not let us go. The image of God implanted in our essential structure pressures us, leading us to repentance or despair.

Sometimes all of this is too much and we try to flee our freedom. Rather than abuse our freedom in aggressive pride of idolatry, we flee from it in sensuality, an inordinate devotion to creaturely impulse and pleasure. Food, sex, comfort, sport—the pleasures of life—become the object of pursuit. We try to bury our self-transcendence in these fleeting things to the neglect of our responsibility to others and ourselves as free creatures. But this curious form of pride cannot satisfy the thirst of our spirits either. We are driven to more excesses in our pursuit of the mutable goods, but we remain depressed, anxious, and despairing because these goods cannot bear the freight of self-transcending spirit.

The sin arising from our rupture with God results in disharmony within the self. And both disharmonies issue into the interpersonal world as domination of or irresponsibility toward others. We try to deal with the deep unease in ourselves by cutting down others, dominating them, or neglecting them. Disrespect and unhappiness toward ourselves leads to disrespect toward and displeasure with others.

After these attitudes toward others are acted out, we are afflicted by an uneasy conscience when we reflect upon our action. The lure toward harmony—our original justice—will not let us go and we suffer pangs of guilt. This in turn adds to the anxiety we experience as our lot as centers of indeterminate freedom. So we get swept up into a vicious circle from which there is no escape. The circle, though it can be controlled by the internal constraints of a sense of duty or by the external constraints of social pressure, is an inevitable companion to our inner selves. We may appear righteous before others, and indeed perform the duties proper to the standards of the upright citizen, but internally we remain caught in the struggle of anxiety, unbelief, self-doubt, failure in our full responsibility toward others, and a persisting uneasy conscience. This struggle can only be assuaged by the inbreaking of the liberating grace of God. The individual can then find a measure of freedom from the reign of sin, but even then the struggle goes on.

If Niebuhr's insights into the predicament of individual human lives are penetrating, his analysis of the life of groups is equally trenchant.[2] In fact, it is his analysis of the life of groups that has had the most impact on secular political thought. The title of Niebuhr's book, *Moral Man and Immoral Society*, though exaggerated, expresses the gist of Niebuhr's argument. The life of the group is more persistently egoistic and unrestrained than that of the individual. The indeterminate freedom of the human spirit is channeled through the dynamics of group life toward its ends. Therefore, there is no "natural" satiation point that limits its ends, as naturalistic philosophies tend to assert. And the larger the group, the more magnified its lust for power, driven as it is by impulses of spirit. The group takes on a will of its own that transcends the individual. The trappings of its power and majesty enhance its claim on the individual for devotion and obedience. Individuals will be inclined to bow to the group's pretensions and to acquiesce to its claims of authority, even when these do not coincide with their moral scruples. Thus, the power of the group tends to dominate individuals within it and presses with inexorable weight the responsibilities of the group onto the individual.

In this situation, less rational self-criticism is possible. Individuals in their reflective life do question the ends and means of the group, but as they act within and in behalf of the group they are pressed by the weight and momentum of the group toward its purposes. Groups will tend toward more unrestrained pride, contempt for others, and claims of moral autonomy than individuals.

Groups will use every kind of power available to pursue their ends. Economic, social, and political power are most usual and visible within domestic society. Military power is most obvious in international relations. Less visible are moral and religious power. Moral power is used when groups clothe their ends in a moral ideology. Every group tends to rationalize its purposes as being consistent with a higher and broader moral purpose. Thus, hypocrisy is the compliment which vice pays to virtue. Religious power is also used. Large groups, such as the nation, are particularly wont to claim that their ends are sanctioned by the Divine will. Sometimes it is even claimed that the will of the nation embodies the Divine will. As more kinds of power are accumulated and concentrated, the possibilities for historical mischief increase. The ultimate evil is one in which all forms of power are gathered together and exercised without constraint by either internal or external balances of power. Totalitarian domination then becomes complete.

Niebuhr found Marxist analysis of human collective life, especially that of class, useful in his own critical interpretations. This is very evident in his early writings. But there are several crucial differences that have vast implications. The most important is Niebuhr's insistence that the fundamental cause of human egoism is not in the external conditions of society—private property or the relations of production—but inherent in the internal conditions of human nature itself. Sin is the universal condition of all individual and corporate existence. There is no segment of human life that is free of it. Thus, there is no proletarian class or representative of it that is miraculously free of destructive egoism because of its position as an oppressed and therefore interestless group. All humans are involved in sin and are therefore equal as sinners before the radical demands of God. Affirming this, however, Niebuhr goes on to argue that there is a great inequality in guilt. The rich and powerful have the resources to realize their sinful pretensions. They *do* realize them, at least partially, and the historical repercussions of their actions are far more destructive than the actions of their equally sinful, but less powerful, poorer counterparts. But as the poorer segments advance in power and prestige, they have a tendency to seek sufficient power to guarantee their security, inevitably at the expense of other life. Although they can and should strive for more power, as they reach it they are as likely as any powerful group to cope with their past and present insecurity by dominating others.

Therefore, all corporate power is to be distrusted. Ideologies such as Marxism that sanction inordinate power lodged in small groups are dangerous, even more so when they sanction such power in the attractive clothing of moral rhetoric. Such idealistic rhetoric covers over the will-to-power that is part and parcel of group life.

The vicious circle of sin that we described above in its relation to individual life operates even more destructively in corporate life since the group has more power than the individual. Groups are inevitably insecure; the larger the group, the greater its sense of insecurity. Groups have enough of an inchoate capacity of self-transcendence to be aware of their mortality in the transiency of history. They are aware of competitors to their ends. They possess something of the ontological anxiety that is present on the individual level. Out of insecurity, they are vulnerable to exaggerated interpretations of threats to their existence and lash out offensively at those threats. They try to dominate their powerful competitors and sometimes succeed in dominating the less powerful. But there are always individuals or associations within the life of groups or nations that raise objections to actions of the collective. These shifting and unstable "prophetic minorities" are the instrument of self-transcendence, whereas the group is the organ of the corporate will. Although these minorities can bring about alterations in policy, they also serve to stimulate an uneasy conscience. This in turn elevates the insecure anxiety of the group and the vicious circle is completed, only gathering momentum each time around. Such an analysis of corporate life illuminates the terrible round of insecurity, destructive pride, and guilt that was so much a part of American life during the war in Vietnam.

With this heavy emphasis on the egoistic character of corporate will and action, it is difficult to arrive at anything but the Hobbesian war of all against all. But that would be a mistake. Groups do have individuals and factions within them who exercise self-criticism. Nations do have prophetic minorities who criticize national policy, and it is a mark of relatively just groups and nations that they are receptive to the words of judgment spoken against them. Such critical self-transcendence cannot persuade the group or nation to abjure self-interested patterns of action. But it can broaden self-interest so that its more irrational interpretations and oppressive actions can be mitigated. It can move policy several degrees in this direction or that, and in the lives of large collectives such movement is historically significant. Further, in democratic societies where parties must compete for political power, policies representing the interests of varying groups can and do come to power. They can then alter the direction of the society significantly and thereby adjust the equilibrium of power. The upshot of this analysis is not that a higher justice is impossible, but that its achievement is more likely where power is accountable to centers outside itself. Internal guidance systems, though significant, are not sufficient. The capacity for rational and spiritual transcendence makes the pursuit of justice in social existence possible, but the capacity for sin makes external accountability of power necessary.

There is no automatic balancing of self-interest groups in social existence. History is the story of the perennial fragility of various uneasy balances. Often the balances break down and idolatrous will-to-power dominates. At other times varied centers of power struggle chaotically for dominance. Indeed, what peace we have is based on the possibility of war. Our world experiences the tragic results of overweening pride among groups and nations. The pain we experience is wrath—the wrath that accrues as the essential structures of life, based upon the law of mutual love, are violated by human pretension. The prophets saw the judgment of God in such human folly. They directed their pronouncements of judgment not primarily against the pagan nations but against the Chosen People themselves. The prophetic tradition sharpened its judgments so much that the ultimate question became: Can history be anything more than judgment when even the best can claim no vindication before the holy fire of God's law?

As prophetism increased the accuracy of its insights into the fallen state of human existence, it also developed hope for deliverance. It progressed from a nationalistic messianism in which God delivers the nation from its enemies to an ethical messianism in which God saves the good who unjustly suffer at the hands of evildoers. The messianic age will set things right. But as prophetism peered even more deeply into the ambiguities of the human condition, it realized that there *were* no righteous to vindicate. Is history simply the story of judgment? The prophetic question had been asked and was answered from the human side by the sound of silence.

Into this perplexed scene comes Jesus of Nazareth. He embodies in his teaching, ministry, death, and resurrection an unexpected answer to the prophetic question of whether God has resources of mercy to overcome his wrath. In demonstrating his answer, the messianic hope is realized. The crux of the answer is that God overcomes his judgment, not by simply abrogating the wrath that is due to us for our disobedience but by taking the wrath into himself. God acts in Jesus the Christ to make vicarious suffering the key to the meaning of history. God's *agape* love, present in the creation and foreshadowed at many moments in Israel's history, is disclosed and demonstrated decisively in Jesus Christ.

Jesus' teaching combines the motif of the Suffering Servant with that of the Son of man who shall come to reign. The Expected One, rather than coming with overwhelming power to turn the tables on the oppressor, comes in suffering powerlessness. In his ministry, Jesus constantly seeks the outsider, the poor, the despised, and the vulnerable for his acts of healing and forgiveness. He demonstrates that God reached out with merciful love toward those who know they are sinners. Indeed, Jesus becomes God's *agape* love.

Jesus remains curiously aloof from the political and religious groups that have their own notions of what the Messiah should be. He disavows participation in power because to identify with any earthly power group is to identify with the distortions that human sin inevitably introduces into the goals of that group. Each group projects its own image onto the Messiah. So Jesus refuses to participate in the claims and counterclaims that are so much a part of corporate existence. The perfect goodness he incarnated could not be channeled through the expectations or programs of the religious and political movements of his or any other day. Perfect goodness—God's agape—can only come through the Solitary One who represents the All. Others, all others, represent only segments of reality. They live up to the expectations and responsibilities of reference groups that shape and sustain them, and rightfully so. But Jesus as God's Messiah stood before the cross as the Solitary One, bereft of all human support. On the cross he took into himself the wrath of frustrated expectation, religious pride and prejudice, political cowardice and intrigue—in short, the sum total of human alienation. As human pride disturbs the essential structures of love, the reaction of those structures to their violation sets off waves of wrath that must land somewhere. And in this case, they landed on the cross and were thereby taken into the life of God himself. As true God, as God's

36

Does Judgment = wrath?

One, Jesus embodies the freedom of God to overcome this wrath by vicarious suffering. As true man, representing all persons, Jesus demonstrates what human perfection looks like under the conditions of fallen existence. In both modes he incarnates *agape*, the kind of love that in a mysterious and hidden way is the essence of God's sovereignty over sin and death.

The vindication of God's agape is the resurrection of Jesus. The victory of mercy over judgment, of love over sin and death, of God over Satan, is realized proleptically in God's raising Jesus from the dead. The Kingdom of God that is inaugurated in the healing agape of Jesus as the Christ will be consummated in the fullness of time. Until then we know that the sustaining of the creation in all its many facets is dependent upon self-giving, vicarious love. That love cannot be victorious under the present conditions of sin, but neither is it completely tragic. When it is active in human actions it ignites now and again, here and there, the fire of God's healing intentions. In all such occasions the Kingdom of God is approximated, fragmentarily now but with the hope of fullness then.

The Word of God is thus disclosed and enacted for us in Jesus as the Christ. It is addressed to all—outsider and insider, rich and poor, failure and success, sick and healthy, oppressor and oppressed. No one is excluded. The offer of forgiveness is made without condition. The problem is, how can we grasp such a reality? Are we not caught up in a vicious circle of sin that feeds upon itself? It is at this point that we need the in-breaking grace of God to free us from inescapable alienation. The liberating grace of God does strike, sometimes in moments of great pain and struggle that have no religious "tag" on them. But in those moments our defenses go down, our self-justifications crumble, and we become open to the word of affirmation and forgiveness. It is given, and all we need to do is receive it in faith. We accept our acceptance. And at that moment we know that the gap of alienation has been bridged and we are in harmony with God, with ourselves, and with others. The freedom that is ours as spirit is satisfied in its quest for a principle of comprehension and meaning that can meet its self-transcending indeterminateness. It needs no idol to hold onto. We can accept our mortality, our incompleteness, and our possibilities with serenity. Following from such self-acceptance we can much more easily accept and love others. We can even allow the agape love so generously given to us to flow through us to others. In the liberating grace of God, the disharmony of sin is healed and overcome.

Unfortunately, such a condition of harmony is not ours to possess. We cannot make it happen. The healing Spirit of God blows where it will. We can only point to it in our lives and in the lives of others, giving thanks for it in full knowledge of its source. But we cannot possess it in another way. We cannot hold onto it and realize it fully in our lives. Although sin's power over us may have been overcome in us in principle, eschatologically, it continues to plague us. We continue as sinners needing further repentance and grace. There may be progress in our spiritual lives; there may not be. The struggle goes on and will go on. But we can live in hope that the final victory is assured. The body of death which is ours will be transformed into a living body. Meanwhile we live in faith that this will be, and so release the love that is active in living faith, directing it toward a world that needs healing.

NOTES

1. Reinhold Niebuhr, *The Nature and Destiny of Man* (New York: Charles Scribner's Sons, 1949), 1: 17. In this chapter so much of Niebuhr's material is used that it would be senseless to mark every reference. The basic sources of the material are *The Nature and Destiny of Man, Reinhold Niebuhr on Politics*, ed. H. R. Davis and R. C. Good (New York: Charles Scribner's Sons, 1960); and *An Interpretation of Christian Ethics* (New York: Living Age Books, 1958). Parts of the chapter are interpretations and extensions of Niebuhr's thought. Experts will be able to see where these additions begin and end. Therefore, since there is no intention of duplicating Niebuhr's perspective in a strict and limited sense, I call the approach "Niebuhrian." It is strongly indebted to Niebuhr, but it departs from him at certain points.

2. Niebuhr, *The Nature and Destiny of Man*, 1:208-40.

3

Love and
Human Moral Striving

It is crucial to preserve the radical, transcendent quality of the love ethic embodied in Jesus. The ethic is an impossible ethical ideal that became possible in the coming of the Christ. What is the content of this ethical norm? First, agape has an initiating, reaching-out quality. It reaches out toward all; it observes no boundaries. It embraces the whole universe of being. But although there is regard for all, there is a strategic reaching out to the lost, the outsider, the vulnerable ones. It initiates a relationship of caring for all, but particularly for the most needy. It takes the first step in drawing others into the orbit of concern.

Second, agape love is disinterested. It is not calculating in the sense that it demands a return before it will act. Rather, there is a kind of heedless abandon in agape love. It acts without regard for the ostensible "worth" of the recipient. At the moment of the loving act, the recipient may not be able to contribute anything to the relationship of caring established. But agape does not demand a guaranteed return. It may wish for one, but its action is not dependent upon reciprocal response.

Third, agape aims at healing; it is concerned with the other's good so that the other may reenter the bonds of mutuality. It does not love in order to keep the other dependent upon the lover. It invites to interdependence, to fellowship, so that the richness of communion becomes a possibility for the other, either in relation to the lover or in relation to other significant companions.

39

Fourth, agape love makes possible new beginnings in relations among beings. Its initiating love begins relationships, and the forgiving character of its love brings reconciliation, restoration, and reunion. By wiping away the burden of anger and guilt in the past, it allows a new beginning. Forgiveness renews mutuality when it breaks down.

Finally, it is important to note that such agape love is not costless. Initiation may be rebuffed or it may draw one into an abyss of dire need on the part of the other. Disinterested care may return empty-handed. Passionate concern for healing may be met with failure. Forgiveness may not be accepted. And in all of these, the receiver may react with anger and hostility to the offer. Persons sometimes cherish their status as cripples; or they may deny in their pride that they need healing. Agape may be, and most likely will be, accompanied by suffering. The lover, for the sake of the beloved, will take into his or her own self the wrath of alienation that is an inescapable result of disturbed mutuality.

These characteristics are evident in both the actions of Jesus toward others and, through them, the actions of God toward us. Agape is not an abstract ideal. Its promise became incarnate in Christ. Thus, since it is the fundamental religious and ethical reality in the Christian revelation, it becomes normative for Christian ethics. That, however, is only the beginning of the problem. How does such a radical ethical demand relate to the ambiguities of everyday personal and social life? How does such an impossible ethical ideal become relevant to a world shot through with the compromises necessitated by finitude and sin? Beyond personal life, how does it relate to the rough and tumble of the economic, social, and political realms?

Our day-to-day lives are shot through with self, family, business, institutional, and national interest, all of which preclude easy interjections of agape love. Caught up in a web of sustaining and demanding social relations, we are called to be responsible to and for them. Only the solitary person or, as in the case of Jesus, the One acting in behalf of the All, can act in a purely agapistic manner. All other actions are qualified by the claims and counterclaims of social existence. All other actions are conditioned by responsibility to and for specific others. Responsibility in these contexts is not outright disobedience of the norm of agape love, but neither is it a simple, direct acting out of its demands. Rather, responsibility in a Christian sense means a way of acting in which the concrete responsibilities of our daily lives are held in creative tension with the lure of agape. Agape prods and lures all moral responsibility toward a broader and deeper care of being. In doing this, it does not end with the personal dimension but extends further into the spheres of social existence. No area of human interaction, no matter how minimal in quality or rough and tumble in means, can be isolated from the scrutiny of that moral norm, even though that norm cannot offer direct prescriptions for action.

The moral agent, squeezed from one side by the responsibility to and for partial interest, and lured and prodded from the other by loyalty to agape love, is thrown back upon his or her own critical judgment in deciding the proper path of action. However, the agent is not left with only the radical demands of love and the unique situation. There are intermediate principles that occupy the middle ground between the ultimate norm and the changing situation. These provide the criteria for discriminating decisions, criteria that are less "radical" in their demands and more immediately relevant to the problem at hand. It is crucial, though, that these "middle principles" be kept in creative tension with both the ultimate norm and the changing situation.

Much havoc has been created in Christian history by the failure to relate properly the radical ethic of the Gospel to more penultimate human moral striving. German Christianity, especially in its Lutheran form, tended to break the tension between the norm of agape love and the struggles for justice in history by separating them completely. In insisting on the authentic radicality and transcendence of the love ethic, Lutheran ethics saw only the tragic impossibility of agape. Agape was relevant only to the personal realm—the social realm was guided by autonomous principles that came to terms with the threat of disorder and evil. This separation short-circuited the Christian struggle for a relatively just or relatively good society. From the sublime pinnacle

41

of divine agape, which Lutheranism saw so well in its traditions of theology and piety, the differences between relatively good and bad social arrangements became negligible, just as the foothills of a mountain range look flat when viewed from a sufficiently high point.

American and British Social Gospel ethics attempted to relate the norm to history, but tended to sentimentalize the norm by making it a simple possibility. Self-giving love could become the governing principle for moral behavior in business, politics, and international relations. The stubborn realities of human egoism were too easily seen as succumbing to an ethics of altruism. This "soft" utopianism was in error both in its inflated assessment of the capacity of groups for disinterested behavior and in its softening of the hard edge of the radical Gospel ethic. The Kingdom of God would come through the long march of persuasive love through institutional life.

Other types of utopianism are not so soft. When Christians grew self-righteous in their assessment of their own virtue and overly confident in their vision of the good society, they did not hesitate to impose that virtue and vision on society. They even used violent means to achieve what they knew was right and good. This is "hard" utopianism. It is more insightful into the recalcitrance of earthly powers than "soft" utopianism, but just as mistaken in its belief that the radical ethic is possible as a direct norm for social life. What makes this viewpoint "hard" is that it is willing to use coercive power to press its vision onto a reluctant society. Marxism—as a special kind of Judeo-Christian heresy—is particularly prone to the danger of "hard" utopianism. It is utterly realistic in its assessment of the self-interested action of its opponents, utterly confident of its own vision of the good society, and more than willing to use coercive power to realize that vision. All of this is carried on with a peculiar blindness to its own self-interest, limited vision, and tendency toward domination.

A diagram (see p. 43) will be useful in elaborating our Niebuhrian approach to relating agape love to various levels of human moral striving.

The norm of agape stands at the pinnacle of the moral

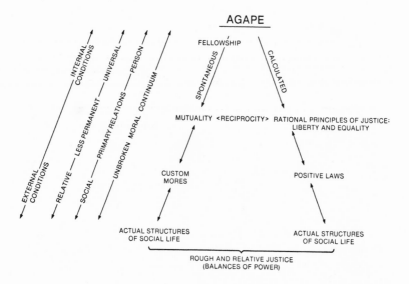

continuum. It interacts with fellowship and mutuality, which in turn need explication before the interaction can be understood. Fellowship, or in Niebuhr's language "brotherhood," seems to be closest to agape love. Fellowship is characterized by a deep mutuality—a fulfilling exchange of contributions to each other's being. Like mutuality, complementarity is the principle of movement. I admire and treasure this quality in you; you cherish this quality in me. We fill each other's cup of being. But fellowship goes beyond mutuality in that it is less calculating. It is usually based on more organic, suprarational ties than mutuality. The life of families and the bonds of old friendships are examples. Fellowship is most permeable by agape love in its initiating, healing, and forgiving capacities.

Mutuality has more of a quid pro quo character than fellowship. It constitutes the primary fabric of human relationships of a personal and small-group nature. Mutual love is the law of life in the healthy relations of marriage, friendship, and primary groups. Mutuality is harmony under the conditions of freedom. But unfortunately, because of both the self-centeredness of sin and the temporality of finitude, the relations of mutuality are fragile.

43

One partner changes, and the earlier complementarity is disrupted. One partner intentionally or unintentionally injures the other, and the relations of mutual respect and fulfilling exchange break down. If left to itself, mutuality would literally "go to hell" because of its tendency to degenerate under the pressures of sin and finitude.

Agape is the healing love that prevents this descent into hell. It initiates mutuality in situations where aversion to risk necessitates one partner reaching out first to the inhibited other. Isolation is overcome. Agape stands by the other amidst changes that upset the calculus of mutuality. It offers healing forgiveness when injury is done. In other words, agape restores broken mutuality. This is the secret of the sovereignty of agape. Without the healing effects of agape, all forms of mutuality, and for that matter, fellowship, would move toward disintegration. Agape is the healing love exercised by human freedom, under the conditions of sin, that deals with the destructive results of that sin.

As the law of mutual love is extended into the arena of justice (rightward on the chart), more rational calculation becomes necessary. Mutuality becomes a reciprocity defined by criteria of fairness. In order to treat each person as we would wish to be treated, we must stipulate the principles of justice that govern such treatment. What is to be distributed to persons in order to ensure that they are treated as ends in themselves, never solely as means? Liberty and equality are the main goods that must be distributed fairly. (The delineation of the meaning of these goods will be postponed until our treatment of Rawls.) Suffice it to say at this point that the principles of justice—liberty and equality— are the rational equivalents of the law of mutual love and that they transcend all social laws and practice. Properly defined, they establish a standard for both law and practice that stretches them toward ever higher achievements.

The definitions of justice, as rational distillations of mutuality, are also in creative tension with agape. Agape serves as a lure toward indeterminate possibility; the principles of justice can always be improved by extending them to more people and by refining their stipulations. They can particularly be pressed to aim

44

at the most needy of the human community. Agape's strategic concern for the least and the lost opens up the principles of justice to include them. But agape also serves as a transcendent point for indeterminate judgment. All achievements of justice in theory or practice fall short of the treatment that is really called for. No achievement of justice can rest complacent. Agape serves also as a standard for discriminate judgment, helping to set definitions and priorities of justice that are most helpful to the least fortunate members of the community. Finally, as agape judges all our forms of mutuality and justice, it leads us to a measure of contrition and humility. All of us fall short in upholding even the demands of mutuality and justice, let alone those of agape love. No one ought to be too haughty or arrogant.

If agape relates to the principles of justice in a creative way, then the principles of justice in turn relate similarly to the positive laws of justice, and they in like manner relate to the actual structures of economic, social, and political life. Thus, we get a moral continuum from the most transcendent "impossible ethical ideal" to the rough and ready world of social reality. Each level on the continuum interacts with the levels above and below it. The changing situation disturbs the present definitions of justice on the levels of positive law and principle, which forces a rethinking of what it means to do justice in each new situation. From the other direction, agape extends and intensifies the principles of justice, which in turn reshape the laws, and so on.

In the ambiguous world of large group relations, the ways in which principles and laws of justice foster just arrangements best are by maintaining a balance of power between self-interested groups and redressing balances when they break down. The relations of groups, if we take the doctrine of sin seriously, are even more fragile than those of individuals. Relations of mutuality are rare and become rarer as groups grow in size and power. The best way to ensure liberty and equality for each interest group, and the members of the group, is to establish and maintain external and internal balances of power. This achievement falls far short of the richness of mutuality that is possible among persons or within small groups, but it is nevertheless a significant

45

achievement of justice and as such is a worthy aim of Christian moral reflection and action. Even efforts at minimal "rough" justice do not evade the moral continuum in which all achievements are held in tension with the final norm. Doing justice in the social realm aims at providing for all persons the external conditions—liberty and equality—needed to realize their own ends. This is the social equivalent of mutual love.

In conclusion, let us explicate some of the unexplained facets of our diagram, particularly those on the lefthand side. Agape as a quality of human interaction is possible only among persons or in very small groups. The character of larger group relations can be described only rarely by mutuality but is more likely a balance of power. Relations of very large groups, such as nations, cannot go beyond self-interested balance of power. This does not mean that the policies of groups or nations cannot be influenced by considerations of agape and mutuality but that the actual quality of relations among them will be characterized by the measure of liberty and equality achieved by a balance of power.

Further, whereas the character of agape is understood, at least by the Christian community, as relatively permanent and universal, the principles of justice (and mutuality) are constantly changing as the historical context changes. Definitions change as the conditions of life change; new possibilities and limitations emerge out of the spontaneities of history itself. And each set of principles is relative to its own cultural and intellectual traditions. These "middle principles" are open to debate and change. Indeed, ethical wisdom is marked by the ability to reason from the transcendent level to the level of middle principles, to arrive at the proper principles, given the changing historical situation. A rigid and unchanging connection between the ultimate Christian norm and specific formulations of middle principles must not be made. Christian ethical reflection must always be open to new historical emergents and be aware of the relativities of cultural perspective. An appropriate flexibility and humility is necessary as we work up and down the moral continuum.

Finally, the impact of agape love has the possibility of shaping the interior sources of human motivation and will in a way that structures of justice cannot. The structures of justice can shape and manipulate the external conditions of human life, but they have much less of a capacity to alter the internal status of human beings. They are not totally bereft of this capacity, but they lack the spontaneity and texture of face-to-face relations that are so much a part of the relations of agape and mutuality. It follows, then, that the reception and impartation of agape love, in its religious and moral senses, and of mutual love are not available to the programs of large groups. The state cannot enhance the level of love in the world. The interior resources of human spirit for faith and love ought to be left to the nurture of smaller voluntary communities. The state has enough to do in its pursuit of justice as fairness, a subject to which we now turn.

4

Rawls on Justice

John Rawls is very helpful in specifying the content of justice for several reasons. Among them is simply the fact that he has so carefully developed a comprehensive theory of justice. Indeed, we will be doing him something of an injustice in that we will use only the broad outlines of his theory and neglect a good deal of the justifying rationale that he elaborates. Further, in terms of the suitability of Rawls for our project, it is important to note that, as Niebuhr, Rawls includes both liberty and equality as the content of what is to be distributed in a just society. Justice cannot be separated from the fair allocation of liberty. Although we will be using the main upshot of Rawls's theory, this does not mean that Rawls's entire worldview is fully accepted. On the contrary, his perspective is colored by a type of rationalistic naturalism that does not capture the heights and depths of the human condition nearly so well as our Niebuhrian position, with its emphasis on the vitalities of indeterminate freedom. Rawls's world is a cool, rational one, bereft of insight into persisting social concupiscence—especially in its more demonic manifestations—or into the creative responsibility that each person has for the use of his or her gifts. Neither the demonic darkness nor the soaring flights of the human struggle are much a part of Rawls's world. This is because the naturalistic assumptions he operates with reduce the range of human willing to natural drives on the one side and rational control and guidance on the other. The full reality of self-transcending freedom is neglected.

Be that as it may, it is important to use the capacities of reason to spell out the nature of the principles of social justice. Rawls has exercised those capacities well, as we shall see.

> Justice is the first virtue of social institutions, as truth is of systems of thought. A theory however elegant and economical must be rejected or revised if it is untrue; likewise laws and institutions no matter how efficient and well-arranged must be reformed or abolished if they are unjust. Each person possesses an inviolability founded on justice that even the welfare of society as a whole cannot override.[1]

All societies must struggle toward defining and achieving justice, however, since all societies embrace an impulse toward both social cooperation and social conflict. A proper set of principles and their accompanying social arrangements do not grow up spontaneously; they must be constructed.

> A set of principles is required for choosing among the various social arrangements which determine this division of advantages and for underwriting an agreement on the proper distributive shares. These principles are the principles of social justice: they provide a way of assigning rights and duties in the basic institutions of society and they define the appropriate distribution of the benefits and burdens of social cooperation.[2]

How are such principles established? The answer to this question constitutes a good deal of Rawls's *Theory of Justice*, which we will have to handle too briefly. Rawls does not want simply to rely on the traditions of Western social justice. Such reliance would be merely an essay in descriptive sociology, not an attempt at a normative theory of justice. Rawls wants to demonstrate that the principles he delineates are universal and necessary and that all rational beings would assent to them. Further, Rawls intends to argue the principles in such a way as to avoid the pitfalls of both intuitionism and utilitarianism. Intuitionism, he believes, is deficient because it comes up with a plurality of principles among which there is no way to adjudicate or order. One is left with no method of setting priorities or weighing these principles against one another. One must simply intuitively strike a balance without adequate reasons for one's choices. Thus, there is a certain arbitrariness in the intuitionist view, which finally precludes rational discussion.[3]

Intuitionism provides one target for Rawls's strictures, but classical utilitarianism is his main target. He believes that utilitarianism has dominated recent definitions of the principles of social justice. Summed up briefly, utilitarianism recommends the greatest satisfaction of the greatest number. In normative economic and political philosophy, justice is defined as an ever-expanding aggregate satisfaction of the greatest number of people. The right is maximizing the good.[4] According to Rawls and other opponents of utilitarianism, such approaches have two basic failings. One is that the quality of what is sought (the good) by humans is not limited by higher considerations (the right). Thus, certain persons may take pleasure in discriminating against others. The satisfaction of these perverse desires must be weighed in the total balance of desired ends. This, Rawls argues, is illegitimate because such ends, if they violate other persons, should have no claim for satisfaction in a just society. "The principles of right, and so of justice, put limits on which satisfactions have value; they impose restrictions on what are reasonable conceptions of one's good."[5]

A second deficiency of utilitarianism is that the quantity of the good—the sum of satisfactions—becomes the primary ethical goal. The greatest balance of good over evil, usually defined as pleasure over pain, is ethically optimal. "The striking feature of the utilitarian view of justice is that it does not matter, except indirectly, how this sum of satisfaction is distributed among individuals."[6] The crasser forms of utilitarianism could countenance the majority's receiving a bonanza of good at the expense of the minority's penury. The total balance of the good conceivably could be improved by such an arrangement. The more ethically sensitive forms of utilitarianism eschew such arrangements in favor of a Paretian stipulation—that the good should be maximized in any distribution with the proviso that no one is left worse off than before and at least one person is better off.

In contrast, Rawls proposes a deontological theory of justice in which the right is not interpreted as maximizing the good. In this deontological theory, the concept of right comes before that of the good. There are kinds of action that are wrong in themselves, and there are kinds of action such as fair distribution of the good that are right in themselves. And these are prior to and independent of maximizing the good; the rules of right regulate the quality and distribution of good. Thus, from this perspective it could never be right for the majority to benefit at the expense of the minority; nor would it be fair for the better-off members of the community to gain considerably while the poorer remain stable.

Rawls believes that all teleological theories of justice, which define the right by some sort of maximization of the good, have tendencies to violate the liberty or desired ends of some individuals for the sake of the greater good of the whole. For this reason, he is skeptical of them. This does not mean, however, that deontological theories are blind to the consequences of efforts at achieving justice. "All ethical doctrines worth our attention take consequences into account in judging rightness. One which did not would simply be irrational, crazy."[7]

Rawls, therefore, aims at arriving at principles of social justice that are rationally defensible (contra intuitionism) and that establish the right prior to and independent of the good (contra utilitarianism) yet take consequences into account (contra the more unrealistic of the deontological theories).

If Rawls will not appeal to self-evident principles or to the utilitarian tradition, how then does he purport to construct adequate principles of social justice? The key to his approach lies in a brilliant stratagem. He sets up a hypothetical contract situation in which rational persons with a set of interests will be forced to arrive at principles that reflect the ancient dictum: treat others as you wish to be treated. Love your neighbor as yourself.

Rawls calls this hypothetical situation "the original position."[8] It is a situation carefully constructed (hypothetically) so that a social contract can emerge among the persons involved, a social contract which will embody the principles of justice that will thereafter be used to guide and assess the practice of the community. Rawls considers this approach to be in line with the social

52

contract traditions of Locke and Rousseau. But his approach to the contract situation is based on the very modern contributions of game theory.

All participants in the bargaining game are assumed to be free and equal rational beings. They are endowed with self-interest; they want to achieve the desired ends of their efforts, whatever they may be. To this "thin" set of assumptions is added the further proviso that is not deducible from the earlier assumption of rational self-interest. The participants must concur that once they have agreed upon a set of principles to govern their community life, they will abide by those principles in the future even if it is not in their self-interest to do so. There can be no renegotiation of the contract later on.

In addition to these rules, the participants are bargaining from behind a "veil of ignorance."[9] This further stipulation helps to ensure that the principles arrived at will be fair, for it is intended "to nullify the effects of special contingencies which put men at odds and tempt them to exploit social and natural circumstances to their own advantage."[10] The participants do not know their sex, talents, class, race, family tradition, ethnic identity, intelligence, ambition, or aversion to risk. Nor do they know their own conception of the good, their religious convictions, or the generation to which they belong. "More than this, I assume that the parties do not know the particular circumstances of their own society. That is, they do not know its economic or political situation, or the level of civilization or culture it has been able to achieve."[11]

In order to avoid having the participants bargain from a position of disembodied rationality, however, Rawls allows them the knowledge of the general facts about human society. "They understand political affairs and the principles of economic theory; they know the basis of social organization and the laws of human psychology. Indeed, the parties are presumed to know whatever general facts affect the choice of the principles of justice."[12] Although there are indeed some problems about the way in which Rawls draws the line between what is known and what is not known—problems which we will discuss later—his description of the veil of ignorance is a further attempt to achieve a fair result in the negotiating process.

Operating within these stipulations, the parties propose, debate, and reach consensus on those principles which will govern their life together. The conditions of the original position press the agents into developing principles of fair cooperation that will aim at treating each other as each would wish to be treated. The stratagem is a way of eliciting the capacity of reason to reflect in an orderly way the law of mutuality at the heart of things. Justice as fairness is indeed a reflection of "the law written in the heart," the original justice that is ours.

Robert Paul Wolff, in his critique of Rawls, sums up the key to Rawls's approach in a more secular way:

> His intuition was that if he constituted the bargaining game along the lines suggested by the contractarian tradition of political theory—if, that is to say, he posited a group of individuals whose nature and motives were those usually assumed in contract theory— then with a single additional quasi-formal, substantively empty constraint, he could prove, as a formal theorem in the theory of rational choice, that *the* solution to the bargaining game was a moral principle having the characteristics of constructivity, coherence with our settled moral convictions, and rationality, and making an independent place for the notion of the right while acknowledging the dignity and worth of moral personality. The constraint Rawls hit upon was so minimal, so natural, so manifestly a constraint under which any person would consent to operate insofar as he made any pretensions at all to having a morality, that Rawls would, if he could prove his theorem, be in a position to say to a reader: *If you are a rationally self-interested agent, and if you are to have a morality at all, then you must acknowledge as binding upon you the moral principle I shall enunciate.*[13]

Rawls goes on to develop the moral principle. We shall first outline the bare forms of the moral principle and then develop them in more detail. Rawls argues that two basic principles would be chosen by those in the original position. "First: each person is to have an equal right to the most extensive basic liberty compatible with a similar liberty for others."[14]

The second principle undergoes revision as Rawls moves through his argument. The first version of the second principle

54

goes this way: "Social and economic inequalities are to be arranged so that they are both (a) reasonably expected to be to everyone's advantage, and (b) attached to positions and offices open to all."[15] But Rawls believes that the second principle is open to varying interpretations. He therefore refines it toward what he calls "democratic equality" and the "liberal principle of fair equality of opportunity." Thus, the revised version of the second principle asserts: "Social and economic inequalities are to be arranged so that they are both (a) to the greatest benefit of the least advantaged and (b) attached to offices and positions open to all under conditions of fair equality of opportunity."[16]

These two principles apply to the basic structure of society. They govern the rights and duties of citizens and regulate the distribution of social and economic advantages. They naturally apply to two more or less distinct parts of the social structure. The first principle defines and secures the equal liberties of citizenship whereas the second deals with social and economic equality.

The basic liberties of citizens are political liberty—the right to vote and to be eligible for public office; freedom of speech and assembly; liberty of conscience and freedom of thought; freedom of the person along with the right to hold property; freedom in the choice of occupation and association, and freedom from arbitrary arrest and seizure as defined by the concept of the rule of law. "These liberties are all required to be equal by the first principle, since citizens of a just society are to have the same basic rights."[17]

Rawls goes on to insist that these liberties be guaranteed by a fair and regular application of the law, that the political process be equally available for participation by all so that they have an equal right to take part in and to determine the outcome of the constitutional process that establishes the laws with which they are to comply and that liberty of conscience be held inviolable. He introduces many reflections on the limit of tolerance that are too numerous to examine here.

However, Rawls does make one distinction that warrants notice at this point. He distinguishes between liberty and the worth of liberty. Liberty may be established in principle, but the worth of liberty may be injured by the inability to take advantage of one's rights and opportunities as a result of poverty and ignorance and a lack of means generally. This lack in the "worth" of liberty is what is pointed to by many socialist critics of "bourgeois" liberties. But this criticism does nothing to diminish the importance of the equal liberties that would be chosen by those in the original position. It would, however, lead to strategies that enhance the worth of those liberties for all. Thus, the first principle leads us to the crucial complementarity of the second.[18]

But before we move to a discussion of the more complex second principle, let us end with Rawls's own final formulation of the first.

First Principle
> Each person is to have an equal right to the most extensive total system of equal basic liberties compatible with a similar system of liberty for all.

Priority Rule
> The principles of justice are to be ranked in lexical order and therefore liberty can be restricted only for the sake of liberty. There are two cases: (a) a less extensive liberty must strengthen the total system of liberty shared by all, and (b) a less than equal liberty must be acceptable to those citizens with the lesser liberty.[19]

Thus, justice as fairness means the equal distribution of basic liberties. This fits well with our Niebuhrian perspective in which mutuality extended into the social realm does mean that justice includes the distribution of freedom. Further, the device of original position used to facilitate the disinterested exercise of reason parallels Niebuhr's assertion that the self in repose has the capacity for such deliberation on justice. And the norms elaborated from such a disinterested perspective do transcend all current practice and therefore provide an Archimedean point for assessment and guidance.

Moreover, the insistence on equal liberties as a priority of social justice fits the Niebuhrian anthropology well. If it is true that the essence of human nature is self-transcending freedom, then the respect by society of that precious quality is crucial. People are affirmed deeply as centers of finite freedom—as ends in themselves—when the social system establishes and protects basic liberties. Perhaps there is even an echo of the Gospel, though certainly not the proclamation of the Gospel itself, in the government's recognition of the inviolability of human freedom, if its exercise does not harm others. If God allows persons to use their freedom for good or ill, and affirms them in spite of ill use, then an echo of that Good News is present in a society's preservation of fundamental freedoms.

Rawls's second principle is yet more complex than the first. If the first principle applies to the liberties of citizenship, the second "applies, in the first approximation, to the distribution of income and wealth and to the design of organizations that make use of differences in authority and responsibility, or chains of command."[20] The distribution of wealth need not be equal, but it must be to the advantage of the least favored persons. This is Principle II*a*. The principle, then, includes a second part, II*b*, which stipulates that all offices and positions be open to all under conditions of fair equality of opportunity. Let us take a more careful look at each of these parts.

Part II*a* is the most discussed and revised element in the whole formula. Rawls carries on a critical debate with two competing ways of justifying inequalities in the distribution of wealth and income. He calls the first of these the "system of natural liberty."[21] This interpretation insists on the equal liberties of citizens, as does Principle I, and it holds all positions open to those with talents. Following from this, persons with appropriate talents and sufficient ambitions occupy the open positions. This approach lifts up the virtue of efficiency, since this will get maximum output from the available talents by raising incentives for the most productive positions. Whatever distribution results from this allocation is just. Rawls rejects this approach, however, because it does not recognize the strong influence of natural and social contingencies on both the initial and final distributions.

> The existing distribution of income and wealth, say, is the cumulative effect of prior distributions of natural assets—that is, natural talents and abilities—as these have been developed or left unrealized, and their use favored or disfavored over time by social

circumstances and such chance contingencies as accident and good fortune. Intuitively, the most obvious injustice of the system of natural liberty is that it permits distributive shares to be improperly influenced by these factors so arbitrarily from a moral point of view.[22]

In short, this system does not adjust or correct undeserved inequalities. It is an approach associated with earlier periods of laissez-faire capitalism and it issues in a kind of social Darwinism. This system lives on through a few commentators such as Ayn Rand, but it does not represent a very large segment of modern thinking.

Rawls then examines and rejects a second interpretation of Principle II*a*, which he calls the "liberal interpretation." In essence, this approach tries to correct for *social* contingencies by adopting the principle of fair equality of opportunity. It compensates for the accident of being born into deprived conditions by offering persons in those situations fair chances to grasp open opportunities. It moves toward compensatory strategies in which undeserved social disadvantage is redressed. More attention is given to the education of poor children than to those of more favored classes. More vocational training is offered to the young of impoverished rural areas than to those of the urban middle class. Child care, with an attendant concentration on basic development skills, is provided for the children of one-parent poor families. Rawls approves of this strategy of redress and later accepts it as his interpretation of Principle II*b*. But as an approach to the whole of Principle II, he finds it lacking, though it is obviously superior to the system of natural liberty. For, even if it works to perfection in eliminating the influence of social contingencies, "it still permits the distribution of wealth and income to be determined by the natural distribution of abilities and talents.... Distributive shares are decided by the outcome of the natural lottery; and this outcome is arbitrary from a moral perspective."[23]

Thus, the liberal interpretation fails because it would allow those who are dealt a meager amount of talent by the natural lottery to be bypassed in any increasing largess of wealth. The parties in the original position, not knowing their own talents, would opt for a principle that would justify continued inequality only if it improved the lot of those arbitrarily deprived of talent. Rawls thinks this objection can be handled by a third interpretation of Principle II*a*, which he calls "democratic equality." In early versions of democratic equality he simply argues that primary social goods are to be distributed equally unless an unequal distribution is to *everyone's* advantage.[24] Later, however, he revises the focus from "everyone" to the "least advantaged." He thereby uses what he calls the "difference principle" to delineate the central thrust of Principle II*a*. The difference principle is described as follows:

> Assuming the framework of institutions required by equal liberty and fair equality of opportunity, the higher expectations of those better situated are just if and only if they work as part of a scheme which improves the expectations of the least advantaged members of society. The intuitive idea is that the social order is not to establish and secure the more attractive prospects of those better off unless doing so is to the advantage of those less fortunate.[25]

The difference principle would be chosen by those in the original position because it would provide a way in which all could share in the benefits of the distribution of natural talents and abilities. The inequality conditioned by the natural distribution of talents would work out to the advantage of the most unfortunate representative individual. In fact, the inequality is permissible because eliminating it would make the least advantaged even worse off than before.[26] Thus, a just system will distribute the primary social goods—liberty and opportunity, income and wealth, and the bases of self-respect—in such a way as to maximize the long-term prospects of the least fortunate. "The basic structure is just throughout when the advantages of the more fortunate promote the well-being of the least fortunate, that is, when a decrease in their advantages would make the least fortunate even worse off than they are. The basic structure is perfectly just when the prospects of the least fortunate are as great as they can be."[27]

There are ambiguities in Rawls's reflections on the notion of the least advantaged. He uses the notion of "representative men" to define the least advantaged. This concept seems to mean typical persons in various social positions or strata.[28] But who are they? Are they unskilled workers, poor one-parent households, dependent children, derelicts, the aged, the structurally unemployed? Rawls never quite answers this question. In a more recent effort, he attempts to define more closely what he means.

> The least advantaged are defined roughly, as the overlap between those who are least favored by each of the three main kinds of contingencies. Thus, this group includes persons whose family and class origins are more disadvantaged than others, whose natural endowments have permitted them to fare less well, and whose fortune and luck have been relatively less favorable.... [29]

Although this newer definition deals with one problem in Rawls's philosophy, it also opens up new ones. It is more realistic in its inclusion of the notion of free responsibility for one's condition than his earlier formulations, where it seemed that talents or a moderate lack of talents determined one's income and wealth. This seems to leave out the idea that people freely elect to use or not to use the talents they are given, regardless of whether they are five- or two-talent types. The freedom to decide whether or not to exercise one's gifts responsibly did not seem to arise. Possession of talents leads to success; lack of significant talents leads to failure. But such is obviously not the case. The element of decision, of resolute will, was negated; this follows from Rawls's naturalistic leanings. In this newer attempt at defining the least advantaged, however, he does introduce consideration of the responsibility factor. There are many persons who are from relatively good families, who have talents, and who have not been plagued by bad luck, but who are downwardly mobile. Rawls then seems to eliminate them from the least-favored status. Earlier he included them since his early definition was based simply on raw economic status. The problem with this new definition is that it would be terribly hard for society to ascertain whether the poor persons involved were "deserving"—affected by these overlapping contingencies outlined above—or "undeserving"—had not exercised a responsible use of their talents. It

would seem better to stick with the first version since it involves
fewer moral judgments on the part of the authorities about why
people are poor. Therefore, whether or not people deserve their
plight as the least advantaged, it would be just that they should
participate in the better conditions made possible by increasing
wealth. Although certain individuals may well refuse such participation, and insist on self-degradation, as a class of people the
deservedly disadvantaged also ought to benefit from the inequalities allowed.

In a most interesting set of reflections, Rawls relates the
difference principle (Principle IIa) to the notion of fraternity in
classical democratic theory. Although the nurturance of fraternity
is generally left to small social units and to the more inchoate
sense of civic friendship in the larger community, Rawls believes
it has a more direct relation to the difference principle as he has
developed it. Adoption of the difference principle would lead to
a heightened sense of social solidarity in democratic societies,
which in turn would complement and enrich the more formal
notions of liberty and equality.

> The difference principle, however, does seem to correspond to a
> natural meaning of fraternity: namely, to the idea of not wanting to
> have greater advantages unless this is to the benefit of others who
> are less well off.... Now wanting to act on the difference principle
> has precisely this consequence. Those better circumstanced are
> willing to have their greater advantages only under a scheme in
> which this works out for the benefit of the less fortunate.[30]

Rawls believes that the difference principle will guard against
some of the negative spinoffs of meritocratic society encouraged
by the principles of both equal liberty and fair equality of
opportunity. Meritocracy in its worst form means an equal
chance to leave the less well-endowed behind to stew in the sure
realization of their inferiority. A sense of fraternity nurtured by
the difference principle would insist on cultural and educational
resources being allotted, not solely according to their return in
productive trained abilities, but also according to their worth in
enriching the personal and social life of the least well-endowed.
This would go a long way toward fostering a firm sense of self-

esteem among the least fortunate of our fellow citizens. It is not difficult to see from a Christian point of view—indeed it is obvious—that there are real echoes of agape love in this interpretation of the difference principle. We should not be overly sanguine about the abilities of government to communicate the sense of fraternity, or of agencies of the government even to approximate the warmth and affirming power of agape, but nevertheless there are characteristics here that have unmistakable connections with the Christian notion of agape love. The most defenseless, the least, and the last become a first priority in the distribution of benefits. Their "deserving" or "undeserving" characteristics are overlooked. Their "usefulness" does not become the main criterion for including them in the orbit of human care.

If the difference principle (Principle II*a*) corresponds to the value of fraternity, and the principle of equal liberty (Principle I) corresponds to the notion of liberty, then the principle of fair equality of opportunity (Principle II*b*) corresponds to the notion of equality in classical democratic theory. It is to this last principle that we now turn briefly. Fair equality of opportunity means more than holding all positions open and discouraging discrimination on irrelevant criteria, though it does include these meanings. It also means further enabling those who have been hindered by social contingencies to compete better for those open positions. If equality of opportunity means that everyone should be able to run the same race for the open positions without unjust discrimination, fair equality of opportunity means that those encumbered by social disadvantage so badly that they are not even near the same starting line as the others are moved closer to that starting line by compensatory treatment. The principle holds that in order to treat all persons equally—to provide fair equality of opportunity—society must give more attention to those born into less favorable social positions. "The idea is to redress the bias of contingencies in the direction of equality."[31] Thus, Principle II*b* includes not only the notion of equality of opportunity but also that of *fair* equality of opportunity wherein social hindrance is redressed to provide more equal chances.

It is significant that Rawls does not insist upon equality of result in such an approach. Everyone running in the race does not have to win the race or even place, for that matter. Rather, the principle of fair equality of opportunity aims at what Rawls calls "perfect procedural justice." There is no independent criterion for the right result. "Instead there is a correct or fair procedure such that the outcome is likewise correct or fair, whatever it is, provided that the procedure has been properly followed."[32] In short, there is no quota of successful finishers that makes the race fair or unfair; but there is a way of ensuring that the race itself has been made fair.

This concludes our explication of Rawls's two principles. However, for Rawls it is not enough to enunciate the principles; they must be put in what he terms "lexical" order. He believes that persons in the original position would insist upon a certain order of priority among principles. The first priority would be the assurance of equal liberty.

> This ordering means that a departure from institutions of equal liberty required by the first principle cannot be justified by, or compensated for, by greater social and economic advantages. The distribution of wealth and income, and the hierarchies of authority, must be consistent with both the liberties of equal citizenship and equality of opportunity.[33]

As enough wealth is generated and distributed reasonably well, which condition Rawls assumes, persons in the original position would not sacrifice a fuller liberty for further economic and social advantages. As long as urgent needs are satisfied, persons want to pursue their purposes freely. It becomes important to secure the free internal life of the individual and his or her self-chosen communities. Further, persons desire the liberty to participate in shaping the political and legal realms in which they find themselves.

> Under favorable circumstances the fundamental interest in determining our plan of life eventually assumes a prior place. One reason for this I have discussed in connection with liberty of conscience and freedom of thought. And a second reason is the central place of the primary good of self-respect and the desire of human beings to express their nature in a free social union with others.[34]

63

Further, the principles of fair equality of opportunity (Principle II*b*) takes priority over the difference principle. And the whole of the second principle comes before the principle of efficiency and that of maximizing the sum of advantages.[35] But this ordering would be followed only if we assume relatively favorable circumstances. There are exceptions to this particular ordering.

> Until the basic wants of individuals can be fulfilled, the relative urgency of their interest in liberty cannot be firmly decided in advance. It will depend on the claims of the least favored....[36]

Only dire social conditions justify the restriction of the rights to equal liberty. This restriction can be accepted only if it is crucially necessary to lift the quality of civilization so that in due course liberty can be enjoyed by all.

> The lexical ordering of the two principles is the long-run tendency of the general conception of justice consistently pursued under reasonably favorable conditions. Eventually there comes a time in the history of a well-ordered society beyond which the special form of the two principles takes over and holds from then on.[37]

Finally, it is important to sketch Rawls's conception of the good society, or the "well-ordered society," as he calls it. First, there would be the maximum amount of equal liberties for all to pursue their own private ends and to participate in shaping the public realm. We have already seen what this means in a more specific sense. The additional elements that are significant here are Rawls's ideas of "social union" and society as a "social union of social unions." Usually the liberal democratic intellectual tradition is charged with being individualistic and privatistic. But this charge is far from the truth for Rawls and, for that matter, for Niebuhr.

There is a sense in which both Rawls and Niebuhr resist the idea that there should be a political notion of the common good that presses toward substantive ends. Public authorities are not to define the good life nor to use their persuasive and coercive powers to realize that definition among the citizens. A plurality of ends must be allowed and perhaps even encouraged. Rawls is very skeptical about perfectionist or organic notions of the state's

64

role. Both those notions of society are teleological—that is, they presume that the social pursuit of the good comes before the principles of right. Perfectionism seeks "to maximize the achievement of human excellence in art, science and culture."[38] Other versions of perfectionism might seek to establish moral and religious ends as paramount, such as seems to be the case in the proliferation of Islamic republics. Organic theories of society tend to project onto the public realm the characteristics of private life, especially the family or clan with its emphasis on blood and soil and the role of the father. Both theories lead to an authoritarianism in which equal liberties are curtailed for the sake of substantive ends.

Rawls rejects both approaches:

> While justice as fairness allows that in a well-ordered society the values of excellence are recognized, the human perfections are to be pursued within the limits of the principle of free association. Persons join together to further their cultural and artistic interests in the same way that they form religious communities. They do not use the coercive apparatus of the state to win for themselves a greater liberty or larger distributive shares on the grounds that their activities are of more intrinsic value. Perfectionism is denied as a political principle.[39]

A society of equal freedom will have a great variety of social unions—voluntary associations—in which persons band together for the pursuit of substantive ends. "We need one another as partners in ways of life that are engaged in for their own sake, and the successes and enjoyments of others are necessary for and complementary to our own good."[40] Perfectionist and organic ends are certainly in order here, as well as many other kinds of ends ranging from the ridiculous to the sublime. However, the public realm is not bereft of common meanings and values. Rawls believes that the commitment to and practice of justice as fairness provides a rich texture of public meaning and value. A well-ordered society as a whole is a form of social union. It is a "social union of social unions" in which the "successful carrying out of just institutions is the shared final end of all the members of society, and these institutional forms are prized as good in themselves."[41]

A second characteristic of well-ordered society is a persisting tendency toward more equality. Equal freedoms, especially in the political and legal realms, will press the claims of the less well-off. The insistence on fair equality of opportunity will be particularly effective. The principle of redress within a system of open positions will unleash much talent that could not be realized under adverse social contingencies, and this expressed talent will be remunerated. Although the difference principle does not press toward the eradication of all inequalities, it does serve to under-gird whatever efforts the least well-off make toward social mobility. Thus, in the application of both principles, there should be a steady movement toward more equality. And further, although significant inequalities may be tolerated, the difference principle insists that the surplus generated by those inequalities will help to increase the prospects of the least advantaged.

A third quality of a well-ordered society is that the commitment to justice as fairness is not incompatible with considerations of efficiency. Although the values connected with efficiency are not given priority over the principles of justice, they cannot be ignored. Rawls is aware that efficiency in the allocation of resources is necessary for the production of surplus which in turn allows the difference principle to function. He takes seriously the considerations about whether or not a system of justice works in the real world.[42] Moreover, in a society that is just in its basic institutions, all the principles of justice would be compatible with the principle of efficiency. Improvements in efficiency would make everyone better off in the proper proportion while the practice of justice would also be efficient. In a non-ideal situation, however, insistence on just procedures would most likely make some of the more advantaged worse off in order to improve the prospects of the least advantaged.[43]

Such a society, Rawls believes, would be stable and strongly legitimated. A sense of fraternity would pervade it, and its public commitment to liberty and equality would give it public meaning and purpose. Beneath the umbrella of a fair society, persons could pursue their conception of the good individually and in the context of social unions.

This completes our explication of Rawls's theory of justice. I believe it provides a suitable complement to a basically Niebuhrian approach to justice in society. While we do not have to agree with Rawls's notions of human fulfillment, which are very much in the rationalist tradition, or with his ultimate grounding of the principles of justice, which likewise lie in autonomous reason, the elaboration of the principles of justice is both helpful and compatible. We shall have occasion to qualify some Rawlsian insights as we construct our own broad principles of the just society, a task to which we now turn.

NOTES

1. John Rawls, *A Theory of Justice* (Cambridge, Mass.: Harvard University Press, 1971), p. 3.
2. Ibid., p. 4.
3. Ibid., p. 34.
4. Ibid., p. 30.
5. Ibid., p. 31.
6. Ibid., p. 26.
7. Ibid., p. 30.
8. Ibid., pp. 17-21.
9. Ibid., p. 136.
10. Ibid.
11. Ibid., p. 137.
12. Ibid.
13. Robert Paul Wolff, *Understanding Rawls* (Princeton, N.J.: Princeton University Press, 1977), pp. 16-17.
14. Rawls, *Theory*, p. 60.
15. Ibid.
16. Ibid., p. 83.
17. Ibid., p. 61.
18. Ibid., p. 204.
19. Ibid., pp. 250-51.
20. Ibid., p. 61.
21. Ibid., p. 66.
22. Ibid., p. 72.
23. Ibid., pp. 73-74.
24. Ibid., p. 62.
25. Ibid., p. 75.

26. John Rawls, "Distributive Justice," in *Economic Justice*, ed. E. S. Phelps (Harmondsworth, Eng.: Penguin Books, 1973), p. 329.
27. Ibid., p. 328.
28. Rawls, *Theory*, pp. 64f.
29. John Rawls, "A Kantian Conception of Equality," in *Cambridge Review*, March 1975, p. 96.
30. Rawls, *Theory*, p. 105.
31. Ibid., pp. 100-101.
32. Ibid., p. 86.
33. Ibid., p. 61.
34. Ibid., p. 543.
35. Ibid., pp. 300-303.
36. Ibid., p. 543.
37. Ibid., p. 542.
38. Ibid., p. 325.
39. Ibid., pp. 328-29.
40. Ibid., pp. 522-23.
41. Ibid., p. 527.
42. Ibid., p. 78.
43. Ibid., pp. 79-80.

5

Implications
for Social Philosophy

EFFICIENCY AND GROWTH

As we sum up our basic principles of social philosophy, it may be wise to begin with the role of efficiency in our perspective. Both Niebuhr and Rawls are fearful that the economic value of efficiency has eclipsed other more important values. Niebuhr thought that, though human culture depends on the ability of an economy to establish margins of welfare beyond the satisfaction of primary needs, American culture is increasingly under the threat of "gaining the whole world" but "losing its own soul."[1] To Rawls it is clear that the principles of justice ought to precede the value of efficiency but that in contemporary society this has not been the case.[2] Where efficiency fits into his scheme of values is a subject of some ambiguity. As Wolff points out, Rawls simply assumes an adequate productive apparatus and concentrates on questions of fair distribution.[3] But later, when Rawls considers nonideal situations in which it may be necessary to curtail some liberties in order to lift the quality of civilization, he reveals the unexamined importance of efficiency in his philosophy. In the original position, in which a high degree of efficiency is *assumed*, persons would then place the distribution of liberty first in their lexical ordering of principles. However, in a nonideal situation they might order the principles differently.[4] Yet Rawls denies participants in the original position knowledge about what kind

69

of society they will be living in. This is clearly a contradiction. The parties in the original position must know what kind of society they live in, whether it is economically efficient or not, if they are to order their principles properly. If they do not know this, they have no way of ordering their principles. The part of the veil of ignorance that covers knowledge of their own society's economic capacity must be raised; and when it is we see that efficiency is extremely important as an instrumental value in the achievement of both principles of justice.

Economic efficiency is one of the most important, if not *the* most important, *instrumental* values in enabling society to achieve its many ends, including the principles of justice. Economic efficiency in the use of resources means "that any given output is produced at minimum cost, which means both that waste and technological inefficiency are avoided, and that appropriate input prices are used to find the cost-minimizing production process."[5] Thus, efficiency points to the way in which resources are marshaled to achieve ends. There is no question that moral considerations often surround the elements of both means and ends, but at the same time there is no doubt that the value and logic of efficiency make their own claim on society's attention. Economic efficiency opens possibilities; the more efficiency, the more the possibilities. Of course, it is quite another question whether the right possibilities will be chosen and realized. But it seems ridiculous to argue that society should have fewer possibilities.

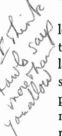

Perhaps Niebuhr and Rawls can be forgiven for their ambivalence about efficiency since they were writing at a time in which the reigning metaphor was "abundance." The writers from the late fifties through the early seventies assumed an ever-increasing surplus of goods. The problems of the distribution of goods—and particularly of abundant leisure—came to the fore. But now the metaphor is "scarcity," often clothed in as much exaggerated rhetoric, only more apocalyptic, as that of the earlier one of abundance. In a society in which increasing numbers of people are born and in which they live longer, in a world in which vast millions need to be fed within the constraints of environment and

70

resources, it is irresponsible to denigrate the value of efficiency. We will need far more efficiency in the future rather than less.

It is illegitimate to contend that humanist goals must take precedence over economic goals, and thereby deprecate the importance of economic efficiency. Economic efficiency is the servant of humanist aspirations and not their rival, and if we fail to achieve a worthwhile civilization the fault lies with all of us, not with those who have created the possibility.[6]

Thus, efficiency is a necessary, though not sufficient, condition for just society. A society without sufficient economic efficiency will have an almost negligible chance of achieving both Rawlsian principles of justice. Nor will it be able to sustain the number and quality of social unions necessary for the realization of more substantive concerns.

We might remark similarly about the value of economic growth, which, like efficiency, is under attack at the present time. We shall address the "limits to growth" question more fully later on, but a few preliminary remarks are appropriate here. Economic growth is "the steady process of increasing productive capacity of the economy, and hence increasing national income."[7] Such a definition does not stipulate toward what ends productive capacity is to be directed; it may be directed toward the production of more human services rather than more maufactured goods. So growth may come in ways that are not energy intensive. In fact, the great growth industries of the future may be directed toward conserving energy or finding new and more efficient sources of energy. If it is assumed that humans have no determinate limit to their aspirations, as our anthropology assumes, that more people will be born and live longer, and that all segments of the population will continue to press their claims for the wherewithal to pursue their aspirations, it will continue to be necessary to encourage growth in order to respond to those many claims and, more important, to respond to them justly. Moreover, the value of growth links up with the value of efficiency since the constraints on us in natural resources must be compensated for by increases in efficiency. Scarce resources will have to be used more efficiently if we are to grow in the future. Further, if undeveloped countries are to raise the prospects of their people, they will need markets for their goods—markets that can be provided by growing economies in the developed world. Stagnant economies will be protectionist and therefore unable to help the developing countries indirectly through trade or directly through aid.

Efficiency and growth are indispensable instrumental values. When they are in decline, the possibilities for an orderly achievement of justice and for enhancement of the quality of life decline with them. The current experience of Great Britain is a case in point. Although it is too complex and difficult to go into the causes of Britain's economic decline, its effects are all too clear. A shrinking economic pie brings increasing industrial strife as organized groups struggle for a relatively greater slice than their competitors, though in the end their slice is smaller in absolute terms. Unorganized persons and those who make moderate claims lose out. Dwindling national income means a waning amount of wealth available for traditional purposes—health, roads, music, arts—and even less for new departures. Both justice and quality of life suffer. The decline may be gentle and civilized, as the slow falling of autumn leaves, but it is decline nevertheless.

Accepting the necessity of efficiency as an instrumental value, we will now move to two further elements of social philosophy with their several subpoints. There is a certain degree of tension between these elements, but there is no contradiction. Indeed, in the constructive sections of Part III, I propose to show how more imaginative attention to all three can contribute to attempts to achieve a better society.

SUBSIDIARITY—PROTECTING AND USING THE "EQUILIBRIUM OF POWER"

The most remarkable thing about most advanced societies is the generally unnoticed fact that such a great segment of our lives is lived out in self-regulated contexts. We live within families, social groups, voluntary associations, economic units, political parties, even loosely defined classes that are in reasonable harmony. Further, human interests are worked out in contexts that offset each other, that is, they are in a rough balance of power in which one group cannot dominate the other and in which equality and freedom are unintentional byproducts. It is very easy to list exceptions to this observation, but it is even easier to point to the thousands of examples that prove the rule. The background conditions for a just society are not primarily a construction of intentional justice, as most idealists and rationalists, Rawls included, are wont to argue. The background conditions—the natural equilibria of power—are a curious amalgam of providence and achievement. It is difficult to see where the givenness of a balance of power and vitalities leaves off and the human achievement begins. Just as humans are an inextricable mixture of nature and spirit, so human societies bear witness to the fact that humans are both creatures and creators of history.

Niebuhr recognized how important this "natural" equilibrium is to the achievement of a tolerable justice in society; he listed it as one of the two main agencies of justice. Roman Catholic social thought has also recognized the centrality of this equilibrium through its principle of subsidiarity. Subsidiarity has meant that individuals and groups should not relinquish proper social policy and commit to the larger community what they can accomplish by their own enterprise and industry. The government, for example, should not transfer to higher and larger agencies functions that can be performed and provided for by lesser and subordinate bodies. The same should be true of private organizations. In societies in which this equilibrium of self-governing entities is highly developed, many economic, social, and political functions are carried out at the lowest possible level.

The importance of this "natural" equilibrium of power—and the principle of subsidiarity—is difficult to exaggerate. At least three very important tasks are performed by these self-regulating and self-governing strata of human corporate life. First, the creative elements of human finite freedom are harnessed in the equilibrium. Creatively, human freedom is worked out in contexts that are close at hand, self-chosen, and in which a chance for effective participation is at its highest. Persons are more creative and productive if their own interest and values lie close to them and are freely chosen. Thus, the subsidiarity principle leads us to propose that the economic tasks of society be performed as much as possible by private enterprises working in the context of free markets. Families ought to be allowed and encouraged to do as much for their members as they can. Educational, social, and political processes ought to be located as near to the people as is feasible so that their participation will be maximized. For the most part, except where there are compelling reasons for public ownership and control, these processes should be owned and controlled by private persons and groups. People will be most creative and productive under such conditions. The argument from creativity presses toward decentralization and localization of social functions.

Second, reliance on the equilibrium of power—observing the principle of subsidiarity—helps to offset and harness the more destructive elements of human finite freedom. Humans abuse their freedom by unduly asserting themselves and their groups. As we argued earlier, the ontological anxiety that is ours as part of the human condition issues in idolatrous pride. And as social groups grow in size and power, the tendency toward self-deification and the attendant domination of others—the historical consequences of sin—grows. In a rough, "natural" equilibrium encouraged by the principle of subsidiarity, however, such consequences are mitigated by the presence of other contervailing centers and kinds of power. There is no automatic harmony in the equilibrium, but where there is a rough balance of power among decentralized, self-governing units, such a situation ought to be used to the hilt for the limitation of the human will-to-power. Where, in economic life, there is workable competition among a significant number of producers in markets that extend from the local to the global, such mechanisms of limitation ought to be preserved and used. Rough balances between owners, managers, workers—both union and nonunion—and consumers ought to be respected. The natural balances among social, political, and ethnic groups that prevent domination of one by the other ought to be encouraged as the least disruptive way of limiting human concupiscence. Thus, a wise society ought to use

74

the natural balances it has as a primary mode of social control over the inevitable will-to-power inherent in groups and individuals. The balance of power resulting from a multiplicity of centers with a measure of economic, social, and political bargaining capacity probably makes for a greater measure of freedom and equality of opportunity—and for that matter, of efficiency—than whatever contrivances are erected in a more intentional way.

Third, protecting and using the natural equilibrium of power preserves a healthy separation and diffusion of different *kinds* of power. Observing the principle of subsidiarity particularly serves to limit the need for omnicompetent *political* power. If most of the economic choices can be made in the context of a competitive market system, if most of the social functions of life can be carried out among voluntary communities, if the most incisive social criticism can emerge from self-constituted "prophetic minorities," if a good deal of higher education can be carried on by private schools and universities, then public, political agencies do not have to be responsible for these functions in any direct sense. As power gathers around these specific, distinct functions, it is dispersed among many centers. Legal, cultural, religious, military, social, intellectual, and political forms of power are distinguishable and often in tension with each other. Dangerous overlaps and concentrations are avoided; political power especially is not made unduly dominant.

The main thrust of the second and third points coincides with what traditionally has been called the "Protestant principle." A wise society will be suspicious of concentrations of any kind of power. And it will be doubly suspicious of overlapping concentrations in which economic and political power, for example, are located in a few hands. The tendency of sinful human beings toward idolatries of pride and power should lead us to be distrustful of accumulations of unlimited power and thus to preserve and use the rough balances that are already present. It is important for society to "let be" if at all possible, for excessive intervention tends to concentrate power in political form and heightens the danger of tyranny.

75

ROLE OF THE STATE

In the preceding we have made no appeal to automatic harmony. Our doctrine of sin dictates no such naive belief. Incessant pride of power leads to breakdowns in the balance of power. Technological change distributes inordinate power to new groups while diminishing that of others. Some segments of the population never have gained enough power individually or socially to be even a part of the equilibrium. The growth of a mature, interdependent society creates many unintended effects in the natural and social world that are not automatically taken care of by market mechanisms. Strong powers tend to accumulate various forms of power, and their overlapping character makes them threatening to the broader society. In short, neither order nor justice is ensured by the free play of various competing centers of power. The harmony we described in the preceding section should be respected, preserved, and used constructively, but it should not be trusted to achieve anything like the just society we envisage.

If our insistence on "letting be" guards against the tyranny of state power, our affirmation of a strong but limited role for the state deals with the continued threat of an anarchy of private powers. Given the reality of finitude and sin, we should be well aware of the perennial tendencies in human society toward disorder and domination. Private power, be it economic, social, or political, has the same predilection as the state for increasing its power vis-à-vis others. Private power is by definition partial, whereas the state can, at its best, express the will of a total society. (We are assuming here that the state is a representative democracy in which there is universal suffrage and in which parties compete for the right to rule. The principle of resistance to government is embodied within the principle of government itself. We are also assuming a legal order that has a good deal of independence from elected political power.)

The government is instituted to promote the common good. Of course, what is included in the common good is a source of great contention. It seems wise to remain rather modest about what is

76

included, considering the dangers of tyranny that accrue to an overly ambitious state, the limitations in the competence of the state itself to decide wisely about the vast complexities involved in the life of a great nation, and the pluralism that inheres in the equilibrium of power itself. Like Rawls, we will avoid perfectionist notions of the state's role.

Nevertheless, there is a heavy agenda for the organizing center, the government. First, in pursuing the common good the government must preserve the health of the "natural" equilibrium of power and vitality. The center must arbitrate conflicts that arise in the society from a more impartial perspective than is available to any party in a given conflict; it must manage and manipulate the processes of mutual support so that the tensions inherent in them will not erupt into conflict, and it must coerce submission to the social process by superior power whenever the instruments of arbitration do not suffice.[8]

Second, the government must perform functions for the whole society that the equilibrium itself cannot. It must provide for defense, internal protection, certain kinds of research and development, foreign policy, and the macroeconomic managing of the economy, among other things. Increasingly the government will be involved in coping with the "neighborhood effects" of the production process on the natural and social environment. This will mean a fair regulation of land use and pollution control, as well as monitoring of the effects of technological innovation, especially medical, on human subjects. These are burgeoning areas for government intervention. Constant vigilance must be maintained in order to fix the boundaries of necessary intervention wisely. No simple rules can be elaborated.

Finally, the government, in all three of its branches, must be involved in correcting injustice where it is found and extending justice where it is necessary and possible. In order to stipulate what this means, we will simply appeal to the two basic principles that Rawls has given us, as well as the lexical ordering he has proposed. Since we developed these matters in some detail earlier, we will not repeat them here. However, there are two further areas of ambivalence in Rawls's thought that should be dealt with here, so that the final form of our normative perspective will be clear. We have already dealt with the confusion concerning the knowledge possessed by participants in the original position about the level of economic development in their society.

The first ambivalence is in Rawls's attitude toward inequality. At times, particularly when he insists on "pure procedural justice," he seems to accept inequality of results as long as the procedure governing competition for open positions is fair. At other times, particularly when elaborating his difference principle, he seems to assume that inequality of condition is inherently wrong and must be justified by appeal to the difference principle. This ambivalent attitude follows from a deficient notion of freedom in his view of human nature.

As we remarked earlier, Rawls tends to argue that the contingencies of environment and natural endowment are determinative in fixing one's wealth and status. Even though he tries to correct this deficiency later, it still remains. He does not account sufficiently for the notion of free responsibility, wherein human agents decide to steward their natural gifts wisely or to neglect them, or wherein they overcome social disadvantages or succumb to them. We would certainly not wish to argue that such contingencies do not *condition* one's life chances, but we argue that they do not *determine* them. Therefore, we have less tendency to view inequality in status and income as *ipso facto* unjust than Rawls does in his explication of the difference principle. This does not mean, however, that justice does not demand the difference principle. One can still maintain that it is just to improve the prospects of the most disadvantaged representative group without charging that more advantaged persons have achieved undeserved positions. If we insist on a more expanded notion of free responsibility among human agents, we can view achievement, and lack of it, as at least partially deserved in many cases. There ought to be no automatic onus for those occupying the more advantaged positions on the scale, just as there should be no automatic onus on those occupying the least advantaged.

A second ambivalence involves the difference principle itself.

78

Rawls varies his language about what the difference principle means in relation to the prospects of the least advantaged. Sometimes he argues that the difference principle means that we must "maximize" the long-term prospects of the least advantaged.[9] At other times he intimates that it means an "improvement" of the long-term prospects.[10] We tend toward the latter version, provided that improvement means "significant improvement." "Maximizing" connotes a lavishness that is unrealistic, in terms both of the political realities and the impossible expectations it may arouse in the least advantaged. There are limits to what is possible and desirable in encouraging incentive, and the language of maximization does not seem to respect those limits. We have a heavy agenda in improving significantly the prospects of the least advantaged, let alone in maximizing them.

Thus, we strongly affirm a vigorous distributive role for the state. Such a role indicates the way in which the political sphere can ensure that all share in the gifts accruing to the whole community. This role does not aim simply at maximizing the aggregate satisfaction of the community or, more crassly, at defusing social unrest by strategies of support for the disadvantaged, although it may perform both these tasks. Rather, it redistributes and redresses because it is just to do so; parties in the original position—being forced to treat each other as they would wish to be treated—would choose such policies. From a Christian perspective, such policies emerge from the "original justice" of humankind. And even more, policies guided by the difference principle and the principle of redress are distinct echoes of the Gospel ethic of agape love. They stretch toward the transcendent notion of universal, disinterested benevolence. But in our perspective they do so within the limitations of a fallen, finite world in which matters of productivity and growth, as well as responsibility and incentive, are taken seriously.

It should also be clearly noted that redistributive policies follow from *both* principles of justice. The distribution of equal liberties to all, and particularly the distribution of fair equality of opportunity, are certainly as important as, and perhaps far more important than, the difference principle in moving toward more

79

equality. Policies flowing from their provenance will tend to unleash more untapped creativity and initiative than the difference principle. Such policies will go a long way toward limiting undeserved inequalities, which rightly provoke the most indignation. Inequalities more closely correlated with free choice are certainly more justifiable, and would not be repugnant in our perspective. Moreover, the difference principle would improve the prospects of people on the bottom rungs regardless of whether their plight was deserved or undeserved. A rising floor of dignity would be provided.

Therefore, our Niebuhrian–Rawlsian perspective embraces a society in which power is as diffuse as possible and in which the natural balances are exploited for all they are worth. And they are worth a great deal in fostering both liberty and equality while at the same time realistically limiting the idolatrous tendencies of the state. On the other hand, we affirm a strong role for the state in pursuing the common good, which includes a strong redistributive thrust among many other important functions. These two affirmations guard against both tyranny and anarchy, the rocks through which the ship of social justice must pass.

The specifically Christian contribution to our perspective can be summarized in the following way. First, the Christian view of human nature emphasizes the sinful propensities of human beings. These propensities are magnified in the life and action of groups. In order to limit the idolatrous tendencies of groups—be they economic, political, social, or religious in nature—it is important to diffuse and balance power as much as possible. Where it is diffused and reasonably balanced, let it be. Where imbalances have emerged because of concentrations of power, make political efforts to redress the balances. In this way societies will be guarded from the destructive effects of idolatrous will-to-power.

Second, the Christian view of human redemption lifts up the role of agape love as the ultimate religious and ethical norm, a norm which can be neither completely triumphant nor wholly tragic within the finitude and fallenness of existence. Since it cannot triumph over the stubborn self-interest of group life, it cannot become a direct norm for governing group life. But since

80

its impact cannot be extinguished completely within history (otherwise history would completely contradict its norm and civilized life would be impossible), agape love makes a crucial difference in human moral striving. It, of course, enters into the moral life of individuals and groups, enriching, renewing, and extending the bonds of mutuality that reflect the deepest law of life. It provides the initiating and healing impetus without which mutuality would disintegrate. In doing so, agape exercises its hidden sovereignty in a world that would go to hell without it. Further, agape enters into the moral striving of society by exerting pressure on whatever achievements have already been made in the principles, laws, and structures of justice. The pressure of agape, operating through individuals and groups, sometimes Christian, sometimes not, works to refine and extend those achievements. It presses them to seek ever more accurate and refined arrangements of justice and to extend those arrangements to an ever-broadening circumference of being. In this task, it makes allies with secular efforts that also move toward the same ends of refinement and extension. (Our use of Rawls is a case in point.) But agape makes its exertions within the limitations of a fallen and finite world, and if it is to have maximum impact it must make these exertions with militance and persistence, on the one hand, and realism and humility on the other. Christians have no blueprint for a just social order. But they do have a view of human nature and destiny that gives them a specific missional perspective within the broader attempts to achieve a higher level of justice in this world.

The achievements of a society governed by the approach outlined above will fall far short of the demands of Rawlsian justice, let alone those of Christian love. There will be no mistaking even this relatively just society for the Kingdom of God. But the relative gains are worth fighting for. We should not need promises of paradise on earth to commit ourselves to policies that serve justice. Indeed, in our perspective we would strongly reject any redemptivist notions of state or society. Such approaches are formula for idolatry and, therefore, the oppression of people by the state. In the short run they may serve useful purposes of social and political unification, but in the long run they sanction tyranny or totalitarianism. And they destroy whatever authentic religious impulses are active in the perpetrators of such redemptivist notions for the simple reason that all political movements are tainted with the will-to-power, and redemption cannot be imposed by power.

We leave the redemptivist, or perfectionist, agenda to the smaller voluntary unions. They are less capable of tyranny and less likely to become intolerant. But, more important, they provide the continuing hope for the maintenance and renewal of society. They are the agencies through which nonheteronomous meaning systems are transmitted and through which the broader political and economic systems gain their guidance systems. Beyond that, they can, and often do, point to transcendent values that judge both their own lives and the life of the broader society. They provide the fertile ground for whatever moral vitality the society can generate. And some of them have the most chance of distinguishing between whatever improvements society can realize and the transcendent fulfillment that eludes even them but to which their symbols point.

CRITICAL REFLECTIONS

Although we have already grappled with some of the tensions that arise within the Niebuhr–Rawls "synthesis" we have constructed, we have not dealt with the objections that would be raised from outside that relatively compatible partnership. I am only too aware of the number of critical approaches that can be made to our "synthesis." In fact, from the beginning I have made no pretensions of fully grounding the normative position I have already elaborated. A good deal of grounding in theological anthropology and autonomous rationality has been included, but I would be the first to admit that our position is *not* fully "critical," that is, cognizant of the complete social and political milieu out of which it arises, and fully grounded, that is, completely argued in a fundamental sense. I will not attempt such a fully critical and grounded theory.

Nevertheless, certain fundamental objections must be met in order to make our perspective sufficiently credible. I will organize the many and varied objections under two basic rubrics. First, the social philosophy elaborated here is not substantive enough; it remains too formal, too pluralistic. Second, it is not generalizable; it cannot serve as a guide for all societies. Let us take up these two rubrics in turn.

First, many commentators charge that the notion of the common good is not expansive enough. The social philosophy is too classically "liberal." It allows individuals and groups to pursue their ends whether they are noble or ignoble. It diffuses power too much and vitiates the "planning capacity" that any rational society needs. It is too pessimistic about the government's capacity to define the "good life" and to press for its realization for all. It allows other large powers, especially economic, to define the good life by default (better the government doing it than General Motors; at least it is under public control). Our perspective, other commentators would assert, allows too many crucial values to remain "formal" when they could be given a more "substantive" meaning. Liberty means freedom from external constraint, but there is no positive notion of what it is for. Equality means "pure procedural justice" rather than an equality of results in which all share equally in the fruits of the society. (Too much inequality of condition is allowed.) The government could and ought to give more content to both freedom and equality.

Moreover, critics from Marxist or socialist traditions would want to pay more attention to the mode of production that a just society would adopt. Wolff makes precisely this point in criticism of Rawls.[11] Such a perspective possesses a normative, substantive notion of what kind of relations of production are just, that is, worker controlled or publicly owned. Our perspective makes no such normative judgments but rather appeals to balances of power and just distribution of liberty and opportunity, along with the difference principle which allows inequality of condition.

Aristocratic critics habitually criticize such a formal system because it does not foster national commitment to excellent ends. The "openness" of its economic, political, and social arrange-

83

ments encourages a vulgarization of values. Mass taste predominates; or, worse, economic imperatives govern the quality of civilization by shaping mass taste.

What all these approaches have in common is a commitment to coherent value systems that could be implemented by the state or by movements of social transformation that would decisively redirect the policies of the state. Some of them are more comprehensive than others, some more revolutionary. But all these approaches desire a society united under a set of public meanings that give substantive direction to its movement. If they locate their set of meanings in the past, they tend to be conservative critics of "superficial liberalism." If they locate their set of meanings in the future, they tend toward what we earlier called "the socialist myth." They intend to make use of all the gifts of modernization—secularization, rational planning, scientific advance, technological competence—without paying the costs of fragmented systems of meaning and eroded traditional community. Modernity without alienation is the socialist intention.

And who would argue with these aspirations? It would be foolish to deny to modern society the fruit of traditional excellence, which conservatism cherishes. It would be irresponsible not to desire a modern society free of personal and social alienation, which is the aim of the socialist myth. The longing for a society in which justice, excellence, and community cohere is a fundamental human hope. Indeed, I am well aware that the social philosophy elaborated in this chapter lacks substantive public content. The freedom I have argued for is basically formal, emphasizing the absence of external constraint. The equality is partial, fragile, and imprecise. The social pluralism precludes an expansive notion of the common good. From a Christian point of view, the values put forth here are provisional, penultimate. Christians have a notion of what freedom is to be used for, what perfect equality might be, and what might overcome the chaos of social pluralism. At its deeper levels Christian ethics moves away from contentless liberalism.

However, changes that are epochal in character dictate a more tentative approach. The religious meaning systems that at one time provided the glue for successive syntheses of culture no longer do so. Christendom, in either its Catholic or Protestant version, is gone. There is no public consensus on a meaning system under which all human endeavors can be organized and ordered. The fact of our existence is pluralism. Even though it can be argued that industrial civilization does provide a system of public values, usually decried in these arguments as idolatrous and reductionistic, it is nevertheless evident that we have a good deal of freedom to forge alternative value systems. I would further contend that those public meaning systems are not as unified and powerful as the arguments assert, and that what we have in modern Western societies is more accurately described as a veritable marketplace of meaning systems.

Moreover, the freedoms that have been painstakingly built up over the centuries in Western societies obviate an *imposition* of new meaning systems. People demand continued freedom in choosing the values that order their own lives. And, as we argued earlier, such freedom is precious and ought to be deeply respected by any society that claims to be just. Thus, in societies where freedom—a value that ought to be inviolable—is present, and the fragmentation of worldviews—a fact that is undeniable—is far progressed, the liberal option is the most defensible strategy. Balancing power, limiting the state, and enhancing social pluralism are proper stratagems for this time and place in history. They provide a context in which justice can be pursued without tyranny. Further, the protection extended to voluntary groups offers the best chance for new meaning systems to arise and to be freely accepted by the broader community. But let us make sure that such new, or, more precisely, renewed, meaning systems are voluntary. Premature impositions of meaningful community turn out to be neither meaningful nor authentically communal. Perhaps we are far from a new synthesis of culture; perhaps we are near. But whether we are near or far, let us allow it to emerge from below, as it were, and reject the temptation to grasp the godlike power to impose it from above.

As to the second set of objections, that the social philosophy projected here is not capable of being generalized, I respond in a properly ambivalent manner. It is true that our approach is undergirded by economic, social, and political conditions that are characteristic of advanced industrial or postindustrial societies. Economic efficiency and growth have enabled those societies to reach a stage in which the imperatives of bare subsistence have been displaced by concerns for the extension and refinement of justice and quality of life. Persons in the original position in these societies would choose the principles that Rawls enunciates, and would do so in the order that he suggests.

But what about societies in which the majority lives at or below subsistence, and in which power is concentrated in the hands of entrenched minorities who dominate the majority? In such instances there are few natural equalibria of power, and the state, far from pursuing justice as fairness, becomes the facade for the rich minority and their allies in the developed world. These situations call for more revolutionary approaches that aim at rapid industrialization and redistribution of land and wealth. Indeed, are not the revolutionary socialisms of the Third World essentially shortcuts to those aims? And is it not morally defensible to concentrate power in a state devoted to those ends and to curtail public and private liberties until those ends are achieved?

The painful response to these queries is the unsatisfactory "Yes, but...." Yes, in many cases revolutionary change is called for, but the perennial question remains: after sufficient political, economic, and cultural power is gathered by the state to pursue its ends, will it allow a limitation of its own power later? Or will it become the new oppressor whose idolatry may be even more thoroughgoing than its predecessor?

Even though we cannot judge such revolutionary efforts by too hastily or too simply appealing to the criteria developed in this chapter, these criteria do provide rough guidelines for judgment. Both technical and moral questions arise simultaneously. Do efforts for constructive change offer possibilities of economic efficiency and growth? Do they offer fair equality of opportunity to their people? Do they observe the difference principle? Do they move toward extending equal liberties to their citizens? Is there a possibility for democratic political life? Do such efforts respect the natural equilibria that may be present? Do they allow a social pluralism that checks the unitive tendencies of the state?

The lexical ordering of principles may proceed differently in developing societies, but it is important that none of them be dropped out completely. And it is indeed an open question which political groups will best observe our criteria. In some cases, moderate change may be by far the best approach. In others, more radical approaches may be called for. There are no simple answers in advance. But it is by no means clear that the principles we have put forth would not be chosen by persons who had the chance to choose.

This concludes the elaboration of our normative perspective, in which we have attempted to be reasonably comprehensive and critical. Let us move now toward examining the case for American democratic capitalism, as it is brought under the scrutiny of our principles.

Too uncritical acceptance of Rawls' two principles — particularly their nature — so they provide w/ option

NOTES

1. Harry R. Davis and Robert G. Good, eds., *Reinhold Neibuhr on Politics* (New York: Charles Scribner's Sons, 1960), p. 227.

2. John Rawls, *A Theory of Justice* (Cambridge, Mass.: Harvard University Press, 1971), p. 101.

3. Robert Paul Wolff, *Understanding Rawls* (Princeton, N.J.: Princeton University Press, 1977), pp. 207ff.

4. Rawls, *Theory*, p. 247.

5. Bannock, Baxter, and Rees, *Penguin Dictionary of Economics* (Harmondsworth, Eng.: Penguin Books, 1978), p. 144.

6. Paul Heyne, *Private Keepers of the Public Interest* (New York: McGraw-Hill, 1968), p. 24.

7. *Penguin Dictionary*, p. 144.

8. Reinhold Niebuhr, *The Nature and Destiny of Man* (New York: Charles Scribner's Sons, 1949), 2: 266.

9. Rawls, *Theory*, p. 78.

10. Ibid., p. 75.

11. Wolff, *Understanding Rawls*, pp. 207ff.

PART II

THE CASE FOR DEMOCRATIC CAPITALISM

The political problem of mankind is to combine three things: economic efficiency, social justice and individual liberty.

> *John Maynard Keynes*[1]

6

Is There Such a Thing as Democratic Capitalism?

Now that we have sketched our version of the problem and elaborated a normative moral perspective, it is time to handle two preliminary issues before we put forward the case for democratic capitalism. First, democratic capitalism must be defined. We must set some marks limiting the subject matter. Second, we will seek to argue that the social system we have described in theory actually exists in fact. This second task logically belongs to the following chapter since many critics of the American social system argue that such a definition as we are about to give no longer describes what we have in practice. They argue that the American social system is neither democratic in any adequate sense of the word, nor competitive. It is rather "corporate" or "monopolistic" or "oligopolistic" capitalism in which democracy is just a word for subtle control by private economic power. So we must take up the defense of our definition in this chapter. What we are arguing for, from a moral point of view, must be shown to exist or the argument is simply beside the point.

IMPORTANT DEFINITIONS

Paul Samuelson, in his famous textbook, *Economics,* asserts that the problems of economic organization are three:

1. WHAT commodities shall be produced and in what quantities? That is, how much and which of alternative goods and services shall be produced? . . .

2. HOW shall goods be produced? That is, by whom and with what resources and in what technological manner are they to be produced? ...

3. FOR WHOM shall goods be produced? That is, who is to enjoy and get the benefit of the goods and services provided? Or, to put the same thing in another way, how is the total of national product to be *distributed* among different individuals and families? ...

These three problems are fundamental and common to all economies, but different economic systems try to solve them differently.[2]

Further, the answers given to these basic questions are limited by scarce productive resources which can be devoted to alternative uses.

Samuelson goes on to assert that the American political economy, which he calls a "mixed economy," is based predominantly, though not exclusively, on a competitive system of markets and prices.

A competitive system is an elaborate mechanism for unconscious coordination through a system of prices and markets, a communication device for pooling the knowledge and actions of millions of diverse individuals. Without a central intelligence, it solves one of the most complex problems imaginable, involving thousands of unknown variables and relations. Nobody designed it. It just evolved, and like human nature, it is changing; but it does meet the first test of any social organization—it can survive.[3]

No one argues that the market system is characterized by "perfect competition," but our mixed free enterprise system answers the three questions of economic organization by relying on its markets for the greater share of its economic choices.

The price mechanism, working through supply and demand in competitive markets, operates to answer the three fundamental problems of economic organization in our mixed private enterprise system. The system is far from perfect, but it is one way to solve the WHAT, HOW, and FOR WHOM.

The dollar votes of people affect prices of goods; these prices serve as guides for the amounts of different goods produced. When people demand more of a good, a competitive businessman can make a profit by expanding production of that good. Under perfect competition, he must find the cheapest method of production, using labor, land and other factors that are relatively cheap and economizing on the use of relatively expensive factors; otherwise, he will incur losses and be eliminated.

At the same time the WHAT and HOW problems are resolved by prices, so is the problem of FOR WHOM. The distribution of income is determined by competitive bidding up or down of factor-prices—wages of each kind of labor, rents of land, royalties of books, and various returns to capital. Anyone possessing fertile land or widely admired crooning ability will be supplied with many dollar votes for his use in the markets for consumer goods. Anyone without property or education and with skill, color, and sex that the market cares little about will receive a low annual income.

Our economy is mixed in two senses; Governments modify private initiative; monopolistic elements condition the working of perfect competition.[4]

Strangely enough, Samuelson does not highlight what for many is the hallmark of a free-enterprise economy—private property. He obviously assumes the existence of such a characteristic, but it is important to include this element in our formal definition since many socialist theories and policies are trying to integrate competitive markets into a state-owned property system. George Dalton gives more direct emphasis to the private property element:

We mean by capitalism an economy-wide or national system in which private ownership of the means of production and market transactions of labor, resources and products are not only present but intimately linked to each other and integrated with all production processes and sectors; that is, they are the dominant or prevailing modes of ownership and transaction. In such economies, the price mechanism is the pivotal mode of allocating labor, resources, outputs and incomes. In addition, we usually mean by capitalism a national economy in which machine technology is importantly present, i.e., a developed economy.[5]

Private ownership includes all sorts of arrangements, from ownership by a single person or family through a broadly based stockholder ownership to worker cooperatives. It simply excludes state ownership as the dominant mode.

Thus, the external marks of capitalism are reliance on a competitive market system as a dominant mode of making economic choices; private ownership of the means of production; economic freedom to enter the market as producer, consumer, investor, or laborer (both organized and unorganized); and a legal order that protects voluntary and peaceful exchange and attempts to maintain the competitive nature of the system. Its internal character—its ethos—is more difficult to stipulate. The driving force of capitalism's economic life is the subject of great debate. (Let us note that the motivation for economic life certainly does not exhaust the number of other kinds of motivation in a society whose economic order is described as capitalistic. Motivations in family, political, and institutional life may diverge sharply from those of the economic order.) Assessments of the entrepreneur's motivation range from the strict rational and systematic maximization of profit in classical theory through the more dynamic theories in which growth becomes the primary objective, to the behavioral theory of the firm, "which drops the assumption that firms maximize something, and instead concentrates on the decision processes of the firm, and the way in which these are affected by the organizational environment."[6]

No doubt each of these assessments has some measure of truth. However, if we stick by the definition of capitalism given above, it would seem difficult to argue that a significant profit is not the primary criterion. "Maximization" may be too strong a term to describe the pursuit of profit in an environment that is not perfectly competitive and in which investors' motivations also vary. Certainly aims of growth and security enter the scene. But in an age in which the scope of some markets is rapidly increasing to world scale, it is impossible to believe that entrepreneurs can be shielded from competitive forces that are real and effective. So let us retain the notion that the rational and systematic pursuit of profit remains a primary spring of economic action in a capitalist economy.

If the above suffices as a rough definition, a similar attempt to define "democracy" is needed. Schumpeter struggles with the questions that surround the various definitions. The classical theories get hung up on questions of the common good and representation of the people. Schumpeter proposes that these questions be made secondary to the election of persons who are to do the deciding.

> To put it differently, we now take the view that the role of the people is to produce a government.... And we define: the democratic method is that institutional arrangement for arriving at political decisions in which individuals acquire the power to decide by means of a competitive struggle for the people's vote.[7]

He goes on to argue that in a democracy the government's powers are limited by a sphere of private freedoms and by a legal order that preserves those rights as well as provides for periodic elections.

Alan Gewirth, in his excellent essay, "Political Justice," gives a more expansive account of the democracy we are trying to define. Gewirth argues that democracy, if it is to be legitimated by valid criteria of political justice, must be based on the method of consent by the people. It is majoritarian rule based on the consent of the governed.

> Government by consent means, rather, that the specific holders of political authority are not independent variables so far as their authority is concerned but are dependent on the votes of the electorate. This entails that the government, as a matter of constitutional requirement, is regularly subjected to a process which passes judgment on it and may transfer its authority to other hands. The right of dissent is thus a basic part of the method of consent. The process culminates in an election, but it also includes free discussion and criticism of the government's policies, and competition for votes among different parties. The government is thus subjected to the various groups within the electorate, and the election, which may be viewed as the culmination of those pressures, determines who is to occupy governmental office in the subsequent period. The government's right to govern depends finally on its winning the election by the constitutionally required majority or plurality of votes.[8]

The minority who voted against the government or those who did not vote at all are also obligated as citizens to the elected government. "Their obligation rests on their having consented to the general rules which determine that it shall be by majority vote that the specific governmental authority is allocated."[9] However, majoritarian rule is qualified by doctrines that advocate the limits of the objects and methods of all governments, including democracies. These limits are called, respectively, liberalism and constitutionalism.[10]

Liberalism refers to equal freedom and both private and public rights, including the rights of universal suffrage, free speech, assembly, religion, movement, choice of occupation, private ownership, and so on. Constitutionalism refers to a legal order that ensures equality before the law and to equal protection by the laws, as well as to an orderly method of consent.[11]

Thus, our definition of democracy includes the notions that government is based upon the method of consent as delineated above, that equal private and public rights are protected, and that both of these elements are anchored in a constitutional framework. Democratic capitalism, then, refers to a polity that encompasses these three elements and an economy in which the dominant mode of economic decision making is based upon a free, private-enterprise competitive market system. There are obvious variations on how much public power, based upon democratic polity, intervenes in the private economic system. But at any rate, in our definition, democratic capitalism is a social system in which there is a good deal of independence of political from economic power, and vice versa.

IS IT REAL?

One of the most serious threats to our project—a moral reassessment of democratic capitalism—is the charge that we are attempting to evaluate something that exists only as a figment in the imagination of mainstream American economists. If this charge were true, our argument would be reduced to the most naive kind of ideology: a moral rationalization for something that no longer exists but that is useful to those who hold power in a new social system that has emerged out of the old. In fact, such an objection is commonplace among many critics of American society who assume that its social system is neither competitive nor democratic. Those who make such assumptions are generally influenced by neo-Marxist or left-wing Keynesian analyses of capitalism, or both. Both sets of analysis agree on what they regard as the crucial characteristic of modern capitalistic economies—they are not workably competitive but are characterized by monopolistic or oligopolistic competition. The answers to Samuelson's What, How, and For Whom questions are made by large private economic powers that are not constrained by competition. Further, they are not adequately constrained by government. In fact, they dictate policy to government. Political power is collapsed into economic power.

One variation on these themes is represented by the rather "rough" Marxism of Paul Sweezy. This author, who has written profusely on economic matters from a Marxist viewpoint, sums up his analysis by asserting:

> With the growth of the giant corporation, capitalism left its competitive stage and entered its monopoly stage. In the competitive stage individual firms grow by reducing costs, realizing larger profits, and investing in increased capacity to turn out products which, being essentially indistinguishable from the products of rivals, can always be sold at or slightly under the going market price. But as some firms prosper and grow and others lag behind and drop out, the average firm in an industry becomes so large that it must take account of the effect of its own production on market price. It then begins to function more and more like a monopolist, for whom the problem of continued growth is radically transformed. Monopoly profits make possible even more rapid growth than in the past, but the need to maintain monopoly prices dictates a policy of slowing down and carefully regulating the expansion of productive capacity.[12]

This situation makes the monopolistic firm move beyond its traditional field of operation to penetrate new industries and new markets; that is, it becomes conglomerate (operating in many industries) and multinational (operating in many countries). The latter tendency forms the basis of Sweezy's theory of imperialism in which the giant monopolies exploit labor and markets abroad to the detriment of the host country. As the monopolies prosper, the poorer countries become even more underdeveloped. But such desperate searches for markets do not stave off the inherent contradictions of monopoly capitalism. The monopolies accumulate more capital than they know what to do with, and, since they must hold output down, there is a stagnation in both production and employment. Waning demand may be stimulated by welfare and warfare spending, but this only deflects the inexorable crisis.

Governments in lands characterized by monopoly capitalism can only reflect the contradictory, and dangerous, tendencies of the economy. The controllers of the giant corporations dictate desired policy to government. "What we have in the United States is a *ruling class* with its roots deeply sunk in the 'apparatus of appropriation' which is the corporate system."[13] But what is dictated by the ruling class cannot overcome the inherent contradictions; it can only provide stop-gap measures.

> We thus have a situation in which the corporate giants control the federal government, and locally based vested interests control the state and local governments. Throughout most of the period when this arrangement has been in operation. . . . it has worked reasonably well for the power-wielders at both levels.[14]

Thus, in classical Marxist fashion Sweezy demonstrates the dependence of the political sphere on the economic means and relations of production. And the economy is based upon giant monopolies that do not behave in a workably competitive way. We do not have anything remotely approximating competitive market systems or representative democracy, although bourgeois social scientists continue to mask these facts.

If Sweezy represents a rather "rough" neo-Marxism in the sense that he continually searches for "real" economic forces which determine everything else, other neo-Marxists are anything but "rough." Revisionist Marxism includes a number of highly sophisticated analysts who come at the issues of modern society from a number of varied perspectives. There are neo-Marxist economists who busy themselves with primarily economic questions. Oskar Lange and Otto Sik come immediately to mind. Both abhor the type of bureaucratic state socialism of the Soviet Union; but at the same time they agree on the fundamental Marxist criticism of capitalism, that is, that it is monopolistic and exploitative and must be superseded by some kind of "socialism with a human face." Neo-Marxism has also emerged among many younger economists in the West who are dissatisfied with mainstream economics. Further, the Marxist tradition provides the fundamental critical apparatus for a significant minority of sociologists, historians, and philosophers. Even some theologians have adopted neo-Marxism as a critical framework. In this world of pluralistic neo-Marxism there is little consensus on prescriptive policies for the future, although these writers tend to be committed to democracy in its Western meaning of civil and political liberty, free elections, and evolutionary change. Nevertheless, there seems to be a consensus among all of them that capitalist economies are not characterized by authentic competition and that capitalist democracies are more or less projections of corporate wishes. What distinguishes theirs from the "rough" Marxism of Sweezy is that they are more subtle in their analyses of the interplay of economics, politics, and culture and more flexible in their prognosis for the future.

Jürgen Habermas, representing the Frankfurt School's tradition of neo-Marxist thought, illustrates this consensus. Although late capitalism shows "surprising vigor,"[15] it is nevertheless beset by inevitable fluctuations of prosperity, crisis, and depression.[16] Monopoly dominates the large, modern section of the economy where we have the significant rapid advances in production.[17] There is a clear and increasing inequality in the distribution of wealth and power.[18] Market ideology serves to maintain the political anonymity of class domination.[19] We have a "formal" democracy in which people can merely assent to or dissent from the agendas shaped by corporate monopoly.[20] Genuine participation in the process of political will formation, that is, substantive democracy, would bring to consciousness the contradiction between administratively socialized production and the continued private appropriation of surplus value.[21] This consciousness will tend toward a crisis of political legitimation. But even more seriously, the erosion of meaning in late capitalism will provoke a crisis of motivation which will enervate the whole system.[22]

Michael Harrington, an American democratic socialist, concurs with the above analyses, particularly concerning the character of the economy and the polity.

> I do not believe the United States is a free enterprise society. I think the people who want us to use this term wish to rationalize and defend rather than describe society.... The United States today does not have a free enterprise society in any kind of Adam Smithian sense of the term. Rather, we have giant oligopolies administering prices, shaping tastes, working together with an all-pervasive government which follows corporate priorities. Therefore, I suggest that rather than using the term "free enterprise" to describe our system we get closer to reality and call it "corporate collectivism." I maintain that corporate collectivism, in its historical thrust and tendency, is not compatible with social justice. Moreover, I am absolutely certain that capitalism—corporate collectivism in its latest phase—is coming to an end.[23]

One does not have to remain within the Marxist or neo-Marxist framework to have similar views of the American economy and polity. Leftwing neo-Keynesians in both Britain and America come in with generally the same verdict: modern capitalism is dominated by oligopoly and government is dominated by oligopolistic interests. Therefore, there is no such thing as democratic capitalism if we mean by that an economic system characterized by workable competition and a polity that is reasonably representative of the whole population's interest.

Keynes, in his classic *General Theory,* observed that the economic systems of the Western capitalist countries were not automatically in equilibrium. This was in contradiction with the classical hope for an overall harmony of supply and demand. Indeed, the Great Depression had indicated that harmony was not automatic. Keynes opened the way for government intervention in managing demand in the whole economy. Even with this provision for intervention, Keynes tended to agree with the neoclassical tradition that firms acted in a competitive manner and could be expected to do so. However, about the same time in the 1930s, two works appeared, one in the United States and the other in Britain, that challenged the classical and neoclassical assumptions about the competitive behavior of firms, assumptions which even Keynes held. R. H. Chamberlain's *Theory of Monopolistic Competition* and J. V. Robinson's *Economics of Imperfect Competition* challenged the notion that the prices of firms are set strictly by market forces. Rather, large firms with a concentrated share of the market could administer prices, could affect demand by shaping tastes, would tend to compete on grounds other than price, and could affect the prices of supply by their massive purchases. A related argument was that a good deal of the economy was already dominated by oligopolistic firms and this concentration was bound to increase.

These two writers, and their many followers at Harvard and Cambridge, reached their conclusions on the basis of classical economic methods rather than on the more heterodox Marxist methods. And although the reasons given for imperfect competition were very different from those put forward by Marxists, some of the main conclusions did indeed converge with Marxism. Free-enterprise market economies were not real, and since the market no longer sufficed to control economic centers of power, only two strategies remained. One was to increase the control of economic life by political means. Unchecked private power should be brought to heel by public power. The other was to promote a doctrine of corporate responsibility on the part of the private powers themselves. Enlightened managers could set a responsible course for their corporations from the inside, as it were. At any rate, the large modern firm could not be expected to maximize profit in a context of effective competition. It might tend to maximize size, as in Baumol's *Business Behavior, Value and Growth,* or growth, as in Robin Marris's *The Economic Theory of Managerial Capitalism.* Or, departing even further from the classical approach, it may not try to maximize anything but rather respond to many kinds of environmental pressures—technological, social, political, and economic, as in the behavioral theory of the firm.

John Kenneth Galbraith has been the most popular American representative of the left-wing Keynesian tradition. Galbraith has had tremendous impact upon the more literate public for several important reasons, among them that he writes so engagingly and that his approach is comprehensively humanistic. Many of his counterparts in the mainstream are limited by a rather myopic, technical perspective, but Galbraith's reflections are what we called in the introductory chapter "value visible." Moral, political, and esthetic values are close to the surface of his economic analysis. He makes no pretense of being a detached scientist.

Whether detached or not, however, Galbraith bases his wide-ranging reflections on one alleged fact: that the classical and neoclassical model of competitive capitalism is an illusion. In *American Capitalism* he speaks of the abandonment of the model in which the behavior of firms is governed by market forces.[24] Rather, he believes that broadly political factors now account for the policies of large firms. The countervailing powers of giant trade unions, cartels of suppliers, huge conglomerate purchasers, consumer unions, and, perhaps most important, government purchasing and regulating agencies all are involved in the interplay of forces with which the corporation must deal. These countervailing powers actually improve the performance of the economy since they limit the predatory tendencies of oligopolies. However, even in this continuing decentralized mode of operation, the danger of inflation is severe because economic factors of efficiency can be ignored. Galbraith ends his book with suggestions that a more centralized direction will be necessary, particularly in relation to price and wage policies.[25]

A little later, in *The Affluent Society*, Galbraith continues his rather optimistic assessment of countervailing power capitalism. It is immensely productive, but the cultural habits of Americans in combination with the power of corporations tend to concentrate wealth in the private sector while allowing the public sector to become increasingly impoverished. We have private opulence and public squalor simultaneously. Galbraith calls for an expanded public sphere so that education, the arts, welfare, urban areas, parks, and so on can get their proper share of the American largess. Thus, both the redistributive apparatus of the state and what Rawls has called the perfectionist role of government should be expanded.

Even more recently, in the late sixties, Galbraith withdrew his view that countervailing power limits the actions of large firms effectively. Rather, the modern corporation appears as the real sovereign of late twentieth-century economies. It has displaced the market as the shaper of social destiny: "So far from being the controlling power in the economy, markets were more and more accommodated to the needs and convenience of business organizations."[26] But the power of the giant corporations had also overcome the countervailing powers Galbraith had seen as operative in the fifties. Stockholders, boards of directors, unions, consumers, and purchasing cartels have all waned in importance before the huge conglomerated and multinational corporations. These giants, with their capacity for technical innovation and organizational expertise, obviate any challenge from new enterprise at home or abroad. Their planning shapes the market, not vice versa. These corporations are under the effective control of the *technostructure,* a bevy of technical experts who manifest the same kinds of characteristics in all advanced economies. Moreover, there is a tendency for the management leadership of the mature corporation in the new industrial system to become interchangeable with the administrative leadership of the state.[27]

After this rather lengthy catalog of arguments against the capacity of the market to constrain large firms, we can see why the liberally educated reading public eschews any proposed defense of democratic capitalism as we have defined it. There simply is no such thing. Large corporations call the shots in national and international contexts. Therefore, if there remains any independent political leverage over private economic power, it ought to be used to plan the real agenda of the people and to coerce private power to submit to that agenda. Therefore, many American liberals continue to call for expanding governmental regulation or even control of American economic life. Without such intervention, a reasonably just society is impossible. Those who worry about the ensuing top-heavy state bureaucracy that such a strategy entails place their hopes in a decentralized socialism of worker-owned or worker-managed cooperatives. Other tougher minded—or, as some would say, callous—commentators agree with such an analysis but argue that private monopoly is preferable to either the statism of traditional social-ism or the chaos of the more idealistic kind. The liberty and prosperity of the majority should be chosen over the statism or chaos that would result from socialist programs.

Such strategies, based on assumptions concerning the death of the market, are not the only options, however, because the assumptions upon which they are predicated are considered by many mainstream economists to be erroneous. There is a vast literature on the extent of concentration and monopoly in modern economies, and the least that can be said about its conclusions is that they are inconclusive. But the most that can be said is that they contradict the assumption that market forces are no longer reliable as a mode of economic choice.

We can begin tracing the counterattack by briefly reporting Raymond Lubitz's argument against the Sweezy assertion that monopoly capitalism will tend toward ever higher rates of profit but at the same time suffer intense periods of depression caused by stagnation, that is, excess productive capacity and rising unemployment.[28] Sweezy, borrowing from 1930s Keynesian anal-ysis, attempts to prove monopoly from these indirect indicators rather than from a direct measurement of concentration. As to the first charge, that profit is rising in relation to wages under monopoly capitalism, Lubitz points out the following:

> Any theory of the tendency of profits to rise must show that real wages rise less fast than labor productivity. If real wages rise and productivity rise at the same rate, the division of national income between wages and profits will be constant.... The historical data for the period of monopoly capitalism fails to show any sign whatsoever of a rising income surplus. It is clear from the record that the surplus, interpreted as the share of property income, has fallen in this century. Employee compensation, the wage share in its simplest meaning *increased* from 54 per cent of national income in 1899–1908 to 69 per cent in 1954–60.[29]

Further, argues Lubitz, the increase in labor compensation per worker-hour in manufacturing rose over the period 1909–14 to 1955–57 by 3.8 times, while productivity in manufacturing rose by only 3.3 times. Thus, profits do not claim the lion's share of productivity's increase. In fact, the share is falling.[30]

The related Sweezy contention that monopolistic corporations are drowning in their own accumulation from high profits and therefore looking desperately for investment opportunities in underdeveloped countries is equally false, according to Lubitz. Rather, he argues that if Sweezy were right about this, corporations would increase their payout dividends. But there is no evidence that this is occurring. Moreover, far from there being an inordinate supply of investment capital, interest rates on corporate bonds have soared as companies bid for scarce investment funds.[31]

As to the thesis that American capitalism is inherently prone to stagnation, Lubitz retorts that Sweezy would have to demonstrate long-term, general patterns of excess capacity and obvious unemployment. And there is little evidence for such patterns.

> It is an old vulgar-Marxist game to "prove" nonobservable tendencies by taking *recessions* as *proof* of the tendency and business cycle *upswings* as *deviations* caused by temporary counteracting forces. Of the entire period of monopoly capitalism that Baran and Sweezy analyze, roughly 1870–1963, they discover problems of "surplus absorption" to exist in *less than one-third* of this time (1908–15, 1929–39, and 1958–63). The rest of the periods were "exceptions." After a century of such Marxist methodology, a certain skepticism on the part of orthodox economists is understandable.[32]

There are, of course, many refinements to both Sweezy's argument and Lubitz's refutation that we are not able to include here. But the gist of the debate has been recorded. The Sweezy neo-Marxist indicators for the prevalence of monopoly capitalism are challenged by Lubitz's more careful empirical investigation. And although many neo-Marxists are more subtle in their economic and social judgments, they tend to rely on similar assumptions about the effects of monopoly capitalism. But if the effects are not forthcoming in reality, is there not good reason to question the existence of monopoly capitalism itself? Moreover, even if business cycles do exist—and of course they do—are they simply attributable to the machinations of monopoly capitalism, or are they explicable on grounds more clearly delineated by orthodox economists, such as failures in monetary or fiscal management?

Or is the fact that we seem to have fewer cataclysmic depressions attributable to the resiliency of a more widely diversified and more massive economy than was extant in the 1930s? Neo-Marxist explanations do not seem to move in these more fruitful directions, but rather keep seeking the independent variables in the economic "contradictions" of an alleged "monopoly capitalism."

The left-wing Keynesians, because they base their analyses more on accepted empirical investigatory methods and less on Marxist ideology, are more formidable. Their arguments point to (1) increasing concentration marked by competition not on price but on peripheral, wasteful differentiation in products; (2) an ability on the part of large corporations to administer costs and prices while they create and shape demand; and (3) a technostructure insulated from the traditional constraints of competitive conditions. The counterevidence comes from many different economists. We can begin with those writers who believe rather definitely that, overall, the American economy is characterized by effective competition and that competitive conditions may be increasing rather than decreasing.

Milton Friedman, for example, takes this line. His famous, or infamous, statement that "the only social responsibility of corporate officials is to make as much money for their stockholders as possible"[33] can only be understood within the assumptions of effective competition. For if competition is real and effective, the pursuit of profit by enterprises will bring about the most good for all. Profit maximization under the conditions of competition will bring together the factors of production in the most efficient and creative way. Enterprises will produce for the consumer the best products for the least money. Those that succeed best in meeting the wishes of the consumer will profit; those who do not will lose. Meanwhile, the resources of society will be allocated best under these free market conditions. Friedman recognizes that conditions of perfect competition are seldom realized in history, but he in no way admits that the American economy is dominated by oligopolistic corporations. "As I have studied economic activities in the United States, I have become increasingly impressed with how wide is the range of problems and industries for which it is appropriate to treat the economy as if it were competitive."[34] Thus, in a competitive economy one can responsibly say that profit maximization is defensible as a motive of business enterprises.

Granting some of the difficulties in measuring monopoly, Friedman nevertheless asserts that "the most important fact about enterprise monopoly is its relative unimportance from the point of view of the economy as a whole."[35] He goes on to point out why it appears that there is more monopoly than there actually is. One reason is that there is a tendency to confuse absolute with relative size. "As the economy has grown, enterprises have become larger in absolute size. This has been taken to mean also that they account for a larger fraction of the market, whereas the market may have grown even faster."[36] A second reason is that cases of monopoly gain more publicity than those characterized by competition. Friedman indicates that the monopolistic tendencies in automobile production would be known by almost everyone, but hardly anyone would know anything about the highly competitive wholesale trade which is twice as important as automobile production. Finally, he explains that the main characteristic of our society is usually taken to be its industrial sector. Many believe large industry constitutes the "commanding heights" of our economy. But Friedman suggests that there may be no commanding heights. The emphasis on the manufacturing sector deflects attention from the reality that it accounts for only about one quarter of output or employment.[37] Perhaps it is because our economy is so diversified and competitive that it is fundamentally so stable

As to the ability of large concerns to administer prices because of their concentrated, oligopolistic character—a point which is crucial to Galbraith's argument—there are several major rejoinders. For instance, George Stigler, one of America's experts in the study and prevention of monopoly, reaches far different conclusions on a major investigation for the National Bureau of Economic Research. He and his coauthor James Kindahl say,

> The main thrust of the doctrine of administered prices is that contradictions in business lead to no systematic reduction of

industrial prices.... A great majority of economists have accepted this finding even though no explanation for this behavior of oligopolists commands general assent. Prices of concentrated industries do not respond to reductions in demand, or so it is believed. We raise grave doubts of the validity of this belief.[38]

The conclusion reached after focusing on "concentrated" industries in the period between 1957 and 1967 is that "'administration' is not a significant phenomenon."[39] It is important to note that in this study, and in the one we are about to mention, vast empirical evidence is gathered and analyzed. In contrast, Galbraith tends to assert a thesis that seems obvious enough to him, and evidently to others, without including any empirical study of his own. Indeed, his list of citations of seminal empirical studies done by others to bear out his thesis is also rather slim.

Nutter and Einhorn, in their update of a very important earlier study called *Enterprise Monopoly in the United States,* come to vastly different conclusions from Galbraith. They compare the economy as it was in 1899 with what it was in 1958. In 1899, 17.4 percent of the national income was gained by monopolistic enterprises, 76.1 percent by those that were workably competitive, and 6.5 percent by those run or regulated by the government. In 1958, the rundown was as follows: 11.5, 66.4, and 21.5 percent. If somewhat broader criteria of monopoly or oligopoly are used, the percentages come out as 16, 62, and 22 percent. From the perspective of this study, then, monopoly has actually decreased while the share of government enterprise has increased decidedly. The authors go on to place government efforts under the monopolistic or competitive rubrics. If this is done, the roughly 22 percent of national income accounted for by the government allocated to the two columns makes the final tally: 18 percent of national income is accounted for by monopolistic and 82 percent by competitive enterprises. Indeed, the share of national income provided for by monopolistic corporations fell by 6 percent from 1899 to 1959. Nutter and Einhorn are very careful to insist that measurement of monopoly is a tricky business. They introduce many qualifications and are not doctrinaire in their conclusions. Indeed, they indicate that the picture can look very different depending on definitions of monopoly, and they provide different percentages for each definition. But their findings point to the prevalence of a high degree of competition in the American economy.[40]

M. A. Adelman, in a study of the growth of concentration, reaches many of the same conclusions. He cautions that the tendency to cite statistics about the largest 100 or 200 corporations and the corporate assets they control is very misleading. First, the industries of big companies are not the industries with the highest levels of concentration. Further, "the huge size of a given company tells nothing about the rivalry it faces, the kind of market it lives in, or its price–output pattern."[41] His conclusion, after cataloging the technicalities involved in measuring concentration, is that the concentration ratio has remained basically the same over the last century. The most interesting problem, he maintains, is why this is so, given the waxing and waning of business cycles, antitrust policies, war, and peace.[42]

A final part of the Galbraithian thesis, which represents a broader spectrum of what we have called left-wing Keynesianism, is that large corporations, through their oligopolistic power, are secure sovereigns of the marketplace because they can generate their own investment funds and their leadership, the technostructure, is so firmly entrenched that it cannot be challenged from inside or outside. Public stockholders are disenfranchised to the point where management need not pursue profitability but can run the business in a manner in which they can comfortably perpetuate themselves in power. Further, because of their great power, these corporations block any new "growth" industries from entering the market to produce new products or to challenge the giants by producing old products. In a slashing rebuttal to this argument, Peter Drucker documents the emergence of realities that "could not have happened" within the framework of Galbraith's "conventional wisdom." First, he traces the wave of recent "takeover mergers." These mergers are

> forced upon a reluctant, and often loudly resisting, management by organizing a stockholders' revolt against it. And the one who takes over is almost invariably a very much smaller company, a total out-

sider—indeed a brash newcomer who did not even exist a few years earlier.... In effect, the "takeover" is far less a merger of businesses than a *coup d'etat*. A guerilla leader, himself owning practically no part of the company he acquires, gets the outside shareholders of large publicly-owned companies to oust their own "professional business management" and put him into the saddle.[43]

Drucker goes on to list the number of old and established giants whose technostructure has succumbed to such strategies, among them Jones and Laughlin Steel, Youngstown Steel, and United Fruit. Drucker then goes on to chronicle the "new growth" companies that have virtually come from nowhere to create new markets for new products and to challenge larger corporations operating in the old markets. Besides the more obvious science-based industries producing new products, such as photocopiers, computers and microchips, he notes the less obvious new growth companies in finance, franchise restaurants, magazine and book publishing, nursing homes and hospitals, and prefabricated housing.[44]

These mergers and new growth industries are both a cause and an effect of competition for investment capital. Established, large corporations are willing to merge because they find themselves under pressures they cannot ignore. "They are unable to attract resources they must have to survive and which they cannot generate just by being big and established."[45]

Although the dramatic examples listed by Drucker may be rather overdrawn, they do throw doubt upon the rather facile allegations of the Galbraith thesis. Indeed, the calmer orthodox mainstream represented by writers such as Samuelson and Dorfman take seriously the theses proposed by the left-wing Keynesians and even those proposed by a few of the neo-Marxists. And though their conclusions are less clear-cut than those of the writers we have just cited, they do bolster the notion that there is such a thing as competitive capitalism. After Samuelson deals with the Galbraith trilogy, he admits that economics will never be quite the same as before.[46] But he qualifies Galbraith's theses sharply and concludes by arguing that the American economy is "workably competitive" and can be made more so.

"Just as concentration in control of share of market was made to decrease from 1900 to midcentury, so by century's end can monopoly imperfections be weakened further."[47] And, dealing with the theory of the firm, Dorfman cautiously opines that the firm must still work at maximization of profit, a sign that the firm is operating in a competitive context. "On balance, the maximization hypothesis is not as firmly grounded in the facts of life as a fundamental hypothesis should be. But substantial and prolonged divergences from the behavior it implies are rare, particularly in industries with many participants. It therefore can still be entertained as a sound working hypothesis."[48]

Even Robin Marris, whose book *The Economic Theory of Managerial Capitalism* continued the Cambridge, England, thesis that there is no such thing as competitive capitalism in the industrial sector, has had a change of heart. Marris, now head of the economics department at the University of Maryland, describes himself as "an old English socialist on the run from the consequences of his own beliefs."[49] He concludes an essay on the present state of capitalism by asserting: "As a matter of fact industrial concentration has barely increased since World War II....So right now, whatever we choose to see as the evils of 'private' sector concentration are not getting worse."[50] Moreover, what concentration there is now "does not necessarily lead to less competition; often subdivisions of powerful conglomerates pose major competitive threats to established oligarchs."[51]

It seems to me—admittedly from a lay point of view—that the mainstream viewpoint is persuasive on this matter of monopoly versus competition. It is no doubt true that the critics, from Marxists such as Sweezy to left-wing Keynesians such as Galbraith, have grasped a measure of truth about the vast reality of the American economy. But I believe that measure is small in relation to the total picture. The American economy today is far more workably competitive than the critics argue. In fact, I am inclined to believe that the tendency in this century has been toward more competition rather than less. There are compelling reasons for this tendency, which may be summed up under three headings: transportation, technology, and information.[52]

111

The great increase in the ease of transport is a crucial factor for increasing competition in the modern world. Ship, rail, and air transportation have vastly improved in recent times and have cut down the kinds of monopoly dependent upon geography. This has been immensely significant because it has meant that competition has been extended from the local to the national and then outward into the world context. Local food stores face stiff competition from regional and national chains that can compete strongly with a notoriously small margin of profit. Further, the consumer now has wheels and can seek out the best product for the least price. But as general food shopping has been dominated by the supermarket, large interstices have opened up for the emergence of specialty shops—delicatessens, ethnic groceries, natural foods, convenience shops. These have proliferated along-side supermarkets.

This widening of the market because of transportation advances has occurred in almost every product one can think of and has resulted in fierce competition that has brought excellent products for low cost to most consumers. The large, diversified companies take part in this competition. Because they do have extensive financial resources and because their competitors are aggressive in developing and marketing new products, they enter into new markets vigorously. Transportation has made local and regional monopolies scarce indeed.

But the broadening of the competitive market to the world scale is perhaps even more important in fostering competition. Even though there are efforts at protectionism on the part of nations, it is impossible for them to seal themselves off from the pressures of a worldwide market. Corporations once holding oligopolistic power in the production of autos, steel, computers, aircraft, textiles, electronic equipment, photo duplicators, tires, heavy equipment, banking, to name but a few, are now facing stiff competition from foreign competitors. There are reasons why older steel plants in the U.S., England, France, and Belgium are closing down. (There may indeed be some unfair "dumping" going on but I suspect that is not the main reason for the difficulties of the older steel-producing operations.) As a world market has emerged, consumers—at least those in the developed countries—have choices of products from many different nations, choices that preclude any simple control of the market by whatever giants may be operating at home. If Detroit will not produce high-quality small cars, Audi, BMW, Fiat, Peugot, or Datsun will. Barring gigantic increases in tariff protection, domestic oligopoly will be increasingly eroded.

Technological advances in research, production, quality control, and marketing play almost as important a role in undermining oligopoly as transportation. New or better products that can compete with or substitute for the old are constantly appearing on the market. This leads to market interpenetration, which reduces monopoly power. Steel is again a good example. A high price for steel creates an incentive for other enterprises to produce substitutes such as concrete, aluminum, plastic, and plywood which can compete with steel for many uses. Large and small companies penetrate each other's market in photo duplicators, computers, watches, cameras, and other products. And it is not true that innovative breakthroughs come only from the giants. Xerox had only $15 million in sales as late as 1960. Texas Instruments came from nowhere. MacDonalds hamburgers were unknown in the early 1960s. Microchips are following the same pattern. A large number of small companies are involved in innovation and production in a highly competitive atmosphere. This market creation and interpenetration operates not only in the production of durable goods, but also in the provision of services. As more of the economy shifts over to services we get more innovation, and therefore more competition, in those areas.

Even as transportation and technology have made for more competition from the producer side, increased knowledge has stimulated competition from the consumer side. The increase in consumers' knowledge generated by consumer research organizations, consumer advocates, the widespread evaluation of goods and services by newspapers, magazines, and television, and ubiquitous advertising, with all its ambiguities, has almost certainly sharpened the critical faculties of most people so that they get more and better products for their money. The tremendous increase in the scope of communication also broadens the consumers' knowledge of products produced around the world which may be available to them. Fewer and fewer people are susceptible to exploitation by monopoly power. They are much more likely to be exploited as consumers by public or publicly regulated monopolies, where they have no choice, than by those operating in the private sphere.

Thus, from my point of view, these worldwide forces effectively counteract tendencies toward oligopoly and monopoly. Recitations of bigness—the top 500 corporations control this and that—are not necessarily demonstrations of monopoly power. The necessary scales of production and the size of the market are crucial factors in assessing their behavior. Competition is and can be an adequate regulator of the economy. The competitive market does provide an effective mode of economic choice. There is such a thing as a competitive market system. Capitalism in that sense is alive.

We have now dealt (it is up to the reader to decide how adequately) with the question of competitive markets, and we must move to a discussion of democracy. Given our earlier definition, can we say that the adjective "democratic" in the political economy of democratic capitalism is descriptive of our actual practice? That is, is the political system based upon consent, is it representative of the majority's wishes and responsive to the rights of minorities, does it preserve a large sphere of private liberties, and is it ordered by a constitutional framework that ensures these elements by law? It would of course demand an entire book to answer these questions fully and adequately. For our purposes, however, a broad and general analysis must suffice.

The critics we have surveyed would be sharply divided on these questions. The division would come over the issue of whether or not political power has sufficient broadly based power in relation to private economic power to constitute an authentic democracy. Marxists and neo-Marxists tend to argue that it does not and that what we term democracy is a sham. Sweezy, Habermas, and Marcuse, among others, would argue, as

114

we indicated earlier, that all we have is "formal" democracy. The external marks are there, but the substance is determined by monopoly economic power. The formal characteristics of elections, constitutions, rights, and so on are important to preserve, but they veil the fact that private economic power decisively determines the political agenda. The existence of these formal "bourgeois" mirrors should not blind us to that fact. Elections are dominated by parties beholden to the monopolists and the candidates put forth offer no real choice. Repression—sometimes, as in Marcuse's view, "repressive tolerance"—blocks any independent political movement that would make a difference. Private life, with its liberties and comforts, is substituted for active, substantive political life. The legal framework tends to protect the interests of the ruling classes. Indeed, the political sphere is simply a projection of private monopoly power dressed up in the high-sounding, but ineffectual, finery of bourgeois ideology.

The democratic socialists we have mentioned—Harrington and Galbraith—and their many compatriots in the intellectual subculture, would not be so pessimistic about political possibilities. There is potential based on universal suffrage for organizing political movements with a difference. Most would even countenance operating within one of the traditional American parties as the Democratic Socialist Organizing Committee actually does. Although the present parties do not offer enough choice, changes may occur that will enable the democratic process to come up with an authentic socialist alternative that will aim at democratizing economic as well as political life. For democratic socialists, the democratic method of consent, the legal protection of private and public rights, and the rights of minorities guaranteed constitutionally are precious. They are not bourgeois formalities but are the result of centuries of human struggle. They cannot be sacrificed in any shortcut to socialism. They constitute protection from and leverage on private economic power.

Regardless of the existence of these important levers, however, government policy is still under too much control by oligopolists. For Galbraith, the technostructure that operates the new industrial state is equally at home in both industry and government; its priorities are the same in either capacity. These priorities lead to private opulence and public squalor. For Harrington, an all-pervasive government follows the agenda of corporate collectivism. So, while there is a vast difference among our critics in their evaluation of political possibility and of the value of "bourgeois rights," both wings tend to agree that *at present* political life is dominated by the needs and wishes of private economic power.

But is this so? To a certain extent, of course, it is because it would be totally irrational for a government to adopt policies that were plainly destructive of its economic apparatus. The government of any state with any kind of economy must be attentive to the needs of its economic engine. To a certain extent, what is good for General Electric is good for the country. Production and employment are crucial concerns for any government, and it would be foolish for it to go sharply counter to the agencies that provide them.

But to a great extent it is untrue that public power fits hand in glove with the agenda of private corporations. First of all, it is remarkable how often the Democratic party is elected to govern when it is invariably opposed by the vast majority of large and small business concerns. The corporate elite are almost always Republican in orientation and support the Republican candidate. Democrats generally propose various regulative and redistributive programs, and these are certainly not favored by most of the corporate elite. Moreover, the election of Carter in 1976 showed that even established Democrats were not immune to voter revolts. Carter was viewed with suspicion by mainstream Democrats and Republicans alike. Political elections do not reflect the wishes of the corporate elite in the majority of cases.

More important, the actual legislative programs put forward since the New Deal are replete with regulatory and redistributive schemes universally opposed by the corporate elite. Indeed, the macroeconomic management of the economy itself with its deficit spending and government programs were objects of scorn by the business community. Social security, progressive taxation, antimonopoly legislation, and stiff taxes on corporate profit historically have all been opposed by private economic power.

But this is all history with which even recalcitrant Republicans have come to terms. What about the record of the government since the Second World War? It has been a record of continuous public intervention into the workings of the economy, in terms of both regulation and redistribution. In regulation we see the inception and growth of the Interstate Commerce Commission, the Federal Aviation Administration, the Equal Opportunities Commission, the Environmental Protection Agency, the Occupational Safety and Health Administration, and the Department of Energy, to name but a few. In the years since World War II we have witnessed several waves of antimonopoly efforts by the Justice Department. These developments make it difficult to believe that political power is simply beholden to the corporate elite.

The record is even more dramatic for efforts at welfare and redistribution. Kirsten Grønbjerg, in a recent book on the extension of welfare, concludes that there has been a significant increase in the perception of the rights of the poor by public authorities. Further, the recognition of these rights in legislation of concrete programs has brought about a situation in which transfer payments to the poor have grown at a very rapid pace. Indeed, if the percentage of our national income devoted to welfare continued to increase at the rate of the 1960 to 1970 increase, the whole budget would be swallowed up by 2016.[53] Although there is little chance of this happening, Grønbjerg's study points out the dramatic expansion of the public sector.

Drucker makes the same point:

> In the fiscal year ending June 30, 1975, welfare spending by all governmental agencies in the United States—federal, state, and local—amounted, according to the Social Security administration, to $287 billion.[54]

He goes on to add other kinds of welfare expenditure to the total and concludes, "The total expenditure for 'public' services, which are in effect, 'transfer' payments from the wage earner to the public sector, thus came to $700 billion, or close to 50 percent of

117

the gross national product of $1,450 billion."[55] This leads him to argue that

> There is no parallel in government history—certainly not in peace-time—to the expansion of public spending in the United States in the last fifteen years.... Fully adjusted for the declining purchasing power of the dollar, which was of course largely caused by this explosion of governmental spending and governmental deficits, we have increased governmental expenditures three- to four-fold with-in fifteen years, or doubled governmental spending, on average, every five or six years. And this even though defense spending—the main expenditure item of 1958—has been going down steadily as a proportion of the budget, as a proportion of national income, and, for ten years now, in real non-inflated dollars as well.[56]

Taking into account that there may be major disagreements about what one includes under welfare or redistributive meas-ures, there must be little doubt that these writers are pointing to real trends. The interests of many different groups, including those of the very poor, have been expressed through political and judicial channels. They have resulted in legislation that appro-priates a good deal of the national income for redistributive purposes. Indeed, with the exception of Sweden, it appears that the United States devotes a greater percentage of its national income to the public sector than any other nation, capitalist or socialist.[57] Although this is not to argue that the programs thus supported are either effective or sufficient, it does indicate that broadly based political power has independent status and lever-age over private economic power. As to the often used interpreta-tion that these are grudging concessions by the economic elite so that the capitalist order can keep going, it would appear that so many and great concessions call into question the fact of that elite's dominance. Certainly the captains of industry do not will such a transfer from the private to the public sector.

A recent book that surveys and analyzes the viewpoints of the corporate elite seems to bear out from the subjective side the fact that we have witnessed a steady encroachment of the govern-ment—which reflects the preferences of the majority of citizens—on the private sector. "While the critics of business worry about the atrophy of American democracy, the concern in the nation's boardrooms is precisely the opposite. For an executive, democracy in America is working all too well—*that is the problem.*"[58]

Therefore, it seems reasonable to claim that our case has been made for the competitive nature of the American economy and for the democratic character of American politics. Our economy can accurately be called "competitive" in the classical capitalist sense, though not perfectly competitive. Our polity can and does allow major interests to be expressed through the democratic process that are independent of the wishes of large corporate centers of power. We have a social system that can accurately be called "democratic capitalism."

BRIEF REFLECTIONS ON
ECONOMIC THEORY

As the inquisitive layperson delves into the debate on monopoly versus competition, he or she is bedazzled by the array of conflicting opinions. In the preceding discussion of the extent of competition in the American economy, we lined up scores of economic "experts" on either side. Like other contested issues, such as nuclear power, DNA and RNA research, limits to growth, and military strength, just to name a few, the experts can be lined up on either side of the issue in approximately equal numbers. This is also the case, I fear, with most economic issues. Unanimity in theory or practice is far from being accomplished. (Incidentally, when economists get testy about the alleged blindness and recalcitrance of their fellow disputants, they tend to accuse their opponents of being "theological" in their opinions, or, worse, of belonging in divinity schools! This of course insinuates that theology has no base in reality and is therefore a congerie of arbitrary opinion. My experience of the worlds of theology and economics leads me to caution the pot from calling the kettle black. Theologians seem certainly as sophisticated as economists in their methodological discussions concerning the role of normative and descriptive distinctions. And they reached such a level of sophistication far earlier than the economists. Further, their mode of reaching conclusions seems no more

119

arbitrary than that of their compatriots in economics. Witness the tremendous advances in the critical investigation of the Bible.)

As one looks beyond conclusions on more or less empirical problems like the extent of monopoly to the level of economic theory, the chaos increases. In the last decades whatever concensus there had been on the level of theory has been shattered. The reigning neoclassical economics has been challenged by "radicals" of both a left-wing Keynesian and neo-Marxist type. Value orientations, with their attendant political implications, have been vigorously inserted into the discussion of economic theory, particularly in its relation to ethics.

The mainstream of American economics—the neoclassical perspective—has been sharply attacked by the radicals. Its anthropological assumptions, especially those implying that humans always tend to maximize their utilities (they want ever more of their varied preferences), have been criticized. Its ethics is unrepentant utilitarianism. Marginal productivity theory is alleged to be oblivious to power relationships. Marginal utility theory is charged to have neglected the social determination of preferences. Neoclassical economics is positivistic in its assessment of human values; it views values as arbitrary, emotion-based preferences that are so subjective as to preclude rational discrimination. Its whole theoretical apparatus is a not-so-subtle apologia for capitalism hidden behind ostensibly value-free "positive science." It is imperialistic in applying its marginal analysis to politics, society, and family. Anyone who has a cursory acquaintance with the radical critique will recognize these arguments and will be able to add many others.

But the weaknesses of "radical" economics are just as numerous, and perhaps even more telling. Much of radical economics, particularly those proclaimed as Marxist, are not economics at all but a system of moral rhetoric that is useful for raising moral issues but has little analytic or prescriptive potency. With its insistence that economics is basically a system of belief, there is all too often a tendency toward the philosophy that "anything goes." There are no empirical problems amenable to reasonably objective analysis; there are only highly politicized subjects that are visible to those with the proper political credentials but invisible to those with "bourgeois" blinders. Further, there is a tendency to use Thomas Kuhn's notion of "paradigm" as a cover for sloppy thinking. Whether or not the paradigm of economics is changing, neoclassical marginal analysis remains the "normal science" of the day; its analytic and predictive capacities have been demonstrated by its usefulness in the work-a-day world. The adoption of many of its methods by Marxist regimes indicates its persisting usefulness; in the sense of day-to-day applicability there is no "Marxist" economics. So goes the neo-classical response.

How do we emerge from this cacophony of ideologies? There are, I suspect, no simple answers. But Paul Heyne, in a fine article called "Economics and Ethics: The Problem of Dialogue," gives us some helpful signposts. He argues that science is a social activity, and the cardinal rule of such activity is the obligation to submit conclusions without reservation to the critical examination of others. Scientific knowledge grows by testing, and it is the scientists who do the testing. And, in Heyne's opinion, the mainstream economists have a better record of openness to criticism than do the radicals. They have encouraged the publication of radical criticism, have paid attention to it, and have publicly responded to it. Although many of their conjectures are just that, they are *warranted* conjectures because they have withstood attempts at critical refutation. "The accusation of official indifference or conspiratorial silence in the face of radical criticism simply cannot be sustained by anyone who pays attention to what economists have actually been doing in the last decade."[59]

My own impression has been similar, even though it is from an admittedly limited (in comparison with that of professional economists) exposure to the economic literature. It is difficult for me to think of Paul Samuelson as a wooden ideologist who refuses to take up serious criticism. It is clear that his economic perspective is based firmly on the neoclassical paradigm; but it is also clear that challenges coming from outside that paradigm are brought into the discussion. Indeed, my impression is that the mainstream tends to soften and qualify its judgments carefully, allowing room for a margin of error. Such recognition of ambiguity seems lacking in the radicals. Indeed, it seems lacking in Galbraith. The more dispassionate, cautious opinion resulting from dialogue with many perspectives seems to characterize those who are alleged to be on the defensive more than it does those who are claiming to bring forth a new paradigm, which is by its very nature uncertain and amorphous.

Thus, I see no "new" economics that provides a better view of the extent of monopoly in the United States than does that relying on traditional methods. Although I would not want my assessment of democratic capitalism to rest upon the philosophical assumptions of many of its neoclassical defenders, I do accept the relative accuracy of their *description* of the American economy. Until the new paradigm becomes clearer, if indeed it appears at all in the immediate future, I can only opt for the "normal science" of mainstream economics.

NOTES

1. As quoted in George Dalton, *Economic Systems and Society* (Middlesex, Eng.: Penguin Books, 1974), p. 18.

2. Paul Samuelson, *Economics*, 10th ed. (Tokyo: McGraw-Hill Kogakusha, 1976), pp. 17–18.

3. Ibid., p. 42.

4. Ibid., p. 56.

5. Dalton, *Economic Systems*, pp. 56–57.

6. Bannock, Baxter, and Rees, *Penguin Dictionary of Economics* (Harmondsworth, Eng.: Penguin Books, 1978), p. 184.

7. Joseph Schumpeter, *Capitalism, Socialism and Democracy* (New York: Harper & Row, 1940; 1975), p. 269.

8. Alan Gewirth, "Political Justice," in *Social Justice*, ed. Richard Brandt (Englewood Cliffs, N.J.: Prentice-Hall, 1963), p. 137.

9. Ibid., p. 136.

10. Ibid., p. 142.

11. Ibid., p. 145.

12. Paul Sweezy, *Modern Capitalism and Other Essays* (New York: Monthly Review Press, 1972), pp. 7–8.

13. Ibid., p. 104.

14. Ibid., p. 119.

15. Jürgen Habermas, *Legitimation Crisis*, trans. Thomas McCarthy (London: Heineman, 1977), p. 17.

16. Ibid., p. 23.

17. Ibid., p. 34.

18. Ibid., p. 38.

19. Ibid., p. 37.

20. Ibid.

21. Ibid., p. 36.

22. Ibid., p. 78.

23. Michael Harrington, "Corporate Collectivism: A System of Social Injustice," in *Ethics, Free Enterprise, and Public Policy* (New York: Oxford University Press, 1978), p. 43.

24. John Kenneth Galbraith, *American Capitalism* (Boston: Houghton Mifflin Co., 1956), pp. 32ff.

25. Ibid., pp. 177ff.

26. John Kenneth Galbraith, *The New Industrial State* (Boston: Houghton Mifflin Co., 1967), p. vii.

27. Ibid., p. 395.

28. Raymond Lubitz, "Monopoly Capitalism and Neo-Marxism," in *Capitalism Today*, ed. Daniel Bell and Irving Kristol (New York: Mentor, 1971), pp. 199ff.

29. Ibid., p. 204.

30. Ibid., p. 205.

31. Ibid., p. 209.

32. Ibid., p. 206.

33. Milton Friedman, *Capitalism and Freedom* (Chicago: University of Chicago Press, 1962), p. 133.

34. Ibid., p. 120.

35. Ibid., p. 121.

36. Ibid., p. 122.

37. Ibid., p. 123.

38. George Stigler and James K. Kindahl, *The Behavior of Industrial Prices* (New York: National Bureau of Economic Research, 1970), pp. 7ff.

39. Ibid., p. 8.

40. G. Warren Nutter and Henry Einhorn, *Enterprise Monopoly in the United States, 1899-1958* (New York: Columbia University Press, 1969), pp. 88ff.

41. M. A. Adelman, "The Two Faces of Economic Concentration," in *Capitalism Today*, p. 145.

42. Ibid., p. 147.

43. Peter Drucker, "The New Markets and the New Capitalism," in *Capitalism Today*, p. 61.

44. Ibid., p. 63.

45. Ibid., p. 66.

46. Samuelson, *Economics,* p. 512.

47. Ibid., p. 531.

48. Robert Dorfman, *The Price System* (New York: Prentice-Hall, 1964), p. 42.

49. Robbin Marris, "The Present State of Capitalism," *The New Republic* 176, no. 21 (21 May 1977): 39.

50. Ibid., p. 41.

51. Ibid., p. 40.

52. Paul T. Heyne, *Private Keepers of the Public Interest* (New York: McGraw-Hill, 1968), pp. 66ff.

53. Kirsten Grønbjerg, *Mass Society and the Extension of Welfare, 1960–1970* (Chicago: University of Chicago Press, 1977).

54. Peter Drucker, *The Unseen Revolution* (New York: Harper & Row, 1976), p. 177.

55. Ibid., p. 174.

56. Ibid.

57. Ibid., p. 178.

58. Leonard Silk and David Vogel, *Ethics and Profits* (New York: Simon and Schuster, 1978), p. 43.

59. Paul Heyne, "Economics and Ethics: The Problem of Dialogue," in *Belief and Ethics,* ed. W. W. Schroeder and G. Winter (Chicago: CSSR Press, 1978), p. 189.

7

The Virtues
of Democratic Capitalism

This chapter is the heart of our positive assessment of democratic capitalism. We will state the affirmative case as strongly as possible. In the following chapter we will take back a portion of what we have given in this chapter as we examine the challenges of and to democratic capitalism. Some of the strengths of democratic capitalism also constitute its weaknesses; indeed, many commentators believe capitalism will be buried by its successes, not its failures. But that discussion is yet to come. In this section we will assess democratic capitalism in the light of the principles of social philosophy we elaborated in Chapter 5. First, democratic capitalism as it is practiced in the United States will be scrutinized in relation to the instrumental values of efficiency and growth. Second, we will examine its contribution to the decentralization of power, to what we called earlier the "natural" equilibrium of power. We argued in our chapter on normative moral values that a just social system will prevent the concentration of power, and the overlapping of different kinds of power, in few centers. This is the "Protestant principle" in our perspective. The propensities of all humans, but particularly those operating in group contexts, are toward self-interested will-to-power. Therefore, power must be checked by power. Moral responsibility of human agents is a necessary element in any orderly social life, but it is not sufficient. Even the "best and the brightest" need to be held accountable by countervailing power. How does democratic capitalism fare in fostering a decentralization of power?

Third, democratic capitalism will be held up to the principles of justice that define the intentional role of the state. We will evaluate the achievements of democratic capitalism in relation to the principles of equal liberty, difference, and fair equality of opportunity. How have these principles been applied under democratic capitalism? We have argued earlier that the refinement and extension of these rational principles of justice constitute, from a Christian point of view, one of the ways by which the ultimate ethical norm of agape works in the world. Every system of justice is pressured by agape toward higher and broader achievements. Of course, agape is not the only element that presses toward greater justice, but it is one that cannot be neglected. Further considerations other than those listed above will creep into our discussion, but this brief description presents the main agenda for this chapter.

EFFICIENCY AND GROWTH

One of the great historical gifts of capitalism has been its relatively distinct separation of the economy from the polity. The logic of economic efficiency was unfettered from the feudalistic sociopolitical apparatus that had smothered the impetus toward innovative production and growth. Even such staunch critics of capitalism as Michael Harrington give it credit for this. "Only with the advent of capitalism and its separation of the political, economic and social systems was there a society that offered individual choice, the possibility of mobility, and an opportunity to rise above the status of one's birth."[1] These gains were made possible by the economic surplus achieved by increased economic efficiency and growth. We should not be overly sanguine, however, about the transition from feudalism to laissez-faire capitalism. It was no bed of roses, as numerous social historians of the industrial revolution have clearly pointed out. The record of unfair and inhuman treatment and of ruptured traditional communities is a sad one indeed. But the alternatives for ordinary people in stagnant, subsistence economies were even worse. And though we should not ignore the fact that a good deal of the human oppression was avoidable, the long-run effects of the transition were enormously helpful to the human project.

The positive long-run effects were made possible by increased efficiency in combining the factors of production, that is, under conditions of free competition entrepreneurs were enabled, indeed, forced, to follow economizing logic. Economic rationality was freed from traditional political and social constraints, and this meant quantum leaps in efficiency and growth. The free play of economic rationality relatively unfettered by other considerations continues to be one of the great, though not unambiguous gifts, of capitalism.

Intellectual critics of capitalism have been eager to point to the negative aspects of economic rationality and to ignore its positive effects: efficiency and growth. It should be stated, conversely, that many mainstream economists and practicing businesspeople are prone to the opposite weakness. But though there is no unambiguous case for economic efficiency and growth, there certainly is an ambiguously positive one. For is not the first task of an economic order to economize, to be as efficiently productive as possible? Its job is to produce the wealth which provides the possibility for civilization in its material and a good deal of its nonmaterial aspects. Without the economic engine, the train and all higher activities on it come to a halt.

Economic excellence is distinct, though not separate, from the political, moral, and aesthetic realms. It aims at so ordering available resources that a maximum of what is desired can be attained. As a business enterprise economizes in the quest for profit in a competitive context, it produces what consumers want. If it is good at economizing, it succeeds in combining the factors of production better than its competitors. It may find new ways of organizing production, it may invent new technologies of production, or it may create new products or market old ones in new ways. If the market in which it acts is reasonably competitive, competition will encourage the enterprise to be ever more efficient so that price comes closer and closer to cost. The ability to economize in this way is a great gift, for it opens up more possibilities for society. Economy in its deepest meaning "is part of the sense of proportion, of the fitness of things, which is an ideal of all human activity."[2]

Without making silly claims for the complete autonomy of economic rationality, it seems warranted to insist upon a provisional autonomy. It is clear to most people that the aesthetic realm, for instance, has its own rationale and criteria of excellence. So do the realms of scientific investigation, scholarship, politics, and athletics, to name a few more spheres of life. We recognize that it is possible to politicize those realms so heavily that their relative independence, with their corresponding criteria, are destroyed or seriously diminished. These realms can lose their reason for being if other considerations become too dominant. So it seems with economic theory and practice. If they are made to bear all the dimensions of human concern, they soon lose any potency of their own or they become so complex as to become completely ineffectual. Indeed, as economizing progresses, enough surplus is created so that those very concerns can be raised, both in economic theory and practice. But though they provide criteria for regulating, guiding, and limiting economic activity, they are no substitute for economizing activity itself.

This hard fact of life—that moral, social, and political gains are curiously dependent on the relative autonomy of economic efficiency—is what has been clearly recognized by democratic capitalism. The provisional autonomy given to economizing has led to what Joseph Schumpeter has called "creative destruction." The opening up of new markets, the development of new technology, and the improvement of organizational forms "incessantly revolutionizes the economic structures from within, incessantly destroying the old one, incessantly creating a new one. This process is what capitalism consists in and what every capitalist concern has got to live in."[3]

Creative destruction has its costs. Obsolete enterprises fail, jobs are lost, regions decline, cities lose some of their industrial base. Even creative new emergents have their ambiguous effects by changing social patterns. Thus, it is crucially important for both private enterprises and government to cushion and mitigate the disruptive effects of creative destruction. Perhaps in extreme cases it is even imperative to halt it. But such extreme intervention should be rare, for if it becomes common economizing itself is seriously hampered. Then society pays the cost of economic inefficiency in higher prices, higher taxes, increasing social friction, and diminished private- and public-sector possibilities. "Higher" values suffer in the demise of the instrumental value of efficiency.

Assar Lindbeck worries about bargaining becoming the primary factor in the system of production, thus severely damaging productive capacity itself.

> The losses in efficiency may be particularly pronounced if, as has already happened in some countries, we get an economic system where contacts and bargaining with government officials and politicians become more important for the successful operation of firms than the ability to pursue effective production, innovation and marketing. A national economy will be in serious trouble if the rate of return on bargaining with public authorities becomes higher than the rate of return on market activities, because managers of firms then start to "chase subsidies and protection," instead of "chasing profits" by attempting to gain higher efficiency in production and marketing. This is exactly what happened a long time ago in countries like Argentina and Uruguay; now some developed countries in the West, such as the United Kingdom, seem to be on the same track.[4]

It is not necessary for economists to denigrate politics in order to make this kind of argument. Inordinate denigration of politics—a strong propensity of the Chicago School of economic thought—does both those economists and democratic capitalism a great disservice. The Chicago economists tend to view political intervention as motivated by greed, narrow and irresponsible self-interest, and parasitical dependence.[5] This image of political motivation is ironically enough the mirror image of that which left-liberal thinkers project upon the business community. Neither projection is true. Indeed, political motivation can represent broader and authentic interests of the whole community. Political power can be based upon numbers, ambition, money, media, and moral cogency. In fact, it is usually based upon a mixture of these elements. But political logic is distinct from economic logic. It seeks to maximize the interest of its base, not by economizing but by appropriating a portion of the economic surplus for its cause. Economic logic must maximize its interest by economizing.

If we have made the case for democratic capitalism's legitimate commitment to economic efficiency, what have been the effects of that commitment? Let us begin with a very broad view. Andrew Shonfield, a British economist who, like Robbin Marris, has experienced a change of viewpoint about the prospects of democratic capitalism, has surveyed the whole field of North Atlantic democratic capitalism. Writing in the late sixties, Shonfield asserted:

> The advanced industrial countries of the Western World have during the 1950's and early 1960's enjoyed an extended period of prosperity for which it is impossible to find a precedent.[6]

He goes on to say that three factors can be identified which account for a good deal of the prosperity. Economic growth has been much steadier than in the past. The growth of production over the period has been extremely rapid. And third, the benefits of the new prosperity were widely diffused. These three factors have been undergirded by better macroeconomic management, a quickening pace of technological innovation, political stability, and a large expansion of trade among the advanced nations. [7] However, Shonfield notes that the United States has shared less successfully in these trends. It has had more recessions and has shown smaller rates of productivity and growth. There are many reasons for this poorer performance: a large military commitment, an aging industrial apparatus undisturbed by war destruction, difficulty in maintaining a technological edge when one is leading but being pursued by competitors who can make use of the technology already developed, and less decisive and skillful macroeconomic management.[8] Regardless of these qualifications, however, Shonfield concludes with an optimistic judgment on the future of modern capitalism.

If Shonfield takes a wide view over a short period of time, Schumpeter takes a wide view over a long period of time. Schumpeter believes that the case for capitalism has to take such a view, for short-run views tend to accentuate the fluctuations and neglect the dramatic achievements over the long run.

Capitalist production, he argues, has grown at the rate of at least 2 percent (his estimate is intentionally conservative) in the past century and can be expected to continue at such a rate or better. The cumulative result of this is remarkable.

> Now these [revolutions in production] each time result in an avalanche of consumers' goods that permanently deepens and widens the stream of real income although in the first instance they spell disturbance, losses and unemployment. And if we look at those avalanches of consumers' goods we again find that each of them consists in articles of mass consumption and increases the purchasing power of the wage dollar more than that of any other dollar—in other words, that the capitalist process, not by coincidence but by virtue of its mechanism, progressively raises the standard of living of the masses.[9]

This conclusion led him to make the famous statement: "The capitalist achievement does not typically consist in providing more silk stockings for queens but in bringing them within the reach of factory girls in return for steadily decreasing amounts of effort."[10]

It seems plausible that the dramatic rise in the standard of living of the masses in democratic capitalist countries is much more attributable to increased economic efficiency and growth than to redistributionist strategies. These strategies should in no way be undervalued; indeed, in many areas they should be stepped up. But the fact remains that adequate living standards for the great American majority are due to the economic efficiency and growth of the capitalist market economy. It has produced an ever-larger pie in which everyone's share is decidedly larger, a not insignificant achievement.

This point has been made by Arthur Okun in his provocative book, *Equality and Efficiency: The Big Tradeoff*. He writes:

> Roughly, at all points on the income scale, family disposable incomes in real terms (that is, corrected for inflation) have doubled

131

in the last generation. As a result of the rising tide of progress, any average or absolute measure of real family income records dramatic improvement. The poverty-line living standard that was out of the reach of 11 percent of Americans in 1973 would have exceeded the incomes of about one-third a generation ago.[11]

As an American economist of liberal inclination, Okun is not overwhelmed by the ethical virtues of capitalism, as the following quotation will indicate. In order for our society to be made tolerably just—and Okun takes as a touchstone of justice equality of result—democratic government must intervene. But even with these provisos, he concedes that capitalism provides the benefits of efficiency and growth that other systems cannot.

Indeed, the most confident prediction I can make about the American economic system is that it will evolve and adapt if its basic framework is preserved and strengthened rather than scrapped. The capacity to adapt gradually is the greatest virtue of our present mixed system. Reforming it and promoting its evolution are feasible objectives, and are far more attractive to me than scrapping it. The alternatives I can see threaten efficiency, and they promise a limited increase in equality only at the expense of dangerous and costly bureaucratization. Although the ethical case for capitalism is totally unpersuasive, the efficiency case is thoroughly compelling to me.[12]

Samuelson values the importance of efficiency and growth highly enough to put charts pertaining to them into the cover pages of his textbook. And the upshot of the diagrams indicates a gradual increase in both over the long run. Although competitors among the major advanced industrial nations have gained on us, the American economy still holds the leading position in real per capita gross national product (GNP). Moreover, if other measurements are used, such as the measure of economic welfare proposed by Nordhaus and Tobin, the trends remain much the same. That index, which includes measurement of pluses such as increased leisure and minuses such as ecological costs, shows slower growth than the GNP, but gradual and steady growth, nevertheless.[13]

It is not necessary to chronicle further attestations to the ability of American democratic capitalism to perform well in relation to the instrumental values of efficiency and growth. Most fair-minded commentators concede this, at least when American performance is viewed in the long run. Further, it seems that improvement of growth rates in lesser developed countries is tied to their improvement in advanced countries. This belies the stock criticism that development of the richer countries is at the expense of the poorer. We shall have another opportunity to delve into the theory of dependent capitalism more thoroughly in Part III. It is enough to say at this point that no less an authority on development than Arthur Lewis throws grave doubts upon this charge.

> When the developed countries are expanding, as in the thirty years up to 1913, the developing countries move ahead; when the developed are depressed, as they were for the nearly three decades that included the two world wars, the developing are almost at a standstill. And when the developed revive and grow faster than ever, as between 1950 and 1973, the developing also grow faster than ever.[14]

Another kind of frontal attack on the growth of wealth occasioned by more efficient production in the advanced countries is leveled by many ecologists, aristocrats, ethicists, and other social critics who argue that the growth of the national product has no positive correlation with the enhancement of the quality of life. Growth, they argue, simply proliferates the material content of our civilization. We get more advertising, more unnecessary differentiation of unnecessary products, more waste, and more vulgar consumer fetishism without any gain in the "higher" values that constitute quality of life. Again, there are disturbing truths in these objections that we will wrestle with later. But it is important at this point to counter some of the distortions that crop up in this popular criticism of capitalist growth.

First, it is not easy to draw the line that demarcates material from nonmaterial progress. Efficient production in a market economy lowers the price of most goods and services, making them available to more people. It seeks out and stimulates new needs and wishes. It creates and distributes an increasing amount of wealth for all classes so that they can purchase the goods and services that are produced. What is produced may be books, journals, classical records, organic foods, travel opportunities, beautiful design, or stereophonic equipment, as well as umpteen different kinds of toothpaste, dog food, cereal, gadgets, clothes, soaps, and toilet paper. Moreover, the surplus created by the economic system may be distributed by various agents to churches, symphonies, museums, drama groups, social clubs, ethnic organizations, colleges, charities, and political causes as well as to business enterprises that cater to their numerous consumer desires. The former part of the listings have to do with "higher" values, yet these goods and services are directly dependent on sufficient economic productivity to make them available cheaply to those who want them. They show up in the GNP.

Second, it is all too easy for intellectual critics to lampoon the economic system and its complicitous middle-class adherents for their doting over refined distinctions in soft drinks, shampoos, Styrofoam decorations, Detroit automobile models, TV quiz shows, and athletic contests. But these critics rarely complain about the elaborate differentiation in gourmet foods, wines, cheeses, books, journals, high-performance foreign cars, and housing arrangements (including summer cottages) that the fecund market also makes available. To the blue-collar worker, gradations in TV programs may mean a lot whereas the vast variety of French wines seems a useless waste. What truck driver knows or cares about the distinction between Stilton and Danish Blue cheese? But he will know the difference between Budweiser and Schlitz. What makes the differentiation in one set of products wasteful and in the other admirable? Further, that despised demon, advertising, is educating the middle and working classes into the tastes for goods and service thus far reserved for the upper class. "Higher" tastes are being diffused much more broadly than ever before. Advertising may create and shape consumer desires to a significant extent, but all that it creates and shapes is not automatically bad.

It would be terribly difficult to argue, rhetoric aside, that the quality of life has declined for the average citizen in the United States. The efficiency and growth brought on by the free market system have created expanding possibilities for that citizen. And these possibilities are not necessarily materialistic in any crude sense. But making fulfilling use of these possibilities is up to the person whose value system selects the possibilities to be pursued. No doubt there is pressure by advertising to buy what needs to be sold. No doubt consumer fads addle the brains of supposedly rational utility-maximizers. But persuasion is not coercion. We have a chance to choose. And I for one am not totally discouraged by the choices that are being made. Every time I am able to get beyond the stereotype of the "mad consumer" that appears in our social commentary to the flesh and blood person, I find that that person is not primarily concerned about procuring more and more low-level creaturely comforts. Usually far deeper concerns about family and personal health and fulfillment come first, followed by concerns about church, city, and country, with a commitment to ever-increasing consumerism far down the line.

There can be little doubt about capitalism's performance in relation to the economic values of efficiency and growth, at least up to this time. The free-enterprise market systems of the North Atlantic community, now joined by other rapidly developing countries, have produced an unmatched diversity and quality of goods and services at low prices. Advances in farming, industrial production of consumer goods, transportation, communication, medicine, and chemicals have been made almost exclusively by the free market countries. There has been a tremendous amount of inventiveness which has pulled living standards up for all. This has indeed enhanced the possibilities of civilization for more and more people. This fact has been undervalued or unrecognized by those critics of democratic capitalism who continue to believe that any fool can perform the economizing task and that those who can are dealing with lower level needs and wants. Meanwhile, of course, they do the more difficult and challenging things that deal with "higher" values. The social wealth produced by economizing does not guarantee a just or good society; but it is a precondition for such a society.

Perhaps in the future new systems of production will supplant the free-enterprise mode. Perhaps such a new system can do away with the injustice and disruption of "creative destruction." But that new system will also have to avoid the centralization of political and economic power in the state if it is to be any improvement on democratic capitalism. It will have to be economically efficient as well as socially nondisruptive. And on top of that, it will have to undergird the civil and political liberties that are now a part of democratic capitalism. It will have to encourage a diffusion of power, to contribute to the decentralized equilibrium of power that is already present. For free market practice does contribute to diffusion of power, one of our principles of social philosophy. It is to this subject that we now turn.

THE DECENTRALIZATION OF POWER—SUBSIDIARITY

In this section we aim to lift up the contributions of the free market economic system to the decentralized equilibrium of power that we consider to be one of the marks of the good society and, we believe, one of the necessary preconditions for the just society. In the next section we will assess the contributions of the state to both this equilibrium of power and movements toward intentional social justice. Here, however, we are concerned with indicating the ways in which American economic practice enhances the unconsciously coordinated equilibrium that characterizes the greater share of our economic, social, and cultural life. We argued in Chapter 5 that such a "natural" equilibrium is extremely important in limiting the will-to-power of private and public agencies. Such limitation partially carries out the "Protestant principle" element of our social philosophy. Although we cannot rely completely on the countervailing power inherent in the natural equilibrium, we must make use of it as much as we can since it cuts down the number of decisions the state must make, and thereby inhibits centralization of too much and too many kinds of power in the state.

It is very easy to point out the many ways in which our economic, social, and cultural lives are regulated and shaped by conscious intervention on the part of political agencies. However, the more remarkable fact is that we live our lives in spheres that are relatively free of such intervention. A good deal of the substance of our lives comes from our involvement in voluntary arrangements that, though unplanned and uncoordinated by the state, yet result in a fairly orderly harmony. Most of us work for private enterprises of a profit or nonprofit character whose decisions are made privately; we buy most of our goods and services from enterprises whose productive activities are basically self-determined; we procure our health care and housing through private arrangements. Many of us attend or teach in private schools. We belong to a startling variety of voluntary associations. We gain our information through a variety of media that are privately controlled, and we pursue our recreation and cultural enrichment primarily through private channels. In this many-faceted texture of life, we have an astounding measure of freedom to choose from among many offerings. And those who offer goods and services are in competition with other producers—they cannot coerce us into the choices we make. Indeed, this unconsciously coordinated equilibrium lends great "worth" to our liberty, to use Rawls's language. Our liberty is not abstract but is very concrete; it can be and is exercised significantly in all the areas listed above. Even the poorest have a measure of choice in these areas, though the "worth" of their liberty is greatly diminished by their lack of economic wherewithal.

But the important observation to be made at this point concerns the extent and vitality of this diffuse but orderly equilibrium. It is difficult to say whether the free market economic system is a cause or an effect of this dynamic equilibrium in the social and cultural spheres of life. No doubt it is a mixture of both; causation goes in both directions. But it is accurate to say that free market arrangements make a very important contribution to this decentralized but coordinated social system.

The first contribution relates to the economic task itself. Under free market capitalism the major economic tasks of American society are performed without direction from the political centers of power. Considering the massiveness of the economic task, this is an amazing accomplishment. The importance of this contribution is stated admirably by Assar Lindbeck. His statements deserve lengthy quotation.

> Most people seldom think about the enormous work which we, in fact, "ask" the market system to do for us: First, to tell producers about the preferences of consumers (via their demand in markets); second, to inform consumers (via prices formed by way of competition) about the lowest costs of providing different goods; third, to give firms incentives (via profits) to produce the goods which consumers want to have and are willing to pay the costs for, to economize in the use of resources, and to create new products and production techniques; and finally to coordinate billions of production decisions of millions of economic agents (via equilibrating market forces) so that the outputs of all firms fit not only the final demand by consumers but also the required inputs of other firms, at home and abroad.[15]

It is precisely the market system, assuming the existence of competition and free entry, that fosters a far-reaching decentralization of economic decisions. Without a reasonably well functioning market system, a decisive centralization of economic decision making would be necessary.

> This is perhaps easiest to see if we try to visualize what the economic system would look like without markets for goods, labor, and capital. For then it would be necessary to have some central agency that determines what the preferences of individual consumers were, or should be; that told firms how and what to produce, qualitatively and quantitatively; that decided to whom different goods and services should be delivered and what new products should be introduced. And in addition to all that, the centralized authority would also have to direct labor and capital to the sector where they were regarded as needed, as well as to see that billions of decisions by millions of different production units and households were reasonably consistent, so that production and consumption would not be disrupted by severe bottlenecks in the economy. Trying to visualize what this type of society would look like helps us to understand what a heavy reliance on markets has saved us from: a strongly centralized command economy, where pluralism could hardly exist because pluralism presupposes decentralized decision-making and a considerable autonomy of households, firms, and other organizations that are engaged in economic activities, including the production and distribution of information and of what we call culture.[16]

138

Thus, market arrangements make possible the achievement of the bulk of the economic tasks of society without undue political centralization. These arrangements limit the number of issues upon which explicit political decisions have to be made and hence on which it is necessary to achieve agreement. Further, the fewer issues on which agreement is necessary, the more likely it is that agreement can be reached while a free society is maintained. The society does not have so great a stake in the continuity and scope of decisive political power that it becomes dangerous and disruptive to countenance the change of government through elections or the challenge to government policy by organized dissent. It is difficult to stipulate at what point so many choices are located in the political sphere that elections and organized dissent become unwelcome. But it is not difficult to see that an inordinate number of such choices will increase political and social strife to threatening levels. When governmental income policies embrace most jobs in major industries in the private sector as well as those in the public sector, as is the case in Britain, every disagreement on economic issues becomes a confrontation with the government, with no mediating third parties. A highly chaotic situation ensues, with an implicit temptation on the part of the government, thus far not fully exercised, to impose industrial discipline by coercive power on unruly groups, be they labor or management. The danger of severe political confrontation, with all its threats to parliamentary democracy, increases as more economic decisions are pulled out of the market context for political disposal.

There are other considerable economic gains facilitated by market systems in addition to the avoidance of political centralization. Innovation is certainly one of these gains. Competition stimulates innovation in production and marketing techniques. Further, if entry to markets is kept open, entrepreneurs ferret out every unsatisfied desire for goods and services that may emerge from consumers and proceed to produce new goods and services for them. Although a lot of chaff is produced in such a process, much of the innovation is helpful and humanizing.

Thousands of firms are born every year into this dynamic and innovative system. Many die, but many do not. These firms, it turns out, are the major source of new jobs. In a comprehensive study of how jobs are created and lost in the United States economy, David Birch shows that small, young companies that employ fewer than twenty people and that are less than five years old are the most important source of new jobs.[17] This fact suggests why government attempts to create new jobs, or stem the decline of old ones, have proved so expensive and so relatively unsuccessful. Therefore, it seems that important gains in efficiency and significant growth in new employment are spinoffs of competitive, open market systems.

Further, as we argued earlier, a workably competitive market economy such as that of the United States provides restraint on private economic power. Producers must compete with each other for the various markets in which they operate. Competition is an effective restraint that would otherwise have to be provided by government regulation or control. And if it is true that competition has not declined in the way that many critics believe, and in fact may have increased, such unplanned countervailing power continues to be an important instrument for taming private power in the majority of cases. In cases where the market fails to limit private power or fails to deal with harmful externalities, government must of course step in.

A more ambiguous function of the market system, but one that is necessary, is its relation to what we earlier termed "creative destruction." As technology moves toward more efficient production, older systems, and the jobs connected with them, are sloughed off. It is estimated that the decline of jobs happens at a standard rate of about 8 percent a year across the United States, showing little variation between North and South, cities and suburbs.[18]

The social disruption connected with this "creative destruction" is caused by the operation of impersonal forces in a market system. Under the social arrangements of the private market, those who suffer losses—owners, investors, managers, workers— are not usually able to stand in the way of change. This is not to say that their losses should not be dealt with in a just and humane way by private business and government. But such creative destruction is utterly necessary for economic health, and under American democratic capitalism, it tends to take place in a depoliticized way. The "losers" cannot veto the economic change taking place, though they understandably try vigorously to do so. Thus, competitive market forces insist on the destruction of low-productivity plants and jobs. But the story does not end there. New plants with new technology are created with better and more productive jobs. Growth is achieved through the continuing destruction of bad jobs and their replacement with good ones. This process in the industrial sector, combined with the new jobs continually created by the birth of thousands of small firms, provides both employment and increased economic efficiency. Again, these gains have their accompanying losses that must be compensated for, but without impeding the process itself.

Britain provides an example of what happens when such creative destruction can be vetoed by the combined forces of unions and government.[19] These forces tend to prevent bad jobs from disappearing instead of financing new good jobs that can survive against international competition. In the short run nonproductive jobs are preserved, which means that in the long run the productivity of the entire economy is hampered. The chain reaction then begins. Organized power demands wages beyond productivity gains. The wages are granted, but the amount they will buy shrinks. Unorganized persons and moderate unions lose out because they can't or won't extract wage gains beyond productivity gains. Recriminations begin. Workers demand comparable wages across the board. Industrial strife increases. Because of all this, domestic industries have difficulty keeping up with foreign competitors. More subsidies for low-productivity industries are demanded. Capital flees the country for better pastures. The government must take over the role of investor, and it must make its decisions on the basis of political considerations which may not make the best economic sense. Meanwhile, the amount of public money available to finance social services remains stationary or declines. The health services, the school system, the publicly financed radio and television service, the arts, parks and playgrounds, and pension and welfare systems all become starved for funds.

Such are some of the outcomes of replacing the creative destruction prompted by market forces with job preservation schemes dictated by political power. This is an oversimplified picture of Britain's continuing industrial decline. There are many causes, among them a deep cultural preference for quiet security and leisure over the more active life. But this picture is not far from the truth. The economic changes necessitated by market forces have been impeded by political power since more and more economic choices are made in the public, political arena and not in the private, impersonal marketplace. Economizing suffers when political decisions replace economic ones. Fortunately, American society has not politicized economic choice to the extent that Britain has, and therefore it allows creative destruction to take place within the competitive market system where the "losers" have less capacity for veto. Moreover, because of the productivity gains of the process, our public sector can cushion significantly its untoward effects through unemployment compensation and job retraining. Further strategies for mitigating these effects are necessary, and we shall speak of them later.

Another contribution of the American market system to the economic task is its ability to direct innovation into socially desirable directions. Charles L. Schultze, in an important effort to catalog the public uses of private interest, puts it this way:

> It is not simply that market incentives and the price system stimulate new technologies in general, but that they tend to direct invention toward conserving those resources which are scarce.... Most economic analysis of the nature of inventions suggests that they tend to occur in very rough conformity with economic needs and scarcities as signaled by prices and profitability.[20]

If, in the future years, market arrangements are allowed to signal accurately the real costs of energy, we can expect innovation in the kinds and use of energy. The same could be said regarding problems of pollution, congestion, and modes of transportation. Unfortunately, our tendency to cushion ourselves against short-term rises in price usually leads us to inhibit the development of the very innovations that increased prices and profitability might make possible.

A final important virtue of market arrangements in achieving economic purposes is that they "reduce the need for compassion, patriotism, brotherly love and cultural solidarity as motivating forces behind social improvement."[21] Thus, in addition to cutting down the need for political direction of economic choices—which leads to centralization and bureaucratization—market systems allow us to economize on the amount of moral consensus needed to run the economic engine.

Interestingly enough, many commentators of different persuasions make this point. However, this is not the time to take up the debate over quality of motivation. The point to be made now is this: Market systems, by relying on voluntary exchange relationships based on self-interest, decrease the need for consensus on the moral, ideological, and social level. They contribute to the decentralization of power by making it unnecessary to have cultural and moral agreement. The economic task is done without such consensus. Economies that do not rely on market arrangements must either presuppose or impose such a consensus. The first option is unavailable to the United States and the second is unacceptable. By relying on market arrangements, we can live more comfortably with our pluralism, and thereby resist the temptation to impose a specific value system on our people.

In summary, then, market arrangements get the bulk of our economic work done without demanding political omnicompetence by the government. This avoids social strife by decreasing the number of economic decisions that have to be made in an already overburdened political sphere. The market reduces the risk of government tyranny, since it obviates the need for the government to have enough power to know about economic matters, decide on them, and make those decisions stick. Its competition provides a needed restraint on private power, freeing the government to deal with cases where competition fails. Further, it shields the government from having to make some most painful decisions regarding obsolescent industries and jobs. Positively, market arrangements increase the likelihood that the

143

economy will be innovative and efficient. So there is a great deal to say for the performance of American market arrangements in diffusing power but yet getting the economic task done well. Ironically, though a number of Western democratic capitalist nations are busy politicizing an increasing number of economic decisions, Eastern European countries like Romania and Hungary are increasing the area of market operations.

> This problem—of encouraging initiatives to innovate—is probably the basic unsolved problem of nationalized economies, along with the problem of avoiding bureaucratization and a strong concentration of economic, political and military power in the same hands.... it is ironic that in Eastern Europe it is considered progressive and even radical to advocate greater reliance on markets, at the same time that in the West radicals regard their opposition to the market system as an important part of their ideology, in principle.[22]

Besides getting the economic job of society done without undue political centralization, the American system is instrumental in an even more important achievement. Its operation creates a rough system of "natural justice" that, though flawed and therefore in need of supplementation, is nevertheless a precondition for the more intentional efforts at achieving a greater justice. Without this rough substratum of "natural justice" undergirded by the free market system, the tasks of intentional justice would become extremely burdensome, if not impossible. For this rough system—unplanned and unconsciously coordinated—distributes elements of liberty and equality of opportunity fairly enough in the eyes of the majority of the population that it is accepted and affirmed. Again, as in the case of economic choice, the government is freed to concentrate on the breakdowns within the system of natural justice rather than to try to order the whole society according to its overarching principles of justice, a task which, if possible at all, would necessitate overwhelming political intervention.

This substratum of natural justice is an important source of the moral legitimation of American democratic capitalism. Indeed, let us recall the fact that we are reassessing the possibilities of democratic capitalism on the basis of moral criteria. In this section we are arguing that market arrangements—capitalism, if you will—contribute to a wide distribution of liberty and equality of opportunity. Again, it is impossible to disentangle the intertwined political, social, and economic contributions to this system of natural justice. But its existence is certainly not unrelated to the presence of free market arrangements.

What are the components of this natural justice for individuals? Rawls, as we have already seen, argues that justice is the fair distribution of liberty and equality. Liberty includes public and private liberties whereas equality includes the distribution of primary goods and opportunity. Let us take this differentiation as the agenda for our discussion. First, let us look at the contribution market arrangements make to the wide distribution of liberty for individuals and groups and then move on to considerations of equality.

There is a certain sense in which the economic liberty encouraged by the American economic arrangement constitutes freedom itself. In market economies such as ours, individuals are free to enter the market when and where they please. We can sell our goods or services to whomever or whatever we wish. In other words, we can choose our vocation. Of course, our freedom is limited by our own abilities and initiative as well as by what the market wants at a particular time. We have to make our choices judiciously and bear the risks of those choices. We have no license to be rewarded for activities that other people do not want. But we have a wide latitude of choice, and as long as the economy remains innovative and open, choices will continue to be wide. Further, on the consumption side, we are free to choose how our money is spent. Money is simply an exchange item, never an end in itself. It can buy many important things from primary goods to goods of "higher" value. It can support activities that are cultural or even spiritual. On the other hand, it cannot buy the most important qualities of fulfilling life: human love and friendship, aesthetic sensitivity, moral earnestness, or religious fulfillment. It can support activities that nurture such qualities, but these activities cannot guarantee the qualities.

The freedom to spend our money as we see fit enables us to live according to our chosen values—to choose our sources of information, to live where we want, to support the institutions and causes we hold dear, to participate in recreational activities we like, and to carry on a family life with as much human richness as possible. The American system, with its considerable autonomy of persons and households, maximizes choices in all of these areas. Again, these choices are limited by our incomes, by governmental taxation, and by what the market offers. But multiple choices and the possibility of their realization are present. The economic freedoms we have are part and parcel of freedom in general, a fact which escapes many critics who believe that economic freedom relates only to lower, "material" needs.

It has also been argued, most persuasively by Milton Friedman, that market arrangements under American capitalism are an important support for political freedom of dissent. They can and do support the freedom of individuals and groups "to advocate and propagandize openly for a radical change in the structure of society—so long as the advocacy is restricted to persuasion and does not include force or other forms of coercion. It is a mark of the political freedom of a capitalist society that men can openly advocate and work for socialism."[23] Conversely, there is little freedom in socialist societies for the advocation of capitalism. Friedman argues that a fundamental protection for dissent offered by capitalism is the existence of a private market economy in which dissenters can earn a living. "No one who buys bread knows whether the wheat from which it is made was grown by a Communist or a Republican, by a Constitutionalist or a Fascist, or, for that matter, by a Negro or a White. This illustrates how an impersonal market separates economic activities from political views and protects men from being discriminated against in their economic activities for reasons that are irrelevant to their productivity."[24] Further, dissenting groups have access to many private sources of money to finance their organizations and causes. In a large pluralistic society such as the United States, many independent foci of support—from wealthy patrons to poor students—are available to causes in lurid variety, some imaginable and others not. Moreover, sometimes it is not even necessary to convince people or financial institutions of the soundness of the ideas to be propagated. It is only necessary to persuade them that the venture can be financially successful since the competitive publisher, for example, cannot afford to publish only writing with which he or she agrees.

The existence on the American scene of private educational institutions and philanthropic foundations provides further sources of public criticism and dissent. All kinds of "subversive" ideas and movements are generated from such contexts. As Schumpeter argued, the wealth of capitalist society allows the expansion of education and the intellectual class, one of whose stocks in trade is criticism. However, we should not exaggerate the extent of the space for criticism offered by private money. Private money can also be withheld from unpopular causes, and private employment can be denied known dissenters. But the private economic sphere does provide an important buffer from public power which can also be discriminatory, and in a much more devasting way if there is no private sphere in which to subsist. One would no doubt rather be a Maoist propagating Maoism in the United States or Britain than a libertarian propagating capitalism in Russia, Cuba, or even Tanzania.

From a moral point of view—Christian or otherwise—the role of such dissent is extremely important. Private support for dissenting organizations in the United States makes possible what Niebuhr called "prophetic minorities." Based upon self-interest or altruistic concerns for justice or a mixture of both, these groups constitute one of the important facets of the conscience of the nation. They can bring the fire of transcendent judgment into the myopic interplay of self-interest. They can pronounce the "No" when it needs to be said, and provide sources of agitation for needed change. Historically, many of the improvements of the American social order have come from these agencies, either through their own activities or through their insistence that the government act. Cause-oriented voluntary associations have been an indispensable instrument of democratic social change, and they have existed because people have had the freedom to dispose of a significant amount of discretionary income according to their own interests and values.

If American market arrangements support the private and public liberties of individuals and groups, they also distribute economic opportunity widely. In fact, they proliferate opportunity and allow millions of agents to pursue those opportunities according to their own interest, abilities, and initiative. A tremendous dispersion of economic opportunity has been the hallmark of American society for the majority of individuals and families. And even in the many cases where there was little "fair" equality of opportunity—where people did not enter the race at the same starting line—there was opportunity to better oneself. This widespread opportunity to better oneself has been and continues to be the great drawing card of America. It is the center of the American Dream. I believe it is *the* most important element that a society, or an economy, can offer. In the eyes of average people it far outweighs strategies of intentional redistributive justice. And the lived experience of the great majority of the American people in the past and present is one of greater or lesser social mobility. A large country socially and geographically, a high degree of freedom, an open and fecund market, and millions of enterprising newcomers have encouraged the dominant American experience of social mobility.

Social mobility has created a social fluidity that has prevented rigid classes from developing. American society certainly does have discernible classes, but membership in them is generally not permanent. The opportunities offered by the social system opens up chances for betterment for the vast majority. As these opportunities are grasped and betterment is experienced, there is little opportunity for class consciousness to develop. The resentment with a capital "R" that has been so much a part of societies with a more traditional past and with less mobility has been avoided in American society. In addition, social mobility and its attendant lack of class consciousness has contributed to the fluidity in political allegiance. The parties have shifting constituencies that are the bane of those who want sharper ideological differentiation in American politics. A healthy market system has inhibited political polarization that follows from rigid social classes.

There has been a powerful "dark side" to the American experience; mobility has exacted its costs, many people have not been able to achieve mobility, there have been serious disruptions in economic life, and sections of the population—black people for instance—were not allowed to participate freely in the quest for betterment. This "dark side" needs to be made visible to American society, and that need is being met profusely. The exploration of the "dark side" in historical research, art, the news media, plays, and movies has been so intense that it has led many Americans, and foreigners for that matter, to believe that the "dark side" has been normative. But if that were the case, there would have been a revolution long ago. At the very least, people would have quit coming to American shores or, as it happens at present, infiltrating our borders. It is not morally lax to insist that a good deal of natural justice has been experienced through the proliferation of opportunity. That has been the normative experience. The "dark side" must be attended to with moral and political earnestness; but if strategies of improvement are constructed for the majority solely out of interpretations of the dark side, serious distortions are likely to occur. More "social problems" are found and targeted for governmental solutions than are actually extant. We have enough difficulty grappling with the problems we really have, without producing issues that do not exist. (This brings to mind the case of the small-town library in Iowa that had to close for lack of federal funds because it did not have facilities for the handicapped even though there were no handicapped people in the village.)

Thus, the market system, decentralized and unconsciously coordinated as it is, generates a wide distribution of economic opportunity. It further rewards the efforts made by individuals to take advantage of the opportunities offered, and it does so without central political direction. A rough system of justice based upon market exchanges distributes income according to the contributions of various agents.

The market, as we have noted earlier, is a system of economic

mutuality characterized by voluntary exchange. One party supplies a good or a service to someone who wants it for the price he
or she is willing to pay. Economic enterprises do the same thing.
There is a competitive context in which suppliers and purchasers
make their offers. Like human mutuality, economic mutuality, if
voluntary and informed, betters the situation of all those involved. Market arrangements reward the excellence by which
one party supplies what someone else wants or needs and is
willing and able to pay for. The greater the want or the need
dictated by demand in the marketplace, the greater the reward
for services delivered well. Thus, in this age able economists seem
to be paid highly, as are doctors, lawyers, executives of large
companies, skilled craftsmen and women, and professional
basketball players, among many others. Many more of us are paid
more moderately. Some contributions to the economy, such as
those made by dishwashers and low-level secretaries, are very
modestly paid because there is such a large supply of people who
can offer these services. Thus, the calculus of economic mutuality
works out to reward most those who supply the greatest wants
and needs best. Income is distributed according to such a system.
There are, of course, distortions introduced by monopoly, by
limiting access to the market, by discrimination, and by other
factors. But in a rough sense, economic reward is proportional to
economic contribution.

Reward is therefore unequal. This inequality results from a
number of things. Tastes and preferences of consumers dictate
unequal rewards; some goods and services are wanted and
needed more than others. But a good deal of the inequality is on
the supply side—the side of the productive agents. Inequality
results from the adverse or favorable social environments that
shape agents. Inequality results from the difference in the extent
of talents given out in the natural lottery. But inequality of income
results also from choices made by productive agents. Persons, in
their self-transcending freedom, must not necessarily succumb to
adverse circumstances or to a two-talent share dealt out by the
natural lottery. People can *decide* to better themselves in spite of
adverse circumstances and modest talents. Likewise, persons

150

from favorable social milieus with rich endowments of talents may decide to waste opportunity. And both sets of individuals are rewarded accordingly. Even more important in explaining unequal rewards, however, is the freedom of agents to choose their vocations, and their attendant incentive and reward systems. The vast majority of people do not want to make the kind of commitments it takes to become rich and powerful. They have other interests that are not correlated directly with an extremely high income. They are not economic marginal-utility maximizers. As some wag has put it, "There is a marginal utility from not bothering about marginal utility."[25] The bulk of American people want a comfortable standard of living, as they themselves define it, and improvements in that standard. But they choose patterns of life and vocations that are consonant with values related to their own and others' human fulfillment, values which are not consistent with those needed to gain very high incomes. Those who go after the high incomes need a different set of values and a good deal of luck.

There is a partial, but by no means complete, justice about this system. In fact, we could conceive of it being affirmed in Rawls's original position, which we discussed earlier. It is quite possible that persons in a position such as the one Rawls elaborates would choose market arrangements to establish a basic reward-for-contribution system. The market would deal out proportional rewards to those who satisfied best the needs and wants of the group. Different inputs garner different rewards according to the expressed needs and wants of the group. Accepting this as a basis, which has further virtues of efficiency and decentralization, the group could then correct the flaws. The least advantaged could be helped through transfer policies so that their prospects would be kept constantly rising. Further, fair equality of opportunity could be promoted through strategies of redress. Initial inequalities of wealth could be mitigated through taxation. The whole system could be made more fair even though it would have a modicum of fairness as part of its basic arrangement.

Participants in the original position assume that they have different conceptions of the good life; the substantive ends that their freedom is used to pursue varies. They do not opt for what Rawls calls "perfectionism," since such an option threatens private and public liberties. The market, then, would be left to distribute income in accordance with the plurality of values— conceptions of the good life—expressed in it. Unequal reward for unequal contributions to the market would be allowed as a basic rule-of-thumb system of distribution. But we need not stop there. The principles of difference and redress could operate within and beyond these arrangements. Equal freedoms could be preserved and extended. And a good deal of these could be had without heavy intervention by a government which would have to presume to have "authoritative knowledge as to what everyone merits or deserves in terms of the distribution of income and wealth."[26] It would also increase monetary incentives that promote efficiency. In brief, we are arguing that market arrangements fit well with Rawls's elaboration of the original position. Participants could well decide to choose market arrangements as a basic system of distribution. Further, we are arguing that American society, with its strong reliance on market arrangements, measures up reasonably well to such a version of the original agreement.

It is simple to list the flaws in the system of natural justice that we have been describing. Significant numbers of people are born into and perpetuate a culture of poverty that inhibits the development on their part of sufficient skills to contribute to the economy. They receive little from the distributive system of the market. Conversely, large numbers of people are born into and perpetuate a system of privilege based upon inherited wealth. Their success in the system is "unearned" to a considerable extent. The blind, sick, very young, and very old cannot contribute to the economy. Large enterprises shape our values and preferences toward their own ends. The values encouraged by them and other agencies are sometimes vulgar and debased. Those with very limited economic wherewithal have less "worth" of freedom; their choices are limited by their low incomes. These are all problems that seek attention. But saying all this, we come back to our contention that this system provides a rough substratum with which to work. It is tolerable enough to be corrected. And it has the great advantage of not needing centralized direction. It separates and diffuses decision making. In doing so, it supports private and public liberties, distributes economic opportunity widely, and distributes economic reward according to contribution.

We have now asserted that the market arrangements that predominate in American society contribute to a decentralization of power by (1) performing the major portion of the economic task without political omnicompetence; (2) supporting a system of rough natural justice that provides a workable, unconsciously coordinated substratum for more intentional efforts at justice. Finally, we wish to suggest that the large American private market supports social and cultural pluralism. This furthers a separation of political power from social and cultural power. When persons and groups have freedom and sufficient economic wherewithal to make that freedom effective, they are able to support educational, social, religious, and cultural organizations that reflect and nurture the values they prize. These conditions are most certainly present in American society and continue to provide one of its decisive defining characteristics.

The role of voluntary associations in sustaining a viable American pluralism has been cogently demonstrated by many commentators, among them James Luther Adams and Robert Nisbet. Supplementing the family, the basic foundation of personal identity, voluntary associations transmit and express indispensable elements of our cultural heritage as well as generate new and revised strands. These "social unions" reflect the fundamental communal nature of reality. Within them, persons pursue with their fellows every imaginable concern, from the ridiculous to the sublime. These agencies in American society form persons according to religious and cultural definitions of reality, and through them religious and moral regeneration are attempted. Aspirations for human fulfillment wisely are left to these groups. In this respect we can even talk of the humility of democratic capitalism. The government is not expected to promote substantive definitions of human nature and destiny; much less is it expected or

153

allowed to "create a new humanity" in accordance with those definitions. Remaking humanity is not a goal of American democratic capitalism. At most, it provides the necessary economic, legal, and political arrangements for individuals and groups to pursue their own conceptions of human fulfillment. There is a loosely defined "civil" or "public" religion that serves to establish a morality for the rules of the game, but it remains essentially formal.

It is certainly not correct to argue that there are no attempts at overarching meaning systems. Urban industrial civilization has its own perspective and ethos which coexist with the smaller, close-at-hand social contexts of the private sphere. This meaning system has many ambiguous characteristics which we will discuss later. At this point, it is important to note that the voluntary social unions of American society provide competing alternative views of reality that are crucial for viable pluralism. The flattening effect of the urban industrial ethos is countered by a plurality of other outlooks. Moreover, besides bearing alternative meaning systems, many voluntary agencies provide other basic services to a significant portion of our population. These networks provide education at many levels, child care, hospitals, homes for the elderly, recreation, charitable and social work, and various other human services. A large number of these services are conveyed in an atmosphere shaped by the ethos of the sponsoring agency. They provide variegated channels of human care.

Although many commentators appreciate the important role of the American voluntary sector, fewer appreciate its connection with the market arrangements that support its independence. Economists friendly to capitalism hearken repeatedly to this connection. Lindbeck, von Hayek, von Mises, and Samuelson all make this point. Indeed, it is impossible to understand the passion of Milton Friedman's argument without being alert to this insight. Not only does Friedman make basically a *moral* argument for capitalism on the basis of its preservation of individual freedom, he further believes that the freedom of voluntarily constituted groups is dependent on market arrangements. If one remembers that Friedman is a member of a minority that has been the object of repeated political oppressions, it is easier to understand why the freedom of voluntary groups sustained by free markets is so morally crucial to him. American pluralism is indeed fostered and supported by the economic system we have adopted.

Free market arrangements, then, can and do contribute to a wide diffusion of power in American society. In getting the major economic tasks done with a minimum of political intervention, in supporting private and public liberties, in spinning out a vast proliferation of economic opportunity, in distributing reward according to contribution, and in sustaining the independence of a plurality of social and cultural institutions and groups, the American economy avoids the need to centralize large amounts of power as well as kinds of power in a few centers. This ability makes a precious contribution to the limitation of idolatrous human will-to-power even as it performs crucial positive tasks. Such an instrument should not be easily dismissed from a moral point of view.

THE INTENTIONAL ROLE OF THE STATE

We have just surveyed the ways in which the unconsciously coordinated market system contributes to the diffusion of power in American society. Simply diffusing power and, for that matter, relying solely on the market to diffuse power are not adequate for the achievement of a better society. There are both technical and moral reasons for this. Technically, there are areas where the market is unable to achieve desired purposes; there are areas of market failure and there are common, public goods that must be provided by government. Further, there are moral reasons for the intervention of government. Will-to-power breaks down the precarious harmonies of the natural equilibrium and the powerful must be restrained by government from oppressing the powerless. The weaker members of society have a claim to a reasonable level of life in an affluent society. Fair equality of opportunity must be extended to those who are seriously disadvantaged. Government, as we argued earlier, can and does exercise the

155

human capacity for justice. It can shape the laws and structures of society to include the rightful claims of the whole community, and especially those of the most disadvantaged. It can become an instrument of a more universal justice and thereby a vehicle of agape's impact on the world.

Therefore, in this section we move from a discussion of the economic arrangement to that of the political system. Democracy, as we defined it earlier, is the polity that combines with capitalism in the American sociopolitical system. It is this mix that we find morally defensible. Without democracy, capitalism would degenerate into a social Darwinism of the survival of the fittest—the fittest being those with the most economic power. There would be no automatic harmony in an unfettered capitalism, although every advantage ought to be taken of the harmonies that are present. The democratic element in the equation turns laissez-faire capitalism into "reform," or "liberal," or "redistributive," or "social market" capitalism. There is no question of the need for state intervention in the achievement of a more just society. The real debate pertains to the extent and mode of intervention—questions which we hope to address constructively in the final chapter. Conversely, we have argued that capitalism, with its reliance on market arrangements, fits democracy well in that it supports the diffusion of power necessary for limited government as well as a high degree of freedom and pluralism. Further, we argued that its capacity for efficiency and growth creates the economic surplus necessary for the redistributive role of the democratic polity. An efficient market system provides the wealth to make the difference principle effective. It also spins out a profusion of opportunities without which it would make little sense to talk of fair equality of opportunity. The existence of many opportunities in a context of freedom makes the effort at fair equality of opportunity more manageable.

It is much less controversial to argue the benefits of government action on behalf of more justice. Left–liberals and socialists, religious and humanistic alike, include such a program at the center of their agenda. My main purpose is to assert that there has been considerable achievement on the part of the American polity in making American society better. If sufficiently demonstrated, this assertion further calls into question the criticism that the American government is simply the tool of the economic elite.

It will be too cumbersome to catalog all the ways in which government has intervened. We will be content to list what we consider the main recent contributions of government to making American society a better society. Following our principles developed in Chapter 2, we will list the main achievements of American democratic government in (1) preserving the health of the natural equilibrium; (2) providing common public goods; and (3) correcting unjust circumstances and extending and refining justice in new areas.

One of the most important intentional roles of government, in addition to the protection of legal and orderly exchange, is the role it plays in limiting monopoly. This is crucial for the ongoing health of market economies. Although there are many examples attesting to the propensity of government itself to become involved in protecting and extending monopolies, the overall record of the American government has been impressive. The tendency of regulatory agencies to be captured by the regulated industry itself notwithstanding, the history of antimonopoly actions by the government is lengthy and laudable. The Sherman Act, the Clayton Act, the establishment of the Federal Trade Commission, and New Deal activism are examples of pre-World War II efforts. In the period since then, the Justice Department has been even more assiduous in its prosecution of the antitrust laws. The prosecution of cement, steel, and electrical equipment cases fall within recent memory. More recently, the Celler–Kefauver Antimerger Act closed loopholes in horizontal mergers. Samuelson, after surveying the performance of the government, concludes,

> In summary, both Republicans and Democrats are spending more and more money on lawyers and investigators to enforce antitrust laws with ever-increasing vigor. Firms no longer dare to use group practices that used to be standard in American industry. . . . While no one would claim that American antitrust legislation and en-

157

forcement have been completely logical or have come anywhere near complete success, one has but to look abroad to realize how much worse off our economy might have been were it not for the omnipresent threat of legal prosecution. American enterprise is kept on the defensive and would never dream of adopting the flagrant devices that are all too common in most places.[27]

Since the 1930s, the macroeconomic management of the economy has been another important role of the government in maintaining the health of the economy. Although Shonfield indicates that the American economy has suffered more recessions than the other Western industrial nations, with the exception of Belgium, the American record, he believes, is still relatively successful.[28] The government has used Keynesian demand management to keep the economy free of disastrous downturns. The debate between those supporting monetarist strategies of management and those supporting fiscal strategies goes on. It is hoped that the techniques of management can be sharpened even further so that severe economic downturns can be avoided or corrected.

A further strategy in maintaining the competitive health of the American economy is governmental insistence on free trade. An open policy on trade allows world competition to press domestic producers that may be monopolistic. Obviously, traumatic changes in industries must be avoided, but long-term policy must be the encouragement of trade. Worldwide specialization is thereby fostered, and developing countries can supply certain goods and services more efficiently than we can at home. In fact, encouragement of trade is one of the crucial ingredients for the development of poor countries. At the same time, protection must be provided against foreign enterprises who are highly subsidized by their governments or who dump surplus goods in open markets. But, broadly speaking, free trade goes a long way toward breaking down or preventing monopoly in the manufacturing sector where monopoly is more likely to be present. And the American government's record on free trade has been basically good.

Another role of the government is to redress imbalances of

power among the various productive elements of the society. This makes for systems of countervailing power which, in turn, increase both liberty and equality of opportunity. One of the key effects of this role has been the legitimation of union power. The right to organize as a bargaining power in opposition to management was not won without a great struggle, but it was indeed won. Working people in most of the main industrial enterprises have been unionized. Their countervailing power, having been established, then interacts with that of stockholders and management in a system of bargaining that is for the most part self-regulating. When real breakdowns occur, government can intervene as a more impartial third party, reserving its entry for the most difficult cases. Although it seems to be true that wages would have risen anyway in the industries that were heavily unionized, the need for organized countervailing union powers is in no way diminished. Union power prevents precipitous management decisions or practices that may bring traumatic changes in the lives of workers or may endanger their health. Unions have been able to ensure that industrial practices respect workers as ends in themselves, not simply as factors of production. These gains have protected workers from some of the ravages of the creative destruction dictated by market forces. Government unemployment benefits have further cushioned the effects of industrial change.

The same might be said about government efforts to help those farmers who are squeezed by the process of modernization in farming. The intention of these efforts has been praiseworthy—to cushion marginal farmers from the effects of changes dictated by market pressures. Unfortunately, the interventions have often led to results the opposite of those intended. The better strategies include those that offer direct loans and aid to marginal farmers to tide them over market fluctuations rather than subsidies that interfere with market forces themselves. These latter interventions have generally benefited large farmers and at the same time created agricultural surpluses or shortfalls.

At any rate, the point we are making is that the intentional role of government has been directed toward cushioning the effects of market forces on those who lose out in the process. Government has provided short-term support and job retraining schemes for many of those who need them. Again, the coverage is only partial and in places must be extended, especially in efforts to support displaced workers and farmers in finding jobs in other areas of the economy.

A final way that government in the United States contributes to the health of what we have called the natural equilibrium is by encouraging the support of an independent, voluntary sector of private organizations. It does this by maintaining a relatively low level of taxation, in comparison with other advanced industrial nations, and by allowing tax writeoffs for contributions to non-profit voluntary associations. The encouragement of social pluralism and vitality by these policies is of paramount value. One of the distinguishing marks of American society is the extent, variety, and vitality of its associational life. Americans are accustomed to having more disposable income for these associational purposes, and indeed to giving more to them, than any other people. Schools, churches, recreational and social organizations, political and ethnic groups, as well as many others are strongly supported by the free choice of Americans. Through these agencies Americans provide for themselves and for their fellows services that in other social systems must be provided by the state. In the following chapter we shall call for a more extensive use of this network to supply the increasing demand for social services. We have a good record in encouraging this sector but can do better.

Besides government strategies to maintain and restore the health of the basically self-regulating natural equilibrium, the United States government has in recent years presided over a significant growth in its role in providing common goods which the market cannot provide. Earlier in the chapter we indicated the rather astonishing growth in public expenditure on federal, state, and local levels. We shall not attempt any comprehensive listing of governmental provisions. We shall mention only several important provisions that strengthen our case for affirming the independence and effectiveness of the American democratic polity.

First, rather than succumbing to the Galbraithian notions of private opulence and public squalor, we point to a number of important instances of public opulence. The prime example is the amount of public support given to education. American schools, from kindergarten to graduate research institutions, are provided better equipment, physical plant, support services, and more highly paid teachers than other nations. Even in this time of economic recession, Americans make a huge investment in educating their young. This is not to say that all is well with American education, but our failures are not primarily for lack of public economic support. Nor am I saying that educational opportunities are fairly distributed, but even our poorest schools are not in their situation simply because of economic neglect. Other factors intervene that are not amenable to solution by simply increasing the amount of money spent.

Second, the United States has made more progress than most nations in dealing with the "neighborhood effects" of the industrial process. "Neighborhood effects," or externalities, are costs and benefits of production that cannot be charged or rewarded to the producer. The best examples of such neighborhood effects are air and water pollution. The costs to innocent bystanders for pollution of the air by steel mills, for example, cannot be measured and charged to the offending mills. Nor can the benefits to the community of beautiful buildings and grounds constructed by an enterprise be added to its balance sheet. It is well known that in modern industrial societies, where interdependence grows by leaps and bounds, such neighborhood effects multiply in number and impact. Air and water pollution are the most crucial neighborhood effects since they influence the life and health of the whole community, if not the whole earth.

One of the major achievements of American government has been the control and abatement of these forms of pollution. The battle is not over by a long shot and there is continuing debate on the mode of government intervention in pollution fighting, but our achievement is noteworthy. The regulation of nonmarket behavior of major industrial enterprises has produced significant improvements in the quality of air in the United States. Steven Kelman of Harvard's Kennedy School of Government gives us a summary of his investigations:

> Carbon monoxide levels in eight representative cities declined 46 percent between 1972 and 1976. Carbon monoxide levels that had been found in urban air were enough to increase the incidence of heart attacks and of painful angina attacks among people with heart disease. There has been a major decline in heart attack deaths in the United States during the 1970s. No one yet knows why, but I predict that studies will show that improvement in air quality has played a role in this decline. Another common air pollutant, sulfur dioxide, which definitely causes respiratory illness and death and is suspected of causing cancer, has now declined to a point where almost every place in the country is in compliance with EPA standards.[29]

Much the same can be said of water pollution. Again, Kelman summarizes nicely:

> There are rivers and lakes around the country—from the Pemige-wasset River in New Hampshire through the Mohawk River in New York to the Wilamett River in Oregon—previously badly polluted, that are now opened in parts for fishing and swimming. Levels of various pesticides in streams and rivers, as well as of phenol—an organic waste considered a good indicator of the presence of toxic industrial wastes—have declined dramatically during the 1970s.[30]

Besides America's pioneering efforts of pollution control, its government involvement in the provision of parks, roads, mass transportation, urban renewal, and the arts is not insignificant. There is, of course, great controversy about what the extent of such involvement ought to be. Massive amounts of money are already devoted to these ends, but progress is not often easy. The United States, especially in its urban areas, still experiences large migrations of poor people from outside and within its borders. These migrations put immense pressure on public facilities and make their proper maintenance much more difficult than in countries with more settled populations. Considering these additional burdens, American performance is better than often thought, though there is still room for considerable improvement.

Even though the facets of the intentional role of government that we have been mentioning contribute to the health of the natural equilibrium and to the provision of public, common goods, they do not pertain directly to the increase in justice in American society. If justice has to do with fair distribution of goods, we must move to the criteria of justice elaborated by Rawls and discussed in Chapter 2. We must assess the performance of American democratic capitalism in relation to the Rawlsian principles: (I) equal public and private liberties; (IIa) the difference principle in which inequalities in the distribution of primary goods are affirmed insofar as they significantly improve the long-term prospects of the least advantaged members; and (IIb) fair equality of opportunity.

With regard to the first principle of equal liberty, we must begin by affirming the presence of a high degree of public and private liberty for Americans. This has been, and continues to be, a huge plus for our society. People can live freely according to their own values—speaking, associating, moving, organizing, and experimenting. Indeed, there is probably more private freedom now than there ever has been. Traditional cultural restraints have eroded, and people can live by about any ethos they choose. Even rural and small-town areas have become increasingly tolerant. Nevertheless, there has been a great deal of room for extending and refining the notion of equal liberty.

The most important agenda we have had as a nation is extending liberty to our large black minority. The history of denial of liberty is too well known to need chronicling here. The treatment of black people has been the American dilemma; promises in the foundation of the nation were denied a significant portion of our population. But great gains have been and are being made. I believe the historians of the twenty-first century will look back to the two decades between 1950 and 1970 as the irreversible turning point of American treatment of our black and other minorities. Of major significance has been the extension of equal public and private liberties. The Civil Rights Act of 1964 and the Voting Rights Act of 1965 are of pivotal importance in this quest. Voting rights have been extended in all areas of the nation, at last giving minorities political power commensurate with their numbers. Private liberties of access to public accommodation, housing, and movement have been greatly extended. Cultural freedom and pride have increased with these liberties. Much is left to be done in this area, but the process is moving forward, on legislative, executive, and judicial fronts. The same can be said of the extension of equal rights to women.

Next in importance in ensuring equal liberties—in this case public liberty—was the weathering of the storm of Watergate. The nation's handling of this challenge to democracy reinforced the notions of freedom of the press, democratic consent, and firm constitutionalism. It demonstrated that no one, not even the president, is above the law. The transition of power from a disgraced president to a caretaker president and then to a newly elected president of the opposing party took place with a minimum of political upheaval. Such political orderliness was remarkable and confirmed our confidence in democratic procedures. If the economic and military elite were really in control of the country, as many radical critics allege, such a transition would have been impossible.

Third, a bundle of recent reforms have increased the "worth" of our public liberty, that is, our equal right to political voice has been given more muscle. One person–one vote patterns of representation have been enforced by American courts. Reforms in campaign financing, in the organization and leadership of congressional committees, and in lobbying procedures have cut down the entrenched power of special interests. The ordinary citizen's vote and opinion now have more worth. The devolution of some power from the federal to the state level has increased political access to many citizens and groups.

Meanwhile, our private liberties have also been refined. Freedom of information, the provision of legal assistance, protection against arbitrary arrest, surveillance, and coercion have increased the fair and equal application of the law. We have great problems in this area, particularly in regard to the right to a fair and speedy trial, that need to be worked on. But the recent

refinement of rights has led many people to believe that the rights
of the accused have become dominant over the rights of society
for security and lawful order. It is more likely, however, that the
rights of both society and the accused are violated by inefficiency
in the judicial system rather than by too few or too many rights
being extended.

The continuing failures in the equal distribution of liberty
notwithstanding, America continues to be an immense island of
liberty. Both the natural equilibrium, with its market arrangements and social pluralism, and the intentional role of government have contributed mightily to this phenomenon. When we
speak of the achievement of a more just society, then, we would
do well to treasure this accomplishment even as we constantly
protect and extend it. Equal liberties are a part of justice, perhaps
the most important part, as Rawls's lexical ordering suggests. The
assurance that people can make freely the decisions that shape
their lives is of paramount importance in preserving human
dignity. From a Christian point of view, such assurance is crucial
in respecting the self-transcending freedom of the human spirit.
As societies preserve and extend equal freedom, they make room
for the creativity and criticism that self-transcending freedom
generates. This in turn fosters a built-in check against the idolatrous tendencies of political power. It provides space in which
individuals and groups can pursue their aspiration toward human
fulfillment without being bothered by the state or by other
would-be definers of that aspiration. It is in this kind of context
that generation and regeneration of nonheteronomous meaning
systems and human community are most likely to occur.

Extending liberty, however, without ensuring minimal economic means is like the recommendation to "let them eat cake."
Thus, the difference principle must operate to provide a rising
floor of support for the least advantaged members of society so
that their long-term prospects will be significantly improved.
From a Christian point of view, this is the way that the democratic polity distributes care for the hungry, unemployed, defenseless, sick, and handicapped members of society. Basic
minima must be provided whether the least advantaged are

deserving or not. (This does not mean that there will not be some who will refuse to be aided, nor does it mean that support systems should be concocted without regard to work incentives.) Christian concern for justice continues to respect the freedom of agents to refuse aid and the crucial role that independence plays in bolstering human dignity. Christian agape is not excessively paternalistic; neither is a Christian conception of justice.

Although American society has a great distance to go in approximating the difference principle, it has made important strides forward. There are many seriously disadvantaged representative persons in our society; it is a waste of time to debate which are the most disadvantaged. Therefore, let us designate several and outline the ways in which government has improved their long-term prospects. We can begin with the plight of one-parent, impoverished families.

Three major programs have been legislated to deal with perhaps the most serious and baffling poverty problem: the fatherless family. Nearly half of all poor white children and two thirds of all poor black children live in families headed by their mother, who is separated, divorced, widowed or was never married.[31] Aid to Families with Dependent Children (AFDC) is the major effort directed at this group, and its aid is considerable.

> In 1972, more than 3 million families (nearly all of them fatherless) received over $7 billion of benefits from that program. The size of the AFDC rolls was one of the fastest-growing U.S. statistics during the sixties, doubling about every four years.[32]

Other important programs include Medicaid, food stamps, and Head Start, which are available to the working poor as well as to one-parent families. Since 1967, Congress has enacted more than a dozen food aid laws and now appropriates more than $9 billion annually to feed the poor. These laws have significantly improved the prospects of the American poor. In 1977 the Field Foundation sent a medical team to revisit poverty areas that it had examined ten years earlier. Its 1967 report had revealed serious incidences of malnutrition. However, its 1977 report, though not deliriously exaltant, made this statement:

There are far fewer grossly malnourished people in this country than there were ten years ago. Malnutrition has become a subtler problem. . . . But in the area of food there has been a difference. The food stamp program, the nutritional component of Head Start, school lunch and breakfast programs, and to a lesser extent the women-infant-children (WIC) feeding programs have made the difference.[33]

The largest federal effort has gone into the food stamp program. It has grown from a $288-million budget serving 2.8 million people in 1968 to a $5-billion budget serving 15 million people today. Further, it seems that practically all food stamps go to people who need them most. As Nick Kotz, a Pulitzer Prize-winning author of books on hunger in the United States, asserts,

The Congressional Budget Office concluded that 87 percent of food stamps go to families living on incomes less than what is needed to buy a decent amount of food alone. The CBO study also showed that food stamp benefits have lifted four million people above the poverty line, including several million working poor. In fact, food stamps are virtually the only government aid offered to the working poor. . . . Middle-class citizens also have benefited. When the unemployment rate rose above nine percent in 1974-75, participation in the food stamp program rose from 14 million to 19 million participants. In fact, food stamps today help more Americans than any other social program except social security.[34]

Government has also made increasingly large expenditures in the expansion of social medicine, particularly through the Medicaid program. Without it, the health care industry would not be showing such a growth trend. Programs in this area make it possible for the poor to gain competent medical care regardless of their ability to pay. More of this care is given in the better equipped and staffed private hospitals than in the old county or municipal hospitals. Indeed, it seems that the very poor and the well-off are able to use the same hospitals. It is the working poor and the lower-middle classes that have a greater economic burden in their access to proper health care.

Other vulnerable people in our society are the elderly poor.

Again, major gains have been made. The right to a rising minimum standard of consumption has been established for the elderly.

> For the first time, legislation enacted in 1966 bestowed some minimum benefits on all Americans over the age of 72, regardless of whether they had ever contributed to the social security system. Since then, the level of minimal entitlements has been increased and the age requirement reduced to 65 through additional programs that supplement the standard system of old-age benefits. Currently, the principle of contribution serves mainly to preserve pride while fulfilling the right to survival.[35]

Those retiring at age 65 will be below the poverty line in old age only if they have been extremely and persistently poor in their working years. While this situation needs serious attention, the very fact that the extension of elderly rights has included more and more people indicates the progress we have made. Social Security and Medicare represent a huge redistribution from today's young to the elderly. Large increases in the Social Security tax have been made with minimum resistance. "In terms of public attitudes, social security is probably the greatest success of any major federal expenditure program in American history. And it has brought the nation within sight of ending poverty for the aged."[36]

All of these government programs are ways in which the democratic polity transfers wealth from those who can afford it to those who need more support. They are the difference principle in action if they indeed do increase the prospects of the least advantaged. In most cases, it would be difficult to argue that they have not increased those prospects, though it is less difficult to argue that the increase has not been significant enough. Concerning the distribution of the burdens of the transfer system, it seems that federal taxes are essentially proportional over the bottom 95 percent of families on the income scale. But taxes on the top 5 percent are genuinely progressive. Although federal personal income tax bills were 11 percent of the average income for all Americans in 1972, they were 27 percent of the income for families with before-tax incomes above $50,000. The progressive part of the taxing system—that in excess of the 11 percent average—amounted to $13 billion, which was more than the total cost of Medicaid, welfare, food stamps, and public housing combined. There is an authentic redistribution from the well-off to the less-well-off.[37]

The difference principle is in the process of being engaged in American society. Questions of life and death are no longer settled in the marketplace. Political intervention has ensured that the inequalities of the marketplace will work to the benefit of the least advantaged. These benefits gradually increase as the overall wealth of the society increases. After all, the poverty line— defined in the United States as one half the average income per head—keeps moving upward as the average income moves upward. So, given our means of definition (a relative one) we will always have the poorest 20 percent. However, the prospects of those in the lowest 20 percent are improving because of transfers. There is little doubt that many in that lowest group are in a miserable state, but there is also little doubt that many have received benefits that have enabled them to lead lives of significantly more comfort and dignity. They have shared in the progress of the nation.

Rawls's Principle II includes not only the difference principle, which we have just sketched, but also the principle of fair equality of opportunity. Equality of opportunity means keeping positions open, enforcing nondiscriminatory practices. *Fair* equality of opportunity means the practice of redress. The injurious results of past injustice or neglect are redressed by differential treatment of the disavantaged so that they can be prepared to run the competitive race with more equal chances of success.

Through legislative, executive, and judicial efforts, the United States has made major gains since the midfifties. Beginning with the school desegregation decision of 1954 onward, long-overdue advances in extending nondiscriminatory treatment to blacks have occurred. In later years such efforts were broadened to include women, Native Americans, the handicapped, and other minorities. The programs are far too numerous to explicate here;

the more important among them are the Civil Rights Act of 1964, the Equal Employment Act of 1972, various interpretations of the Fourteenth Amendment, and efforts by the Equal Employment Opportunities Commission and Fair Employment Practices Commission.

Although we are far from achieving a society of authentically open positions in which the hiring, promotion, and compensation of persons is based solely on their job performance, we can see the principle of equal opportunity working. As Arthur Okun has written:

> In fact, the principle of equal employment opportunity was established as a right and removed from the sphere of the marketplace a decade ago. That action has been followed by a significant reduction of racial discrimination in labor markets. Black women have scored particularly impressive gains. The average earnings of black women aged 18 to 44 rose from about two-thirds those of their white counterparts in 1959, to more than 90 percent in 1969. . . . The gain for black males is also significant, although it is much smaller and their position underlines the large remaining disadvantages. During the sixties, the earnings of black men in the age groups under 45 advanced from roughly 60 percent to roughly 70 percent of the corresponding white earnings. . . . I believe the record dramatizes the general point that political decisions about fair play can change economic behavior. It further illustrates the general possibility that what is good for equality may be good for efficiency. The narrowing of racial differentials during the sixties implies a gain of nearly one-fifth in the wages and salaries of blacks. That gain approached 1 percent of the national income.[38]

Many of the same things could be said about the progress of women and other minorities. Although the kind, extent, and seriousness of discrimination against women is far different from that against blacks, the cause of nondiscrimination has been advanced with at least equal vigor. In fact, the movement for equality of treatment for women will most likely be more far-reaching and persistent than that for black people, primarily because of the number and power of women. Added to the efforts of government are the efforts of many private organizations who press for nondiscriminatory practices within their own bailiwicks. Indeed, given the present momentum of efforts to achieve open positions, it is hard to predict anything but continuing advance. The number of women, black, and other minorities who are appearing in formerly closed positions in the media, schools, businesses, professions, sports, entertainment, and government attests to the vigor and irreversibility of political efforts to achieve equality of opportunity. Elliot Zashin, in a very balanced article on the progress of American blacks in the last two decades, ends with the following conclusion, which, although it applies only to blacks in his article, could well apply to the progress of other minorities and women.

> The gains of the past two decades have placed blacks in general much closer to equality—however defined—than ever before in our history. We cannot return to conditions which prevailed before the 1960's; blacks are too conscious, civil rights legislation barring overt discrimination is too much a part of our practice, and blacks have achieved enough of a political foothold to prevent a return to a not terribly benign neglect. But I do not think that one can say objectively that black inequality is no longer a major problem in American society, nor can one say with confidence that the forces set in motion by the developments of the last two decades will— say, in two or three more decades—eliminate virtually all the handicaps that have been the legacy of racism and discrimination. We must confront the issues posed by continued black inequality, or the effects of past racism and discrimination will persist many decades into the future.[39]

The historical burden—the effects of past racism that Zashin talks about—on disadvantaged groups is precisely what must be corrected by the principle of redress, the moral demand to offer a more *fair* equality of opportunity. Chances to compete for open positions must be made more equal. The arbitrariness of being born into severely disadvantaged conditions must be redressed by improving those conditions or by differential treatment accorded those harmed by such conditions. The first alternative is a long-term one that reverts to the impact of the difference principle and its transfer payments, aid-in-kind, and subsidization. It also reverts to the principle of equal liberty, especially the assurance of political power commensurate with numbers. The second alternative, differential treatment for severely disadvantaged, is more appropriate to the present discussion.

A good deal of controversy has surrounded various schemes of affirmative action, primarily because affirmative action has led to quotas and timetables and has attached itself to group membership rather than individual considerations. The deFunis and Bakke cases, as well as the many court cases ordering quotas for police departments, schools, and so on, are examples of an ongoing controversy. It seems that the conflict surrounding these efforts stems from the appearance of unfair discrimination against nondisadvantaged persons. Requirements for preferential procedures and outcomes for disadvantaged groups seem to punish qualified persons of majority status.

Be that as it may, strong programs of redress go on. The most important have developed around the issue of education. Busing, integration, and remedial and preferential entrance strategies have all focused on more roughly equal chances for education. Without proper tools with which to compete, open positions are of diminished value to the severely disadvantaged. It is in this area that I believe we have made the least progress. And a good deal of the difficulty is that we have adopted strategies that seem to punish persons and groups that are neither severely disadvantaged nor distinctly advantaged. Approaches must be found that offer differential treatment to needy persons without overtly disadvantaging that middle range of people. Further, disadvantage must be defined not by sex or race or ethnic identity, but by economic and social deprivation. We will outline several of our proposals in the final chapter. Right now it is difficult to measure the results of recent efforts at redress even though they remain the most visible and controversial of the whole range of state intervention.

The intentional role of the state has indeed taken up many of the concerns of justice as we earlier defined it. Entitlements under both main principles have been extended to more and more people through broadly political means. Considerable progress has been made in the fair distribution of liberty, access to primary goods that improve long-term prospects of life, and fair equality of opportunity. Sometimes this progress has had to be made in the face of opposition from private economic power. Just as often, the resistance has come from the political weight of those who can by no stretch of the imagination be called the economic elite. Considering the massiveness, messiness, and diversity of American society, the efforts at more justice by political means has not been distressingly ineffectual. We have made more progress than many nations who are much smaller and homogeneous. But there is no room for exultant self-congratulation. Extremely serious challenges remain.

In summary, we have argued that the American market economy and democratic polity in combination constitute a morally defensible social system. The market system—capitalism, if you will—possesses many characteristics that are extremely valuable to any viable social system. It has given America an efficient and growing economy. Through efficiency and growth it has raised the living standards of the masses of people. Without the production of wealth at a sufficient level, other higher considerations of the human project recede from the horizon. Further, market arrangements both reflect and support human liberties, social pluralism, and a rough system of reward-for-contribution. And they do these things in an unconsciously coordinated manner, thus cutting down the need for political omnicompetence. These are extremely positive spinoffs that have moral significance. They preserve respect for humans as ends in themselves, as centers of self-transcending freedom. They encourage voluntary human community without which human fulfillment is impossible. They provide the free space for religious aspiration. They support dissent that checks abuses inherent in concentrations of private or public power. All of this lends American society a diffusion of power that places checks on idolatrous will-to-power. American society is far from deification of the nation, of business, or of any competing social group. Our idolatries move in different directions, as we shall see later.

The fragile and flawed equilibrium reflected and supported by market arrangements is always in danger of falling into anarchy. Chaos is ever nearer to us than tyranny, and this is both the bane and blessing of American life. But societies that pursue justice seriously cannot tolerate the kinds of anarchy that oppress humans. Therefore, the American democratic polity is constructed as an instrument to correct the chaotic arbitrariness that emerges in the bubbling turmoil of the natural equilibrium. That equilibrium itself is regulated, managed, and ordered. Common public goods are provided, and justice as fairness is pursued. All of this is a part of the intentional role of American government. Democratic government has established a range of rights that are removed from the more arbitrary outcomes of the economic and social marketplace. And this has made for more justice. But our argument is that these political achievements have not been incompatible with capitalism. Indeed, the robust fecundity of the natural equilibrium, of which market arrangements are a fundamental part, has been the indispensable substratum upon which a higher justice is constructed.

Democratic capitalism has been an undervalued social system, especially by the liberal intellectual community, both religious and secular. We have attempted to challenge that underassessment by emphasizing the values and achievements that are often overlooked. In avoiding the tendency to damn with faint praise, we have probably praised with all-too-faint damnation. But the time is coming for that. We now turn to the challenges to democratic capitalism, challenges that arise because of its practical and moral failures.

NOTES

1. Michael Harrington, "Corporate Collectivism: A System of Social Injustice," in *Ethics, Free Enterprise, and Public Policy* (New York: Oxford University Press, 1978), p. 45.

2. Paul Heyne, *Private Keepers of the Public Interest* (New York: McGraw-Hill, 1968), p. 21.

3. Joseph Schumpeter, *Capitalism, Socialism and Democracy* (New York: Harper & Row, 1940; 1975), p. 83.

4. Assar Lindbeck, *Can Pluralism Survive?* (Ann Arbor: University of Michigan, 1977), p. 14.

5. See, for instance, Yale Brozen, "The Ethical Consequences of Alternative Incentive Systems," in *Can the Market Sustain an Ethic?* (Chicago: University of Chicago Press, 1978), pp. 18ff.

6. Andrew Shonfield, *Modern Capitalism* (New York: Oxford University Press, 1969), p. 61.

7. Ibid., pp. 18ff.

8. Ibid., pp. 330ff.

9. Schumpeter, *Capitalism*, p. 68.

10. Ibid., p. 67.

11. Arthur Okun, *Equality and Efficiency: The Big Tradeoff* (Washington, D.C.: The Brookings Institution, 1975), p. 69.

12. Ibid., p. 64.

13. Paul Samuelson, *Economics*, 10th ed. (Tokyo: McGraw-Hill Kogakusha, 1976), pp. 191-97.

14. W. Arthur Lewis, *The Evolution of the International Economic Order* (Princeton, N.J.: Princeton University Press, 1973), p. 67.

15. Lindbeck, *Can Pluralism Survive?*, p. 8.

16. Ibid., p. 9.

17. "Small Is Beautiful in Creating New Jobs," an article describing a study carried out at Massachusetts Institute of Technology by David L. Birch and published as a report, "The Job Generating Process," *The Observer*, 22 April 1979.

18. Ibid.

19. Walter Eltis, "The Union Veto on Economic Growth," *The Sunday Times*, 17 September 1978.

20. Charles L. Schultze, "The Public Use of Private Interest," *Harper's* 254, no. 1524 (May 1977): 47.

21. Ibid., p. 45.

22. A quotation of Assar Lindbeck in *The Political Economy of the New Left 1971*, cited by George Dalton, *Economic Systems and Society* (Middlesex, Eng.: Penguin Books, 1974), p. 166.

23. Milton Friedman, *Capitalism and Freedom* (Chicago: University of Chicago Press, 1962), p. 16.

24. Ibid., p. 21.

25. Heyne, *Private Keepers*, p. 19.

26. Irving Kristol, "A Capitalist Conception of Justice," in *Ethics, Free Enterprise and Public Policy*, p. 65.

27. Samuelson, *Economics*, pp. 529-31.

28. Shonfield, *Modern Capitalism*, pp. 3-18.

29. Steven Kelman, "Regulation That Works," *The New Republic* 179, no. 22, issue 3333 (25 November 1978): 16.

30. Ibid.

31. Okun, *Equality and Efficiency*, p. 111.

32. Ibid.

33. As reported by Nick Kotz in "Feeding the Hungry," *The New Republic* 179, no. 22, issue 3333 (25 November 1978): 20.

34. Ibid., p. 21.
35. Okun, *Equality and Efficiency*, p. 18.
36. Ibid., p. 108.
37. Ibid., p. 103.
38. Ibid., pp. 78–79.
39. Elliot Zashin, "The Progress of Black Americans in Civil Rights: The Past Two Decades Assessed," *Daedalus* 107, no. 1 (Winter 1978): 260.

PART III

THE CHALLENGES
AND POSSIBILITIES OF
DEMOCRATIC CAPITALISM

Introduction to Part III

In the preceding chapter we sought to demonstrate that the combination of democracy as a polity and capitalism as an economy is morally viable and that democratic capitalism as practiced in the United States is pressing toward an approximation of the just society. Moreover, we have admitted to serious problems facing American society. Some of them can be attributed to the fact that any society as large, diverse, and changing as American society is bound to have an unending series of challenges. The implications of this commonsense observation often escape those critics who are inclined to attribute the struggles that beset us simply to the moral failures of democratic capitalism. Even allowing for that observation, however, it is true that we face issues that do flow from the peculiar combination of democracy and capitalism. In addition to challenges coming from the kind of society we live in—its largeness and diversity—and from democratic capitalism, we face those stemming from the dynamics of modernity, the struggles common to all societies of a science-based, urban, industrial character. Therefore, the sources of the challenges facing American society today are not easily designated. But what is more certain is that these challenges must be faced, at least in the foreseeable future, within the limits and possibilities of democratic capitalism. Thus, it is fair for the commentators who analyze them to lay these challenges at the doorstep of the social system we have been calling democratic capitalism with the demand that it face up to them.

In Part III we intend to "face up" to these challenges. We will take up in turn what we consider to be the most serious issues elaborated by the critics—state them, reflect critically upon them, and suggest constructive responses. We will pursue the third task in a manner consistent with our general argument, that is, that democratic capitalism may have constructive ways of meeting these challenges which avoid both political centralization and moral callousness. If democratic capitalism has been and is a morally legitimate social order, as we have argued earlier, we should grapple with the challenges before us in ways that conserve the gifts and possibilities of that order, while at the same time dealing imaginatively with its flaws.

It would be well at this point to enter some disclaimers. Some of the issues facing American society are so complex that I can only respond to them with the general intuitions of a layman. Those issues will receive only brief comment, no matter how much they really deserve. Also, the issues are so numerous that some important ones must go by the wayside. But it is hoped that the most serious challenges are included. We shall order our discussion according to the framework we have been using. We shall discuss challenges to the values of efficiency and growth, to the existence and performance of the natural equilibrium of power, to the approximation of the Rawlsian principles of justice, and to the cultural substratum of American society.

8

The Challenges Surrounding
Efficiency and Growth

A good deal of mystery surrounds the economic performance of nations and empires. Like their more general fate as political entities, nations' economic achievements seem to rise and fall without clear causes. Historians puzzle about this waxing and waning, but their verdicts appear too long after the fact to be useful in solving present dilemmas. The waning of industrial productivity seems particularly to beset Great Britain, which had once experienced both empire and industrial supremacy. Spending time in Britain illuminates the nature and symptoms of industrial decline and exposes one to a vast array of reflections about its causes. But there is little consensus on causative factors and even less on the way to stem the long decline. Although the plight of Britain should not be unduly exaggerated, it exhibits certain unpretty symptoms. Industrial strife, inflation, falling living standards for those who can least afford to bear them, shrinking support for crucial public sector endeavors, moves toward protectionist economic nationalism, and resurgent class consciousness are all effects of decline in economic productivity. But what of its causes? Is it the existence of an aging industrial apparatus, the heavy taxation that dampens incentive, monopoly conditions in industry that would horrify most Americans, a wealthy upper class that refuses to invest in Britain, the power of the unions to veto creative destruction and to extract wage gains without gains in efficiency, heavy government regulation of and involvement in the economy, or a deep-running cultural disposition for security and leisure? All of these, and a host of others have been suggested by the pundits. And how to turn things around is a question that stimulates an even greater diversity of responses.

We do not bring up the "British sickness" in order to luxuriate in our exemption from it but in order to face up to the fact that we may be experiencing some signs of it ourselves. It is no secret that many of our Western European competitors such as West Germany, France, Sweden, and Denmark, as well as Japan have outstripped us in productivity. In turn, their living standards have approached or surpassed our own.[1]

For many, no increase in living standards would not be a great hardship. In fact, it is usually members of those fortunate segments of the population who attack the instrumental values of efficiency and growth. But they rarely foresee the full repercussions of long-term declines in efficiency and growth. Here, the British experience should instruct us. When the pie no longer grows larger by gains made possible by increases in productivity, people begin insisting that it be divided up more equitably, and their notions of equity are highly partisan. Declining wealth sets off the politicization of the whole distributive mechanism, and those with political power make the gains, regardless of their economic performance. More and more economic decisions are made on political grounds, which further decreases economic efficiency. Such politicization, rather than increasing efforts at impartial justice, actually makes such attempts less feasible. Historically, the extension and refinement of justice accompanies economic achievement, not vice versa. Like it or not, it seems that, barring heavily authoritarian solutions, a society must have enough economic surplus to "play" with in order for a higher degree of justice to be secured.

Thus, our decline in economic efficiency is a serious matter. We will need more efficiency in the future rather than less. The factors of production will have to be combined even more effectively than in the past. We have mentioned some of the symptoms already present in Britain that give reason for our increased commitment to economic efficiency. In addition to these, several more reasons come to mind. For one, we will be facing heightened competition from abroad. Western Europe and Japan are no longer lagging behind. And right on their heels are the newly emerging industrial powers of Taiwan, Hong Kong, South Korea, and Brazil, to name a few. Further, the long-run potential of many Third World countries as producers of both manufactured and agricultural goods is great. We will need to increase our efficiency in specialized fields in order even to maintain the standard of living we have, let alone improve it. And, to some degree at least, the economic development of the underdeveloped world is dependent on the health of the developed economies, especially America's. Severe downturns in economic performance will be accompanied by protectionist measures which will only impede the growth of the poorer nations. Finally, Peter Drucker points to the demographic "sea change" that will demand increased economic efficiency in the future. As the median age of the developed societies goes up, more and more people on pensions will be dependent upon increased productivity on the part of the working generation. Because of these vast changes in age ratios, more elderly will be dependent on fewer workers. And the only way that the implicit promises of pension funds can be made good is by increasing efficiency.[2]

Great debates surround the elaboration of policies designed to increase productivity and avoid chronic inflation, unemployment, trade deficits, and so on. It is difficult for a layperson to gain clarity from the confusion of the economists. But it seems likely that increased efficiency in the American economy will not be stimulated by protectionism, by more governmental control of the economy, or simply by "liberating" private enterprise. Improvement of our productivity may be increased in the following ways, which go with the grain of market arrangements rather than against them.

The United States should continue to press for lower direct and indirect tariffs both at home and abroad. Comparative advantage on the part of many countries will then be sifted out. We will be pressed to locate our own markets and to compete vigorously to

183

maintain them. Economic nationalism should be discouraged even though we will find it necessary to cushion the effects of world competition on old and declining industries. But the cushioning should come in the form of generous support for older workers who are made redundant and of moving and retraining allowances for younger workers in affected industries. Propping up declining industries and regions by various subsidization schemes seems wasteful and ineffective. This does not mean that those regions and peoples should be neglected. It is rare that an area offers nothing that is economically viable, be it natural beauty, a disciplined workforce with relatively low wage expectations, proximity to natural or agricultural resources, or some other advantage.

Many economists, among them Stigler, Lindbeck, and Drucker, believe that competition, and the efficiency it creates, can only be maintained by stopping and reversing "the strong tendencies to mergers of firms, the development of ever larger conglomerates, and the practice of interlocking directorships in the corporate sector."[3] These economists would break up the largest corporations and capital funds into smaller units. Such drastic strategies would be very difficult to execute, however. Perhaps increasing vigilance in monitoring monopolistic practices combined with open trade policies are more feasible options.

In the future it may be important to restrict the detailed and highly selective government intervention that seriously hurts the efficiency of market arrangements: extensive selective subsidies, capital grants, price and wage regulations, import controls, and licensing and rationing systems. In particular, the sort of taxation schemes that favor corporate farming over family farm operations should be eliminated. Policies should increase efficiency and at the same time keep the market open to new participants.

The challenge of increased efficiency certainly applies to the microeconomic realm as well. Better management of productive resources, particularly in the knowledge and service sectors of the economy, is especially important since the American economy will be moving heavily in those directions. Good management along these lines does not mean manipulation and exploitation of

184

workers, but rather the creation of healthy organizational environments and practices that elicit higher productivity from workers because they find their work satisfying and challenging. The challenge to do this applies to private and public sectors and to all forms of ownership. Enhancement of the entrepreneurial spirit will also be important, especially among smaller firms where job creation is at its highest.

It may also prove advantageous to abolish the corporation income tax to encourage investment in future productivity. At the same time, corporations would be required to attribute their income to stockholders, and stockholders would be required to include such sums on their tax returns. Other personal and corporate loopholes should be closed, such as the percentage depletion on oil and other raw materials, tax exemption of interest on state and local securities, favorable treatment on capital gains, and numerous other deductions now allowed.[4] Further, savings for necessary capital formation could be increased by allowing banks and savings and loan institutions to give as high a rate of interest as they determine feasible.

But perhaps the most important step we need to take in facing up to the challenge of efficiency is increased investment in what some economists call "human capital."[5] Great economic, not to mention human waste, is perpetuated by allowing large segments of our population to languish in dependency due to their lack of marketable skills. Much larger investments in this disadvantaged section of society must be made. We will have more to say of this later. At this point we can only say that dependent people are a great drag on economic productivity. They demand tremendous amounts of services and contribute little to economic life. Much more attention to schooling of various sorts and at various levels, to health care, and to early career counseling and family services are needed for the class culture of poverty to be broken and the economic potential implicit in it to be free. (It should be noted that we are speaking here of this problem in relation to the economic need for efficiency. The fuller human dimensions of the problem of dependent poverty go far beyond the concerns for economic performance.)

185

Heavier taxation on inherited wealth and on the consumption of the very wealthy should be legislated to help finance investment in "human capital." Taxation should be directed at "being wealthy" rather than "becoming wealthy," however, since the initiative involved in the latter is economically useful.

These strategies are consonant with the gifts and possibilities of democratic capitalism. But they bracket for the moment the more serious question of social and cultural vitality. They assume that people will be motivated toward economically productive endeavors, an assumption that can be seriously questioned, as we in fact shall do a little later. Governments and firms cannot create the cultural wellsprings that provide the energy for and the guidance of the broader society and upon which the whole social project is curiously dependent.

The suggestions above entail action by both private and public sectors. Naturally, they entail wise microeconomic management of monetary and fiscal matters. They also include wise government decisions about research and development priorities, and perhaps even a measure of indicative planning. But they should not lead toward policies that require more coercive governmental roles in economic choice, policies that may in the long run be neither efficient nor supportive of the valuable characteristics of market arrangements.

Be that as it may, there has been little evidence in the past forty years that democratic capitalist societies are doomed to chronic and deepening lapses of economic efficiency characterized by disastrous unemployment and unused capacity. Indeed, the evidence seems to be on the other side. American democratic capitalism, as well as other varieties of the species, has been remarkably productive in this period of time. Capital is used far more efficiently in these systems than in more centralized economies.[6] The American economy particularly has absorbed millions of new entrants into economic life: women, immigrants, products of the postwar baby boom. Indeed, a good number of the 5 to 7 percent unemployed are people who are temporarily unemployed while taking time to find better work. (Incidentally, the real rate of un- and underemployment in centralized economies is not only disguised by poor reporting procedures but also by policies of overmanning and coerced labor. Those who are chronically unemployed can easily be deemed "social parasites" and put into forced labor camps.) On the other hand, chronic inflation is a worldwide problem that affects all economies and is of utmost seriousness. Without getting into the proposed strategies to counter inflation, we can say that being able to grapple with it effectively is closely related to a more efficient economic performance. And working with market forces will most likely be more effective in combating inflation than wage and price policies, which tend to work against market forces. Combined with sound monetary and fiscal policies, increased productivity is our best weapon.

Hardly anyone argues with the need for increased economic efficiency, although many question its placement in the American ordering of values; however, there are those who seriously question the other instrumental value of growth we have been examining throughout this study. One group of objectors, whom we shall call the ecology contingent, believe the value itself is out of place in a limited world. The other group, whom we shall call Marxists or neo-Marxists, charges that the growth achieved by the democratic capitalist lands is immorally extracted from the underdeveloped world. Both groups place the moral issues surrounding economic growth at the door of capitalism and demand that it respond to them. And since we have tried to make a case for the moral viability of democratic capitalism, such serious charges must be answered.

The arguments of the ecology group are too diverse, numerous, and well known to report in detail here. Critics from this group vary widely in their analyses and prescriptions, from romantics such as E. F. Schumacher and Theodore Roszak to hard-nosed realists such as Victor Ferkiss and Robert Heilbroner. But all raise a fundamental question about growth as a goal of contemporary economic life. The contours of their question are relatively simple. They observe that we are living in a finite environment; there are limited amounts of space, water, land, resources, and, above all, clean, cool air. Industrial civilization is built upon the

187

notion of continuing economic growth, and since growth must use up the limited elements listed above, we are on a collision course. There are limits to growth, and we are fast approaching them. If we do not repent of our folly soon, we will be faced with convulsive change that will alter life as we know it now or destroy it completely. Moreover, growth in production and consumption leads to a style of life that is intrinsically unsatisfying and rapacious. Our commitment to growth is immoral, then, because it robs future generations of their chance to a full life by selfishly using up their resources now and because it leads to disharmony in our relations with each other and with the natural world. From a Christian point of view, we are poor stewards of God's creation because we do not care enough for its future. We dominate it and exploit it for the sake of obscene affluence in the present. The natural world will communicate God's judgment upon us by collapsing its intricate balances and altering irrevocably the quality of life of future generations.

There is a good deal of credibility to this argument. There can be little doubt that humankind's technical capacity has been able to realize human greed to an extent that earlier generations could not. It is undeniable that there are limits in the natural environment. Agressive human intervention into our habitat has despoiled too much of it. But does this augur for the curtailment of growth and technical progress? I seriously doubt that it does. American democratic capitalism has possibilities in dealing with the issue of growth that have already been exercised to some small extent, with the promise of more to come.

First, in beginning to respond to the issue, it is important to indicate that there is a good deal of mystery about where the limits are, and those who claim to have definitive knowledge on that subject are deluding themselves. Even the Club of Rome has retracted some of its earlier dire predictions. Most professional economists have been highly critical of its projections.

Few who have looked into the equations and sources of the Forrester–Meadows Club of Rome works can agree that these have realistically captured the likely pattern of the future. Not only have they conceptual flaws and factual inaccuracies, but in addition, they ignore completely what scarcity will do to changing relative prices, and what these differential price changes will do to encourage substitutions and to relieve shortages.[7]

It is difficult not to see these Malthusian expectations in much the same light that we now see the great alarms of the early sixties concerning population growth in the United States. About the time that the hysteria was reaching its peak, the birthrate was falling precipitously. It seems more likely that we will face a serious problem of declining births among the educated classes rather than the opposite. European countries such as Sweden, France, and West Germany are already worried about their failure to reproduce themselves. People do not blindly overbreed in relation to available resources and opportunities.

Turning to limits to economic growth by the emergence of scarcities, it seems that market arrangements provide as reliable a set of indicators as do political mechanisms. In fact, in areas where there is private ownership of scarce elements, the market will signal scarcity very powerfully. Vested political interests, on the other hand, can disguise scarcities by enacting special subsidies or controls. The price of gasoline in the United States is a case in point. We have been and are being shielded from paying the world market price for gasoline. Our consumption is far above what it would be if we were made to pay the going rate. Market arrangements will serve the same purpose of signaling scarcities in other crucial areas. As prices go up, a rationing system goes into effect and the quest for substitutes or more efficient use is begun in earnest. However, common property resources, such as water and air, for which no rent is chargeable and to which everyone has access will be overused and abused. These neighborhood effects must be dealt with by political and legal means.

Robert Solow believes that the market can be aided in signaling *future* scarcities. Through such policies as graduated severance taxes and conservation subsidies, the market could discount future profits at the same rate as the society would wish to discount the welfare of future inhabitants of the planet. Further, there could be organized futures trading in natural resource products.[8] These approaches would help the market signal future scarcities more quickly than it normally does. Future claims could be reinforced in this way.

However, we know that the market, even with increased sensitivity to the future, cannot handle crucial externalities connected with air and water pollution—elements that cannot be made private property in any meaningful sense. Government must step in; indeed, it already has. The United States is one of the most advanced countries in limiting air and water pollution, and its efforts have had noticeable effect. American cities have significantly cleaner air than a decade ago. American streams, rivers, and lakes are being reconstituted. The question of how much more regulation is needed is intensely debated, especially in times of economic stress. But we should certainly not turn back. Even discounting the apocalyptic qualities of the ecological group's strictures, they are pointing to real issues. Even if the limits of growth are far in the future, there are intrinsic reasons for maintaining the highest possible quality of air and water.

Granted the need for government intervention, though, there is good reason to consider carefully the *kind* of intervention. Many mainstream economists believe that we rely almost exclusively on the most expensive and bureaucratic kind of intervention. Charles L. Schultze, for instance, distinguishes between two basic kinds of intervention.

> Society can go about dealing with market failure in two quite different ways. It can try to isolate the causes of failure and restore, as nearly as possible, an efficient market process. Or it can take matters completely into its own hands, supplant the market process, and directly determine the outputs it wants. In other words, social intervention can be *process-oriented*, seeking to correct the faulty process, or *output oriented*, seeking to bypass the process and determine outputs directly by regulation or other device.[9]

Schultze goes on to argue that social intervention has almost always been output oriented, and this has been a costly bias. It taxes the ability of government to make complex output decisions, and it stretches thin the delicate fabric of political consensus by unnecessarily widening the scope of activities it must cover.[10]

190

It would be more effective, these economists argue, to use the incentive structure of market arrangements to get the desired outcome rather than to try to regulate the outcome directly. Thus, in the case of air and water pollution, the government could institute pollution charges rather than try to make thousands of decisions based on detailed considerations it cannot possibly know or keep up with over time. Speaking of water pollution, Schultze suggests,

> If the polluting side effects of industrial activity were priced, several consequences would follow. Depending on the size of the effluent charge, firms would have incentives to reduce pollution in order to increase their own profits, or to avoid losses. The higher the charge, the greater the reduction; hence, the fee could be adjusted to achieve any desired set of water-quality standards. Firms with low costs of reducing pollution would reduce their waste discharges by more than firms with high costs of production, which is precisely what is needed to achieve any given environmental standard at the lowest national cost. Even when the standards were met, firms would still have incentives to look for ways of reducing pollution still further because they would be paying a fee on whatever residual pollutants remained. And again, most important, there would be strong incentives throughout industry for the continuing development of new technology of a pollution-reducing character.[11]

This kind of strategy is by no means the sole answer. It would have to be introduced gradually as a supplement to direct regulation of outcomes. Later it could replace many of the regulations. But certainly some highly dangerous effluents and pollutants will always have to be controlled by regulation rather than incentive. The same can be said about the effort to provide safe conditions of work. In the case of certain less health-threatening conditions, incentive policies could also work in effecting safer conditions of work. But incentives are out of place when it comes to highly threatening practices. The assurance of care for human life at the workplace must be removed from market considerations. After all these qualifications, though, the potential role for an incentive-oriented approach is considerable, and its absence is very costly.

Thus, both strategies of controlling pollution could go a long way in further reducing our despoilation of the environment. If the incentive-oriented approach were increased, we could do better than we have so far, which is already rather well. And this approach goes with the gifts of democratic capitalism rather than against them. Incidentally, it is important to remember that pollution control becomes an issue only after societies have gained a certain level of wealth. Before that, increase in production without regard for externalities seems to be the priority. For example, the Swedes complain bitterly about Russian pollution of the Baltic. But the Russian offense is less related to general callousness than to the level of affluence achieved. Thus far democratic capitalist countries are in the forefront of environmental concern.

Incentive approaches will work in other ways than in coping with market externalities. As energy sources become scarce, their price will rise dramatically. We are presently experiencing this phenomenon with oil. Such raised prices will stimulate innovation in finding substitute sources of energy and in using the energy we have more efficiently. And if market arrangements have been brilliantly innovative in the past, there is little reason to believe that innovation will suddenly stop. In fact, a few predictions are in order. In the future we will be able to improve dramatically the efficiency with which we consume our present sources of energy. We will look back with bemusement on the crudity of our present wasteful technologies in transporation, heating, and manufacture. Our present technologies represent the stage of development when one of the factors, energy, was cheap and plentiful. When present sources become scarcer, technology will change to cope with the waste if we are made to pay for it. Why should we lose over half the heat generated for heating our homes and places of work? Why must airplanes use so much space for taking off and landing, so much fuel, and pollute so much? When one views the difference in efficiency between American and European cars, is it not likely that American car manufacturers can improve their products immensely?

Further, as the price of energy rises, the search for substitutes will be intensified. Nuclear fission looks like it will not be the best substitute for both economic and environmental reasons, although for the short run we will be partially dependent upon it. But there may be revolutionary potential in nuclear fusion, as well as in solar sources. Much more can be done also with the immense coal deposits that we already know exist. And who is to say how much oil there is in the world? No one really knows.

At any rate, because of both pollution and scarce resources it is unwise to extrapolate from current trends. There is too much uncertainty about sources, the immensity of natural forces are probably underestimated, technical change is too dynamic, and substitute sources may come from highly unpredictable directions. Given the innovative propensities of both governmental and private enterprise, the struggle for environmental quality and adequate sources of energy cannot be expected to end in abject failure. Indeed, under continued prodding from ecological groups, our society can continue to improve its record in environmental concerns, especially if it considers wisely the kind of interventions it makes. The most difficult problems we face are in the international arena where no polity is available to deal with cross-national issues of pollution and supply. In that arena we must work patiently toward international consensus.

Finally, it appears that the *kind* of growth American democratic capitalism will be experiencing may be less taxing on the environment than that which we have had up to this point. Daniel Bell, in his *The Coming of Post-Industrial Society*, has argued persuasively that modern economic systems—especially in democratic capitalist countries—are expanding in the service and knowledge sectors rather than in the manufacturing sector.[12] Less energy is used and less pollution is generated in those sectors even though their output is a significant part of our society's growth. Moreover, emerging life styles in American society seem to be moving from consumption of manufactured goods toward more time- and service-intensive pursuits. Thus, the kind of future growth may prove to be considerably different, on both production and consumption sides.

These strategies no doubt seem terribly partial, incremental, and reformist. They operate within the continuities of democratic capitalism. They do not flow from radically different philosophies of life from what we already have. They may seem complacently optimistic to the more fervent in the ecological group. But we have seen some signs of significant progress, and there is good reason to hope for more. Indeed, it seems terribly pessimistic to think that after centuries of economic and technical progress, everything has suddenly changed and humanity is doomed to be the victim of its incompetence in controlling and correcting the consequences of its own ingenuity. It seems more likely that if doom is to come it will continue to come in the ruptures of human-to-human relations, not human-to-nature relations. What's more, the ecologists, with a few exceptions such as Heilbroner in his *Inquiry into the Human Prospect*, rarely draw out the full conclusions that their demands for the curtailment of growth would entail. Wholesale lapses into authoritarianism, wars of redistribution, pervasive starvation in as yet undeveloped parts of the world, and closure to many human aspirations would be the probable results of decisional or coerced curtailment. And those consequences obviously have moral dimensions, as do the consequences of continued growth. Therefore, it seems that growth must continue until there are clearer signs that we cannot cope with its effects. We must not be stampeded into drastic solutions on the basis of uncertain predictions about the future. And it appears that the combined efficiency of social intervention and market mechanisms give democratic capitalism as much of a chance of avoiding doomsday as do the instruments available to more centralized systems.

A second serious moral challenge to American democratic capitalism comes from those who believe that our economic growth has been primarily obtained by unfair exploitation of weaker, underdeveloped countries. This viewpoint constitutes for many people the single most important objection to democratic capitalism. The viewpoint emerges with many variations, from the pronouncements of hard-line Marxist ideologues of the Eastern bloc to the milder moral exhortations of church bodies. Concerning the latter, any cursory acquaintance with their "social justice" materials will quickly indicate the extent to which the churches have been influenced by the "theory of dependent capitalism." Millions of morally sensitive people believe that American capitalism is the greatest source of oppression of the poor on the face of the earth. This alone, regardless of how the social system works at home, is enough to delegitimate the system in their eyes. This perspective then, with its moral and political challenge to democratic capitalism, must be dealt with or the moral viability of capitalism evaporates.

Most theories of dependent capitalism derive from Lenin's theory of imperialism and are taken up again and again by contemporary Marxist commentators. Persuasive to many people, they are then further promulgated in less ideological form by many critics who are not Marxist in any consistent sense of the word. Be that as it may, the theory has entered the debate on the role of the American economy in the world and commands the assent of a great portion of religious and secular proponents of international social justice. Indeed, it would be fair to say that it is *the* dominating frame of reference for the "progressive" edge of theological social ethics. Thus, this moral objection to democratic capitalism deserves to be handled in some detail. Though our response will be insufficient from a specialized point of view, it will provide a needed segment of our more general assessment of capitalism and its challenges.

It will be useful to elaborate the theory of dependent capitalism in its orthodox form. Paul Sweezy can serve as a good representative of this part of the Marxist tradition, and his view deserves to be reported at some length. He states the thesis of his comprehensive argument in the following way:

> It is absurd to picture the world before, say 1500 A.D. as being in the condition of the Third World today. The truth is—and this is the key to understanding the whole of modern history—that *the underdevelopment of the Third World is the product of the very same historical process which resulted in the development of the advanced capitalist world.* The two, development here and underdevelopment there, are the opposite sides of the very same coin.[13]

He then begins to elaborate the thesis. He chronicles the forays of the Spanish, Portuguese, Italians, and British into unexplored parts of the world after 1500. They conquered and looted. Then they colonized and drained riches from the colonies into their own home economies to finance capitalist development. (Distinctions are not very important here. Sweezy designates as "capitalist" the great Catholic monarchies with their feudal social systems and mercantilist economic policies. Evidently any expansionist imperial power is "capitalist" in this kind of thinking. Babylonia, Egypt, Greece, Rome, and the Turkish empire are also, by this definition, "capitalist" powers.) Nevertheless, Sweezy presses on.

> After the conquerors and the looters came the investors, the traders, the bankers, and the administrators and advisors—all those who make it their business to turn the colonies and semicolonies into lasting sources of profit for the metropolises. As a result of their efforts, a characteristic pattern of economic relations developed between the center and the periphery. The periphery came to specialize in producing raw materials needed in the center and to provide a market for the latter's manufactured goods. Ownership of most of the businesses in the periphery fell into the hands of the capitalists of the center and most of the profits flowed into their pockets. The underdevelopment of the periphery was thus frozen, perpetuated, and deepened, while the center was enabled to continue with the aid of the wealth drained out of its satellites.[14]

Further, the fundamental pattern of the center exploiting the periphery applies within countries as well as in the international sphere. In the United States the Northeast has exploited the South and West. Manhattan lives on the exploitation of Harlem. Rio lives by the surplus it extracts from the shanty towns encompassing it. As a rule of history, then, capitalist development inevitably produces development at one pole and underdevelopment at the other. Once this is clearly grasped, so the argument goes, much else falls into place in a coherent and intelligible pattern. "Trade, investment, and aid are precisely the means by which the advanced countries exploit the underdeveloped and maintain them in their underdeveloped condition!"[15] Multinational corporations are the current instruments of exploitation by the metropolis. The only way that nations, including the developed, can get free of this terrible round of exploitation is through revolutionary changes in their social systems. Revolutionary socialism is the only chance for a just and peaceful future.

Now this argument is compelling intellectually in its clarity and simplicity, and morally in its cutting denunciation of ill-gained riches and undeserved poverty. Its theoretical and moral neatness can be attributed to several key notions. At the heart of the Marxist perspective is the labor theory of value, rejected for over a hundred years by mainstream economics, that assumes that only direct human labor creates value. In this perspective, management skills, entrepreneurial initiative, interest, rent, and the profits that come from these are really a form of theft. Since value can only be produced by labor, the real source of profit under private property systems must be the exploitation of the laborer. When this viewpoint is stretched to apply to the economic relations among nations, it casts every relationship between developed and less-developed nations as a zero-sum game. Every gain by the developed nations must be at the expense of the less-developed since the developed nation provides capital, technology, and management expertise whereas the undeveloped provides the labor. Whatever return is gained by the former is immoral exploitation. In this scenario, we always gain immorally while the less-developed nations lose undeservedly. Further, the argument vigorously generalizes on a global scale; indeed, it is my suspicion that since Marxism failed miserably in analyzing and predicting the movement of industrialized countries, it raised its theory to the global level where complexities and unpredictabilities make it more difficult to falsify. People seek coherent theories for understanding a very complex set of international relations, and since the Marxists have missed the mark in interpreting the development of the industrialized world, they magnify their theory to apply to world history and try to provide that coherence sought by many people, especially the morally concerned. Marxist interpretations have been more than *attempts* at providing intellectual and moral coherence. They have become the motivating interpretations for many revolutionary movements throughout the world, movements which must be respected since they claim to represent a good portion of the world's poor.

Nevertheless, I find those interpretations unconvincing, and I fear that reliance on them will not improve the plight of the poor. Indeed, there is good evidence that as revolutionary socialist regimes come to power they face economic, social, and political problems that were not accounted for by their Marxist theory, but which are accounted for by less doctrinaire economic thought. As they face these problems, they either become intolerable oppressors and malfeasants, or they begin to adopt policies that are more in line with conventional economic thought. Thus, while the Marxist model of dependent capitalism may provide necessary revolutionary fervor, it does not provide the analytical and prescriptive potency needed to wrestle with the complex challenges they face.

Other accounts of economic relations are more credible, though not as simple and morally stimulating. W. Arthur Lewis, in his *The Evolution of the International Economic Order*, gives an alternative interpretation of the causes of underdevelopment and, following from that, a different prescription for improving the situation. First, Lewis contradicts the notion that the industrial revolution in the capitalist countries was dependent on the raw materials of the Third World. He points out that the developing industrial nations of the West were virtually self-sufficient in the raw materials of the industrial revolution and that therefore trade between the First and Third Worlds simply did not amount to much.[16] But Lewis does not deny that a fateful division of the world occurred in which the Third World became the exporters of tropical agricultural goods and raw materials while the First World developed an industrial base. Why did this happen, especially since at that point in history industrialization did not demand the tremendous investment in technology, management expertise, and capital that it does now?

Lewis notes that the favorite explanation for the fateful division, demonstrated by Sweezy above, is a political one in which the exploiting nations prohibit industrial development.

198

Lewis admits that nations such as Britain tried to do this. But the political domination explanation just will not wash, for the world was not all colonial in the middle of the nineteenth century. Brazil, Argentina, and all the rest of Latin America were independent political entities which were free to industrialize but did not.

India, Ceylon, Java, and the Philippines were colonies, but in 1850 there were still no signs of industrialization in Thailand or Japan or China, Indo-China or the rest of the Indonesian archipelago. The partition of Africa did not come until 1880, when the industrial revolution was already a hundred years old. We cannot escape the fact that Eastern and Southern Europe were just as backward in industrializing as South Asia or Latin America. Political independence alone is an insufficient basis for industrialization.[17]

The author, who, by the way, is a West Indian who has had a distinguished career as an economic historian in both First and Third World universities, then turns to economic explanations for division of the world into developed and underdeveloped countries. He eschews the simple morality tales of the Marxist perspective by noting that the classical economists of the eighteenth century had already pointed to the real economic causes of the division.[18]

What these classical economists had seen was that industrial revolution is dependent upon a prior or simultaneous agricultural revolution. In order for industrialization to take place, agriculture has to be capable of producing the surplus food and raw materials consumed in the industrial sector, and it is the affluent state of the farmers that enables them to be a market for industrial products. High productivity in agriculture also allows a greater portion of the rural population to stay on the land and not flood into the cities, thus creating great pressure on the urban infrastructure and making it necessary for government to borrow heavily to sustain a burgeoning urban population. Moreover, power in these countries—and for that matter in Central and Southern Europe—was still in the hands of landed classes, who benefited from cheap imports and saw no reason to support an emerging industrial order. They could respond to the other opportunity the industrial revolution had opened up in other countries, namely to export agricultural products.[19] Incidentally—and this is not part of Lewis's argument—it would be interesting to trace how Catholicism reinforced these patterns and unintentionally impeded the development that would have meant quite a difference.

Lewis summarizes a much more complex argument that we cannot report in detail:

> The principle cause of the poverty of the developing countries, and of their poor factoral terms of trade is that half their labor force (more or less) produces food at very low productivity levels. This limits the domestic market for manufactures and services, keeps the propensity to import too high, reduces taxable capacity and savings, and provides goods and services for export on unfavorable terms. To alter this is the fundamental way to change Less Developed Countries/More Developed Countries relations. But this takes time.[20]

This interpretation is certainly not as dramatic as the Marxist interpretation. And though it is also a bit too simple, it grasps a more accurate insight into why the world is the way it is. Many other economists, such as Samuelson, Harry Johnson, Gayle Johnson, and Luther Tweeten, have similar analyses. They, and Lewis, also have prescriptions that we shall mention later.

All of this is not meant to exonerate the powerful, industrialized West. We are Niebuhrian enough to believe that a great imbalance of power among nations will lead to domination. And there is no scarcity of documented instances of unjust treatment of weaker countries by stronger ones. Political and economic power combined to create monopoly conditions where resources and labor could be extracted from host countries on highly unfavorable terms. American domination of Central America and Cuba are cases in point. Indeed, as many economists have pointed out, the theory of dependent capitalism has a good case with respect to foreign direct investment in petroleum and other extractive industries. Monopoly conditions prevented the host countries from getting a decent price for their nonrenewable resources. But even here the case is somewhat ambiguous. For what constitutes a just price for a natural endowment that was worthless until the multinationals found it and marketed it in the developed West? Caveats aside, however, there is a good deal of historical guilt involved in our relations with the Third World. Our relations with them must be improved so that they have more independent bargaining power in relation to the more powerful nations of the world. But such improvements will not be made if the causes of poverty in the Third World are constantly attributed to economic exploitation on the part of the First. (It is curious that the left always overestimates the capacity of the United States for mischief in the world while the right overestimates its capacity for "good," that is, for ordering the world according to American blueprints.) It is most likely true that the Third World is dependent because it is underdeveloped, not underdeveloped because it is dependent.

Conversely, the affluence of the First World is based not primarily on exploitation of the Third, although there is a measure of that, but rather on a complex set of social, political, and economic factors that have given it, at least at this point in history, very productive economic engines. Trade among the First World nations has pressed toward specialization, which has increased the efficiency of those economic engines. Indeed, Shonfield indicates that the prosperity of capitalist countries since the Second World War has been enhanced dramatically by trade among themselves.[21] Further, even in unbalanced relations among the First and Third World nations, it is clear that the zero-sum game is not the only result. Developing nations have benefited from economic relations with the developed. At least the research of Canadian, Australian, and other economists, for example, suggests that foreign corporations bring more into economies in technology, capital, and access to world markets than they take out in the form of earnings. These studies indicate that there is little difference in the corporate behavior of domestic and foreign firms; on the contrary, foreign firms are given higher marks in terms of export performance, industrial research and development, and other economic indicators.[22] Thus, the record is mixed. It would be naive to think that First World economic incursion has not seriously affected many nations adversely; but it is equally naive to think that significant benefits have not accrued to host countries. An accurate reading would have to include a case-by-case examination of countries and multinationals.

But if democratic capitalist countries cannot be simplistically blamed for the past misery of the world, as the theories of dependent capitalism allege, what of the present and future? Where is the present economic order moving? Robert Gilpin, in an excellent article entitled "Three Models of the Future," outlines three competing interpretations of the evolution of the international economic order.[23] He examines the "sovereignty at bay" thesis, associated with the views of Harry Johnson, that sees the multinationals as instruments of world economic integration. Gilpin argues that this perspective neglects the continuing power and importance of the nation-state and its capacity to shape the economic future by political decision. He then examines the theory of dependent capitalism and concludes that it is too conspiratorial—it overestimates the unity of the developed world and underestimates the capacity of the Third World to act on the stage of history by forming producer cartels and by bargaining with competing economic blocs for aid and advantage. Moreover, the theory does not provide a realistic portrayal of the role of the multinational; it sees it only as an exploitative tool of imperialism. Rather, Gilpin opts for a third interpretation of the world economic order, which he calls "benign mercantilism." Neither unimpeded free market dynamics nor collapsing capitalism will characterize the future. We will see, according to Gilpin, a world economy composed of regional blocs and centers of power, in which economic bargaining and competition will predominate.

> Through the exercise of economic power and various trade-offs, each center of the world economy would seek to shift the costs and benefits of economic interdependence to its own advantage. Trade, monetary, and investment relations would be the consequence of negotiations as nation states and regional blocs sought to increase the benefits of interdependence and to decrease the costs. This in fact has been the direction of the evolution of the international economy, from a liberal to a negotiated system, since the rise of large and rival economic entities in the latter part of the nineteenth century.[24]

Such a scenario seems most likely after the recent emergence of other important economic blocs to challenge the hegemony of the United States. But since the United States is still by far the largest economic power in the world, and since many of the other powerful centers of economic power are dependent upon its military might, it follows that such a benign mercantilism will be strongly influenced by American political and economic policy. It will be crucial, according to this interpretation, to prevent "benign" mercantilism from degenerating into a more malevolent version, in which countries and regions participate in beggar-thy-neighbor policies. In such a situation the Third World would suffer from the economic nationalism that would follow.

Thus, the world is more complex than the theory of dependent capitalism allows. The good guys and the bad guys are not always clearly identifiable. And certainly the facile separation of the world into oppressed and oppressors is not helpful to realistic strategies of improvement, though it may be immensely satisfying as moral rhetoric. Democratic capitalist countries, especially the United States, are not fated by the force of historical necessity to be vicious exploiters of the world's poor. Our gifts can be used for good, even as our power can be used for all. We are not sentenced to be the world's oppressors, just as we have not in the past been primarily responsible for its poverty.

Complexity and ambiguity, however, do not excuse the democratic capitalist nations from the challenge to improve the lot of the world's poor. From a moral point of view, we are summoned to efforts to universalize the possibilities of human fulfillment to all beings. This is the burden of Christian agape and, for that matter, of Rawlsian justice. And in relation to the world's hungry, agape can take the form of the difference principle in international relations. The inequalities among nations, regardless of their source, should be used to enhance the long-term prospects of the disadvantaged. We should not become sentimental about the ease with which this can be done, or we will quickly fall prey to cynicism or despair. Nation-states, as extremely large entities, are least able to engage in disinterested action on behalf of others. This means that strategies meant to enhance the prospects of the world's poor must also be in the broad self-interest of the developed world. Conversely, the problems of the poor countries must not be cast in oversimplified theories which do not encompass the subtleties of the challenges facing them or account for the element of tragedy in the histories of all nations, developed and undeveloped alike. And, ironically enough, the democratic capitalist powers of the world seem to be the only ones able and willing to activate the difference in principle in international affairs. They are able because their economies have been productive enough to offer generous aid. At the same time, their economies are powerful enough to dominate unduly the economies of the lesser developed countries. The centralized economies have not been productive enough either to dominate or to offer sufficient aid. Moreover, the ideological commitment of Marxist socialism is not to aid but to revolution. Hence, Russia, for instance, has a weak record in foreign aid but a remarkable commitment to insurgency.

American strategy in relation to the developing world, then, should take some of the following directions. First, we should continue our good record of emergency aid to nations and peoples who experience serious crises, regardless of their ideological commitments. This is one of the rare ways that nations can really exhibit disinterested care for all. Crisis intervention does not solve the long-term problems of poor nations, but it does respond to dire need and becomes a symbol of the unity of the human family. Churches, of course, are even more obligated to act in this fashion, offering humanitarian aid wherever needed as a direct expression of Christian agape. Churches should be less eager to engage in questions of political strategy where their competence is limited. As an ambassador of one of the African nations once put it, African nations themselves have difficulty sorting out which foreign political groups to support in the turmoil of nation building. How can churches based abroad claim to make these decisions wisely? It would be better, he suggested amid the protests of the white church people, to confine yourselves to increased humanitarian aid. Now this advice should not be taken as a universal rule, but churches should commit themselves to political groups only when issues are extremely clear and moral principles grossly violated. The good intentions of the churches are no substitute for wise policy. As to national policy, the United States should create a commodity reserve program for emergency food relief. Commodity reserves are the first line of defense against hunger and are needed to deal with food shortages arising from unpredictable weather or pestilence. Such a program ought to be internationally supported and administered, but even if other nations hold back, this nation has the resources to shoulder responsibility. In the latter case, emergency aid would be provided as a grant channeled through charitable agencies, where possible, to ensure that benefits actually get to the hungry. The reserves should be managed in such a way as not to depress prices at home or to create undue dependency among recipients.[25]

Second, our foreign policy ought to support political leadership in the less-developed countries that genuinely represents the interests of all their people, but especially their poor. This is easy to say, but infinitely more difficult to do. But in some instances— in Central America, for example—we have supported political leadership that represents only a small rich segment and that positively oppresses the poor. It is altogether clear that the forces of national independence are irreversible at this point in time. Revolutionary socialism has captured the spirit of national liberation in many places in the world; it is one of the major shortcuts to development and growth. In other places, such as South Korea and Taiwan, right-wing governments use more capitalistic approaches to development. Both approaches tend to be authoritarian. But the key issues are whether either approach increases the prospects of the ordinary people, enhances the spirit of national identity and independence, and holds out prospects for the long-term increase in the democratic rights of consent, public and private liberty, and fair equality of opportunity. Evidence for and against either form of authoritarianism is very mixed and must be measured on a case-by-case basis. We should be less harsh in our judgments of left-wing authoritarianism and more demanding toward right-wing governments, simply to redress the imbalance in our record. Regimes who most adequately meet the criteria listed above will tend to be legitimated by their people, and therefore more stable. And this stability is in the long-term interest of democratic capitalist nations. On the other hand, casting our lot with repressive minority regimes is destructive of our long-term political and economic interests, not to mention the moral commitments we have to the improvement of the prospects of the poor. Moreover, as governments representative of their people gain strength, they will deal with multinational firms in ways that are more advantageous to the host country but yet not neglectful of the possibilities that multinationals can offer. This is happening on a massive scale already and will doubtless occur increasingly often in the future. Developing nations are facing a world in which political and economic hegemony have broken down, and their governments will be able to choose alternatives in a more competitive environment. This should be to their distinct advantage. Nation-states and multinationals will have to adapt to this new environment, as they already have begun to do.[26]

Foreign policy for the foreseeable future will be constrained by the political interplay of the great powers and the economic interests of the United States and its competitors, so we should expect no miraculous changes. But we can hope that the United States as a leader of the democratic capitalist nations can put its weight behind the authentic interests of the poorer nations.

Third, we should work to remove trade barriers to imports from developing countries. Luther Tweeten offers important advice in this regard:

> Overall benefits to developing countries can be enhanced by removing trade barriers jointly with other developed countries through multilateral trade negotiations. International commodity agreements to stabilize prices of developing country exports such as sugar can also be beneficial. Buffer stocks may serve as a useful device to stabilize prices under commodity agreements, but care must be taken to avoid high minimum prices that generate burdensome surpluses.[27]

Since we have been committed in principle to free trade, we

should attempt to be true to our principles. Open door policies with regard to goods from the Third World may be the most important thing we can offer in the economic realm. Such policies will enable developing countries to identify and pursue their comparative economic advantage. And, as those countries experience growth, they will in turn provide us with markets for our specialized goods and services.

Fourth, the United States should gradually raise the proportion of its GNP for foreign aid from the current 0.25 percent to the United Nations target of 0.7 percent. A portion of this should be used to help nations develop their industrial base, but the major effort should aim at improving the agricultural base of developing countries. There seems to be wide agreement on this latter point. Lewis, for instance, argues bluntly that

> The most important item on the agenda of development is to transform the food sector, create agricultural surpluses to feed the urban population, and thereby create the domestic basis for industry and modern services. If we can make this domestic change, we shall automatically have a new international economic order.[28]

Although the burden of increasing food output rests primarily with the developing nations themselves, the United States can be of immense help since it is in the forefront of agricultural research. It can aid in the transfer of appropriate technology and research, and it can support indigenous research efforts. Again, Tweeten has important insights:

> Aid would be provided with continuity and mainly as grants, with per capita aid allocations greatest to nations with lowest per capita income. Accordingly aid would be restricted to the purchase of items conducive to economic development such as fertilizer, fertilizer plants, irrigation equipment, and plant breeding expertise. Incentives and penalties would be provided to encourage countries to develop sound family planning, land reform, human rights, and economic development policies. If the U.S. balance of payments problem continues severe, recipient nations might be required to spend a high proportion of aid on U.S. products.[29]

In concluding this discussion of growth, it is important to note that the growth of the developing world is dependent to an important extent upon the continued efficiency and growth of the developed nations. Inputs from the developed world will continue to be needed just as its markets will be needed for the products of the developing nations. Economic recession bodes ill for both parties. In this regard the observation so often made by critics of American growth that 6 percent of the world consumes 37 percent of its goods and services needs to be put into perspective. Without that consumption, there would not be demand for Third World goods nor sufficient demand to stimulate American production of abundant, low-priced agricultural goods. Moreover, it is rarely added in this observation that the same 6 percent *produces* at least 37 percent of the world's goods and services. The United States is one of the few nations that produces more food than it consumes, a fact that should not lead to waves of self-congratulation but should dash the insinuation that we are parasites on the rest of the world's bounty. There may be good ethical, religious, and aesthetic reasons for trimming the kind of consumption we now engage in, but there are fewer good economic reasons for such strategies. In fact, the economic repercussions of broad cuts in consumption may be just the opposite of what was intended.

THE FUTURE
OF MARKET ECONOMIES

We argued earlier that American democratic capitalism is built upon and encourages a wide dispersion of power. Because of the decentralization of power, a rough "natural" equilibrium that is essentially self-regulating ensues. Many of the tasks and functions of society are performed by this unconsciously coordinated system. We have spent a good deal of space arguing that this is so in the economic sphere; we have tried to show that indeed our market arrangements are competitive and can be trusted as the major vehicle of economic choice. We have admitted that there is no automatic harmony in this system and that it needs public intervention for both practical and moral reasons. This system, intricately bound up with market arrangements, undergirds many of the values we cherish and should therefore be maintained and extended as much as possible. In this way, the state cannot and need not become omnicompetent.

Many critics believe, as we have already indicated, that there is no such thing as this unconsciously coordinated system. The whole thing is dominated by large private centers of economic power. We have argued against that view of the American past and present. But what of the future? One of the main trends of the future will be the shift from market direction to political direction, or so many commentators believe. A host of these commentators argue that there will be an inevitable replacement of market choice by political choice. The fact that the equilibrium did and still does exist is of little consequence; in the future it will no longer. We will either be forced by historical necessity to replace the market with conscious political choice, or we will finally wise up and freely decide to do so.

Let us examine an example of the former view, proponents of which do not necessarily welcome the coming politicization of life but are resigned to its ambiguous arrival. Daniel Bell, for instance, represents such a view. He argues that *economizing* logic—a characteristic of competitive market arrangements— is being replaced by *socializing* logic. In the postindustrial society he describes in detail, there are more common public services developed, more social goods such as air, water, neighborhoods, and land that must be protected, and more intensive concerns for social justice to be considered. Interest groups develop around each of these items and demand that decisions concerning them be made in the political arena. Market arrangements are either incompetent or inappropriate to deal with them. So the political sphere grows, encompassing even more of our lives. The political realm, as it becomes burdened with increasing responsibility, will reflect these social claims. It provides a specific locus of decision, as against the more dispersed role of the market, and thus becomes a visible point at which pressures can be applied. Further, it sharpens conflict on values since each interest group has a different set of priorities according to its own ordering. Politics will increasingly become a cockpit of haggling.[30]

Bell summarizes this line of argument in the following:

> It seems clear to me that, today, we in America are moving away from a society based on a private-enterprise market system toward one in which the most important economic decisions will be made at the political level, in terms of consciously defined "goals" and "priorities." . . . Today there is a visible change from market to non-market political decision-making. The market disperses responsibility: the political center is visible, the question of who gains and who loses is clear, and government becomes a cockpit. . . . Whether such a change will represent "progress" is a nice metaphysical question that I, for one, do not know how to answer. This is a society that has rested on the premises of individualism and market rationality, in which the varied ends desired by individuals would be maximized by free exchange. We now move to a communal ethic, without that community being, as yet, wholly defined. In a sense, the movement away from governance by political economy to governance by political philosophy—for that is the meaning of the shift—is a turn to non-capitalist modes of social thought. And this is the long-run historical tendency in Western society.[31]

Schumpeter came up with a similar conclusion. He believed that the very success of large capitalist corporations would "automatize progress," undercutting the need for a function of the entrepreneurial classes.[32] Further, capitalism's hedonist affluence will undermine its own ethos of self-discipline and striving. Its very commitment to education and civil liberty multiplies its critics who demand a "rational," centralized direction of economic life. Some form of socialism will emerge out of the self-defeating success of capitalism.[33] Many Marxist interpretations reach similar conclusions from a different set of causes.

Some versions of historical necessity look for a long, gradual process of transformation that can be reasonably humane. Others, such as those of orthodox Marxism, anticipate that the transformation will be cataclysmic. Still other theorists, such as Robert Heilbroner and anti-Utopians in the environmentalist group, predict a drastic downturn in the human project as expansionist industrial civilization collides with natural limits. But their sentence of doom is pronounced upon both industrial capitalism and socialism.

Our response to these announcements of historical necessity is rather brief. They extrapolate too much from trends they observe at the time and do not allow enough for the unpredictable changes that are a part of human history, changes generated by the serendipity of the historical process or by human choice itself. Although most of these efforts point to challenges that must be dealt with, they do not account for the new paths that are shaped by responses to the challenges. For example, national governments can try to inhibit or even reverse the tendency for political choice to supplant market arrangements. In recent years we have seen countries such as France, Israel, and Britain cut down on the role of political control over their economies. West German and Japanese varieties of democratic capitalism are certainly sharply distinct from their centralized predecessors, Nazi Germany and Imperial Japan. Even many Eastern European countries are extending the sphere of market arrangements and limiting the role of the state. There seems to be little evidence that the public sphere must necessarily swallow up the private. A different outcome may emerge as we experiment more with different *kinds* of intervention which, as we have already discussed, allow the market mechanism to operate more accurately, but yet achieve desired effects. In the following chapters, we will suggest some ways that public goods can be achieved in this fashion.

A second group of intellectuals believes that the market system is doomed. This group does not believe that it will be ended by the force of historical necessity but rather by the realization of people under capitalism that it is fundamentally irrational and rapacious and that social systems can be guided far better by political planning and control. Theorists in this group range from neo-Marxist revisionists and non-Marxist socialists through ecological humanists to European-oriented aristocrats. The Marxist socialist viewpoint has already been dealt with. It assumes that what is being reflected in contemporary democratic capitalism is the agenda of monopolistic private economic power. Thus, it

211

argues that government must intervene decisively in economic life so that "production is for use, not profit" and priorities are set "according to need, not greed." The assumption here is that the real preferences of people and groups are not being expressed because of the domination of economic and social life by monopoly power. Political channels can better express the people's wishes and needs than distorted market systems.

We have already developed our response to this perspective in Chapter 6. In essence, we argued that the American economic system is workably competitive and that people's values are expressed in the demand–supply dynamics of the market. This implies that it is extremely difficult to make profits by providing something that is of little or no use to people and that under competitive market conditions one finds it difficult to pursue one's own greed without in some way answering someone else's need. There are serious flaws with the system, we admit, when people do not have enough economic wherewithal to register their preferences. But redistribution of enough wealth to do so is not inconsistent with democratic capitalism and is in fact being done. Further, we argued that the centralization of too much and too many kinds of power in political hands tempts government to idolatrous pretentions. But, enough; we have already made our case in this matter.

Likewise, we have registered our arguments against those who call for a comprehensive political philosophy—most particularly their own—to order a vastly expanded political realm. Consensus on such a philosophy is nowhere evident, and any premature imposition of a unitive vision will lead to authoritarian paternalism. Given our present state of fragmented meaning, a pragmatic liberalism is preferable over well-meaning perfectionism.

However, granting all this, it is unlikely that the scope of American governmental responsibility will wane. Governmental functions in an increasingly interdependent world will expand, especially if we move toward regional economic blocs whose relations are politically negotiated (albeit in the context of international market forces which cannot be ignored). Neighborhood effects of the industrial process will have to be dealt with.

The health of the equilibrium itself will have to be maintained by vigilant antimonopoly policy. Macroeconomic management will continue to be a high priority in a world economy endangered by inflation and unemployment. Government involvement in pressing toward a higher degree of justice will be necessary. There is little evidence that we will need less-able political leadership, particularly as we deliberate about the proper kinds of public intervention in society.

Accepting these necessary roles, though, should not destroy our sense of proportion. The most important and greater share of our lives are rightly lived within an essentially self-regulating, free social system. The primary economic, social, and religious tasks of our society are fulfilled in this system. It is a precious asset. It is creative, resilient, diverse, and basically stable. American democratic capitalism undergirds it and lives by it. And we can choose to protect it and extend its usefulness, as we shall propose in the following chapters.

NOTES

1. Lester Thurow, "The Myth of the American Economy," *Newsweek*, 14 February 1977.

2. Peter Drucker, *The Unseen Revolution* (New York: Harper & Row, 1976), pp. 27ff.

3. Assar Lindbeck, *Can Pluralism Survive?* (Ann Arbor: University of Michigan Press), p. 19.

4. Both Friedman and Drucker make such suggestions. Milton Friedman, *Capitalism and Freedom* (Chicago: University of Chicago Press, 1962), pp. 174ff., and Drucker, *Unseen Revolution*, pp. 44ff.

5. See particularly Harry G. Johnson, "The Economics Approach to Social Questions," in *On Economics and Society* (Chicago: University of Chicago Press, 1975), pp. 17ff.

6. Drucker, *Unseen Revolution*, p. 121.

7. Paul Samuelson, *Economics*, 10th ed. (Tokyo: McGraw-Hill Kogakusha, 1976), p. 815.

8. Robert Solow, "Economics of Resource and the Resources of Economics," *American Economic Review* 64, no. 2 (May 1974): 12–13.

9. Charles L. Schultze, "The Public Use of Private Interest," *Harper's* 254, no. 1524 (May 1977): 48.

10. Ibid.

11. Ibid., p. 56.

12. Daniel Bell, *The Coming of Post-Industrial Society* (New York: Basic Books, 1973), pp. 121ff.

13. Paul M. Sweezy, *Modern Capitalism and Other Essays* (New York: Monthly Review Press, 1972), p. 18.

14. Ibid., p. 20.

15. Ibid., p. 21.

16. W. Arthur Lewis, *The Evolution of the International Economic Order* (Princeton, N.J.: Princeton University Press, 1978).

17. Ibid., p. 9.

18. Ibid.

19. Ibid., p. 11.

20. Ibid., p. 26.

21. Andrew Shonfield, *Modern Capitalism* (New York: Oxford University Press, 1969), pp. 46ff.

22. Robert Gilpin, "Three Models of the Future," in *World Politics and International Economics,* ed. C. F. Bergsten and L. B. Krause (Washington, D.C.: The Brookings Institution, 1975), p. 53.

23. Ibid., pp. 37-60.

24. Ibid., p. 60.

25. Luther Tweeten, "The Hard (and Sometimes Hopeful) Facts About This Hungry World," *Worldview* 21, no. 12 (December 1978): 24.

26. Lewis, *International Economic Order,* pp. 44-46.

27. Tweeten, "The Hard Facts About This Hungry World," p. 24.

28. Lewis, *International Economic Order,* p. 74.

29. Tweeten, "The Hard Facts About This Hungry World," p. 24.

30. Bell, *The Coming of Post-Industrial Society,* pp. 364ff.

31. Ibid., pp. 297-98.

32. Joseph Schumpeter, *Capitalism, Socialism and Democracy* (New York: Harper & Row, 1940; 1975), p. 134.

33. Ibid., pp. 143-63.

9

The Challenges of Justice

We have already discussed a good deal of governmental intervention in relation to efficiency and growth and in relation to maintaining the health of the natural equilibrium. Now we move to challenges facing American democratic capitalism from the principles of justice themselves, especially as they relate to the internal life of American society. As has been our practice, we will use our interpretation of Rawls's principles of justice to take up the challenges one by one.

LIBERTY

One of the major objections to the American system of justice is that we have many liberties established in principle, but in actual practice these liberties are mere abstractions. We may have the political liberty of consent, but we are not given sufficient choice among real alternatives. We may have the power of the vote and the freedom to form associations, but we and our associations have little weight in the political process compared with that of large corporate economic interests. In principle we are equal before the law, but those who have wealth and power have access to legal defenses that gives them a huge advantage over ordinary citizens. As we move down the economic ladder, we find these shortcomings becoming more pronounced, and even basic

215

private liberties of vocation, movement, association, and abode are severely compromised by lack of economic means.

The "Worth" of Liberty

Rawls makes a distinction that helps us understand this challenge a bit more clearly. He distinguishes between liberty and "worth of liberty." The former involves the establishment in principle of equal public and private liberties. The latter indicates the ability to take advantage of these liberties.

> Thus liberty and the worth of liberty are distinguished as follows: liberty is represented by the complete system of the liberties of equal citizenship, while the worth of liberty to persons and groups is proportional to their capacity to advance their ends within the framework the system defines. Freedom as equal liberty is the same for all; questions of compensating for a lesser than equal liberty does not arise. But the worth of liberty is not the same for everyone. Some have greater authority and wealth, and therefore greater means to achieve their aims.[1]

At this point we will not suggest ways by which the severely disadvantaged can gain more worth of liberty; that subject is better handled under the difference principle and fair equality of opportunity, to the discussion of which we shall come presently. But the issue of worth of liberty is a serious one for ordinary citizens who are not severely disadvantaged.

One of the most important aims in this regard is the continuance of efforts to diminish the linkage between great economic power and political and legal power. Without denying that great economic concerns have a right to a voice in the political process (their fortunes certainly do affect the broader society in important ways), the political process should represent more decisively the interests of the whole community. To this end the direct political power of private centers of economic power should be diminished while the political power of ordinary citizens and their representative associations should be enlarged.

American democracy has already taken some important steps in this direction: limits of campaign contributions and lobbying,

216

disclosure laws, and congressional reforms that diminish the entrenched power of corporate interests. Further, election reforms should make campaigning for political office briefer and less expensive. Harassment of unpopular political parties and persons should cease, although in certain extreme cases surveillance should be maintained by competent, accountable national authorities. As much political power as is feasible should be devolved to lower levels. The practice of patronage should be limited so that tyrannical political units can more easily be challenged. Proportional representation should be assiduously guarded by the courts. And, above all, lower courts should be more efficient so that the rights of both individuals and society are better maintained by a swift and accurate judicial process.

These steps represent an important agenda for our social system, and we have only touched on them here. It only remains to say that the practices we have inherited are improvable—we need not think of wiping the slate clean and beginning again. In spite of all the flaws in our system of equal private and public liberties, its promise remains alive. Considering the massiveness and diversity of American society, a surprising level of quality is maintained.

American democratic polity does express the broad-based interest of the whole society in a roughly effective way. From the lower-middle class upward, the claim for public and private liberties cannot be persistently ignored. Although we cannot be complacent about our performance, it is not accurate to speak of gross systemic injustice in terms of equal liberties for this great segment of the population. But we can speak less confidently about the treatment of the severely disadvantaged, whose plight we will address shortly.

Industrial Democracy

Before we move to that subject, however, another serious challenge needs to be considered. It is difficult to decide whether it should be discussed under the guarantee of public liberty or under the intentions toward more equality, for it has ramifications

217

affecting both liberty and equality. At any rate, the issue under discussion pertains to what is called "industrial democracy" or "democratization of economic life."

This issue is very important because it represents one of the major objections against democratic capitalism raised by a broad spectrum of left-wing critics. These critics, running the gamut from revisionist Marxists through New Left radicals to democratic socialists, affirm the tradition of political liberties practiced by democratic capitalist societies. But they maintain that the political principles of consent and participation should be applied to economic as well as political life. "Participatory democracy" not only should be extended further into political life, it should be introduced fully into industrial life. These theorists exhibit as much hostility toward the bureaucratic socialism of industrialized socialist countries as they do toward capitalism. And certainly the more moderate among them, the democratic socialists, do not want to short-circuit democratic procedures in their effort to overcome capitalism by introducing "industrial democracy."

Thus, the latest version of the socialist dream is a decentralized socialism in which "the workers" own, control, or manage the enterprises in which they work. Or, at the very least, they participate in ownership, control, or management of those firms. And this participation should be founded on rights guaranteed by the political and legal order.

John Cort's theories represent this viewpoint perfectly:

> It makes some sense to say that what we need is simply to extend democratic process from the political arena, where it has been continually corrupted and weakened by industrial and economic oligarchy, to the world of the factory, office, bank and industry, so that the workers begin to own and control directly the means of production upon which their working and consuming lives depend. A key word here is "directly." It is not realistic to think that you can control state-owned factories through elected congressmen and/or the president. Watergate should have taught us how far an elected official can wander from the mind and will of the people.[2]

A good start in this direction, Cort believes, could be made by enacting the following changes in the American economic system:

218

1. A much stronger role by government in the ownership and control of elements in our economy that involve a significant public interest.
2. A provision that corporations doing business with the federal government be required, as a condition of that business, to give a significant percentage of their voting stock to their employees, redeemable on termination.
3. A provision that the boards of directors of such corporations must include at least two members elected by the employees and at least two consumer representatives appointed by public authority.
4. Enactment of the old CIO plan for industry councils representing labor, management, consumers and government in a comprehensive system of economic democracy.[3]

This mild, reformist start would move toward a full-blooded decentralized socialism in which workers control the enterprises in which they work, whether or not they actually own them.

This latest version of the socialist hope is very broad-based, if not among American labor unions, at least among American left–liberal intellectuals. It is even more prominent among the left wing of the social democratic parties of Britain and Europe. The model of Yugoslavia is often designated as the goal toward which Western industrial countries ought to strive. Efforts at such worker-controlled enterprises in Britain and the United States are celebrated as flashes of the future. They may fail now, as they often do, but in the future they will humanize the industrial system.

As were other previous versions of the socialist dream, such as that public ownership would solve the most important industrial problems, this alternative is seductive. And, from our perspective, it certainly ought to be tried, if the arrangement can be shaped by voluntary agreement. But it ought to be experimented with as a test model for a long time before the vision becomes extended by law. Even then it should not be made compulsory across the board. There are many problems with the self-management, "industrial democracy" proposals that need to be explored.

First, there is a lingering romanticism in these proposals that assumes that all unpleasant drudgery can be abolished from

219

work. In worker-controlled enterprises, the tragedy of boring repetitive labor could be assuaged by participation in decision-making processes. Or, even better, all such labor could be transformed by the creation of "work gangs" who would share in a larger productive process than is traditional on mass-production assembly lines. The Volvo experiments in Sweden are an example of this practice. There is much to be said for such experiments, and they ought to be widely attempted. In fact, they have been tried by many American enterprises with varying degrees of success. (Surprisingly enough, American workers involved in a Volvo-type experiment said they preferred the traditional way because they didn't have to involve themselves so fully in the process. They could converse or think about something else under the old system; under the new one they had to devote full attention to production. It is conceivable that workers themselves prefer the former system.) Although the workplace can indeed be further humanized, however, it is unlikely that drudgery will come to an end in the industrial process, or, for that matter, in white-collar or professional pursuits. If one looks closely at any job or vocation, there are boring, repetitive chores that contradict the young Marx's vision of creative workers externalizing their being in their products. Moreover, there will be, at least for the foreseeable future, many jobs that are difficult, unpleasant, and even dangerous. Every effort should be made to improve the quality of the workplace, but it will probably be automation—at which the capitalist world has excelled—that will eliminate the most dangerous and repetitive jobs.

Second, there is a serious question about whether such decentralized socialism can be efficient. In large enterprises, which seem to involve the most serious incidence of dull, grinding labor, there seems to be the necessity for some chain of command in order to get the work done. It is an illusion that the central government in Yugoslavia does not make the basic decisions as to what, how, and how much is to be produced in the factories. The workers may have some local control over management personnel and practice and the conditions of work, but one cannot have a planned economy and decentralized production decisions at the

220

same time. In nations with market arrangements, someone must be free to make decisions about the direction of the firm without facing the possibility of veto at every level of participation. This seems to be the problem with putting representation from local community, political, and consumer units on the boards of directors of firms. It they have real veto power, every other consideration besides economic efficiency can intrude itself into the decision-making process. Could one imagine any political unit allowing a firm to move out of its jurisdiction for greener economic pastures if it had any real power to halt such a move? Indeed, it seems that the large gains in productivity have been achieved by specialization of function. Investors invest wisely, boards of directors oversee managers, managers manage, workers work. Each one of these agents is accountable to someone for some specific responsibility. They are paid to exercise a specialized skill well. Further, unions exert direct countervailing power, and communities exert indirect power. In this arrangement there is a chain of command, but at every link in the chain there is responsibility to someone else. No one is free to ignore the demands of efficiency. And in a competitive system, players in the game are free to move from one team to the next and from one level to the next, as they indeed often do.

Can a fully participatory system along decentralized lines get the work done? The evidence is certainly not weighted in its favor. If the Yugoslavian experiment is so successful, why are there hundreds of thousands of Yugoslav workers seeking new lives and work in capitalist countries? If such schemes are both profitable and productive, as even left-wing proponents agree they must be, why have they not proved more successful for governments that have tried them repeatedly, such as the Labor government in Britain?

For many supporters of worker-managed socialism, such questions about efficiency are beside the point, since they are more interested in the moral quality of the mode and relations of production. But the issue of efficiency has moral dimensions. When it flags, workers' wages go down, their pensions are threatened, the public sector has less wealth to distribute, and social and political strife increases. These repercussions are true whether the systems are socialist or capitalist. Among pension systems in democratic capitalist nations, the moral imperative for continuing economic efficiency is paramount, as Peter Drucker has pointed out. The promise of future high living standards implicit in pension systems can only be fulfilled if productivity increases.[4]

Ownership of the means of production has also been a crucial item of contention, the argument being that private ownership precludes workers from receiving the full share of the wealth they produce. But since ownership is now separated from management, and since ownership itself is a highly varied phenomenon, this argument has less credibility. Indeed, it seems that workers own a broadening share of American industry itself through their massive pension funds. At least this is the burden of Drucker's insight into the revolutionary impact of "pension fund socialism." He estimates that by 1985 pension funds will own from 50 to 60 percent of the equity capital in the American economy.[5] Workers own an increasing share of the economy, even as the proportion of the GNP going to them has increased over the years.

These observations do not satisfy the objections of the true believers in decentralized, worker-controlled socialism, for they still do not answer the demand that workers "participate in all the decisions that shape their destiny," or, in stronger versions, that "workers control directly the means of production upon which their working and consuming lives depend." The assumption here is that if persons provide some indispensable element in a highly interdependent system of production, they have the moral right to participate in or control the direction of the whole system. Does such an assumption hold water? I doubt it seriously, because it allows for no proportional relation between the responsibility to and for an enterprise, on the one hand, and the "say," "vote," or "claim" a person or group has, on the other.

This proportional relation can be illustrated from the experience that many of us had of the student ferment of the late 1960s, when students demanded full participation in the decisions of schools. It soon became clear that their commitment to the running of the school was much less intense than was necessary for full participation. Structurally, they were committed to the school for the short term, not the long haul. They were not accountable to the various constituencies of the school. They had a difficult time understanding the internal necessities in the workings of the school and, what's more, found it all tedious. It was also very doubtful if they had, or even could have had, the required competence to make judgments about educational priorities. They were an indispensable element in the educational process, but the scope, intensity, and time span of their responsibility to and for the school were rather limited. Therefore, their claim for full participation, let alone control, was far out of proportion to their responsibility. It would be foolish and perhaps even immoral, however, to deduce from this that a school should not consult with its students. Students cannot be treated as inert elements in a chemical formula. They must be heard, understood, and respected as ends in themselves. The fact that they are a part of a "social process," however, does not give them a moral claim to control that process.

Industrial life, of course, is different. Nevertheless, the same principles hold. I do not find it immoral to suggest that persons be paid fairly for discrete services offered, be they workers, managers, or teachers. A person can be paid for specific services in a complex process without having a claim to control over the process. If, in addition, the person is free to offer his or her services to other bidders, or to change the service offered, I fail to see the immorality of it all. Further, in large enterprises the worker is likely to have union power guarding against unjust treatment.

It is unlikely that anyone anywhere has full control over the conditions of his or her productive existence. Interdependence and specialization of function preclude such grandiose hopes. Freedom is being able to choose one's dependencies and limitations, not being able completely to control or escape them. In economic life, the existence of many options under competitive conditions guards that freedom better than schemes for "industrial democracy."

223

In summary, it is important to take seriously the authentic note in the challenge of "democratizing economic life." That is the summons to develop environments in which workers at all levels—and that includes managers—find their work challenging and satisfying. And this cannot be done without a spirit of voluntary cooperation of all parties. In order to develop these environments, it would be healthy if American democratic capitalism were to evolve even more in the direction of varied forms of ownership and management in a free, competitive context. The search for more efficient and humane organizational modes should go on. Companies such as IBM have gone quite a distance in shaping such organizational modes. The treatment of IBM employees, and their subsequent morale, rivals anything achieved so far by socialist regimes. It is difficult to predict what forms will be created as organizational experiments go on. But I have confidence that more good models will emerge from free competitive contexts than from enforced participatory schemes.

EQUALITY

Income Distribution

Certainly one of the most serious objections to democratic capitalism is the obvious inequality in the distribution of income and wealth in democratic capitalist countries. Without getting into comparisons between socioeconomic systems, we must face the challenge of those who argue that the present distribution is unacceptable on moral grounds. In responding to these critics, it does not help to point out, as Friedman does, that capitalist countries probably have less distance between the privileged political minorities and ordinary people than do Communist societies, or that countries that are more capitalist—the United States and West Germany—have less inequality than those of more aristocratic background, such as Great Britain and France.[6] The critics respond by pointing approvingly to those mixed economies such as Sweden and Israel that have indeed intentionally achieved a greater equality in the distribution of income and wealth. They believe that the United States should move much more decisively in that direction. People compare themselves with others within their society, not with those who fare worse in other systems.

What are some of the relevant facts about the distribution of income? Samuelson sums up his investigation in the following way: the lowest 20 percent received 6 percent of the 1973 income; the second lowest received 12 percent; the middle 20 percent received 17 percent; the second highest 20 percent received 24 percent; and the highest received 41 percent of the income. Put another way, the lowest 20 percent got 6 percent of income, the bottom 40 percent got 18 percent, the bottom 60 percent got 35 percent, 80 percent got 59 percent, and, obviously, 100 percent of the population got 100 percent of the income. Absolute equality would mean that the lowest 20 percent would get 20 percent of the income, 40 percent would get 40 percent, and so on.[7] It is obvious that American society is far from achieving equality of income. Further, there is no sharp trend toward more equality. "Scholars find that inequality is definitely less in America than it was back in 1929, but little different today from 1945."[8]

There are important qualifications to add to this picture, however. The first, which we have emphasized before, is that since the GNP has continued to grow over the years, the absolute amount that each segment of the population received has grown accordingly. "At all points on the income scale, family disposable incomes in real terms have doubled in the last generation."[9] This does not respond to the questions regarding distribution. But other qualifications do, some of which we have already mentioned. A good deal of inequality is the effect of choice. We choose jobs and vocations on the basis of criteria other than income. We look for intrinsic meaning, possibilities of leisure, security over risk and uncertainty, and pleasant surroundings or geographical location in preference to higher income possibilities. We eschew those attributes necessary for getting rich. Certainly these choices affect the distribution of income. Further, studies of income in relation to the life cycle verify that lifetime incomes are less unequal than those of any one year. Students and elderly people who may have relatively low incomes now, will not have or have not had such throughout their lives.

Harry Johnson sums up these qualifications:

> Observed inequality in income is to a large extent a by-product of the success of the modern economic system in providing opportunities for free choice and self-fulfillment. [The explanation for these observed inequalities] rests firmly on various recent developments in micro-analysis of functioning of labor markets, most notably the life cycle theory of the consumption function, the concept of human capital, the analysis of the implications for career choices of varying attitudes toward risk and toward future versus present consumption, and the detailed theory of leisure as a consumption good.[10]

These qualifications mute some of the criticisms of inequality in America, but not all by any means. How do we sort out and respond to the remaining objections?

First, there is a set of objections based upon an assumption that all people should receive equal incomes regardless of their contribution. In fact, the more idealistic and radical of this set insist that income should be related solely to need and not to contribution. But this set does not really provide formidable opposition. Most commentators representing this viewpoint quickly give it up for practical reasons—it would destroy all incentive and initiative—or for moral reasons—it would demand so much governmental power to enforce such equality that all vestiges of human freedom would be snuffed out. No, the notion of reward for contribution has great ethical appeal. It shows up as an implicit assumption even among the harshest critics of democratic capitalism.

> When authors distinguish between the deserving and undeserving poor, or the deserving and undeserving rich; when Marxists challenge marginal productivity with a theory that attributes all value to labor input, directly or indirectly; or when egalitarian economists rest their case for altering the verdict of the market on allegedly scientific comparisons of the "utility" of income to different people, they are all paying homage—as supporters or detractors—to the initial presumption that income *ought* to be based on contribution to output.[11]

226

No one argues that those who clearly *cannot* contribute to the economy—the aged, sick, handicapped, severely disadvantaged —should receive nothing. Those persons should be covered adequately by the difference principle. Concerning those who *can,* however, there are still charges of unfairness in distribution, charges that transcend the qualifications we introduced above. These charges have to do with distribution that is not proportional to what is deserved. Proper desert is distorted in two ways: first, the market rewards goods and services in a way that is ultimately not fair; and, second, productive agents are hindered from receiving their due because of personal circumstances they did not choose.

Regarding the first objection, we can admit that it holds a good deal of truth. No one should regard the verdict of the market as God's. Publishers of some pornographic magazines receive more reward than teachers; successful rock musicians reap more income than players in symphonies. The list could go on ad nauseam. According to inherited moral and aesthetic sensibilities and traditional standards of excellence, not to mention deeply held religious commitments, the market is often out of whack. But, unless we admit to the thesis of monopoly capitalism, which we don't, we are left with the notion that the market is roughly registering the values and tastes of the consumer. Without large doses of unwanted authoritarian paternalism, the verdicts must be respected as reflecting the present status of taste and value. No self-respecting Christian or humanist can approve of many of the judgments of the market. But what are the alternatives? Whose values and preferences are to set priorities of production and consumption? What is a frivolous whim to you may be of burning importance to me. Are we willing to coerce people in their ordering of values? I, for one, am not. I believe there is ample room, and more than ample cause, for nurturing people in noble, life-enhancing values. The persuasion of the market is *not* coercion. We have the opportunity and the challenge to form people so that higher quality tastes and values will be reflected in the dynamics of the market.

Therefore, within certain limits that rule clearly destructive activities out of bounds, we should continue with the market as the basic mechanism that deals out reward for contribution. We should argue with it, lampoon it, shape it, compensate for it, and, above all, try to nurture people in ways that may in many instances go counter to the direction of the market. But, when all is said and done, the market is a better indication of wants and needs, and the rewards accruing to those who satisfy those wants and needs, than a centralized system with all its practical and moral liabilities. In a very basic sense, it is more democratic than other options in stipulating reward for contribution. In our society professional cricket players should not earn as much as basketball players; nor should dishwashers earn more than plumbers.

The second objection concerning unfairness in distribution has to do with undeservedly high or low income, not because of the preferences reflected in the market, but because of the undeserved status of the productive agent. Again, there are important truths to the charges. People born into miserable social circumstances they did not choose and cannot easily escape are dealt out very low rewards for very meager contributions. They are pushed by circumstances beyond their control toward a life of low expectations. This is arbitrary, and therefore unfair. As a whole this insight is true, particularly of those in severely disadvantaged circumstances, and we shall propose strategies that fall under the difference principle and the principle of redress. But even here care must be taken not to reduce people to their environments. People and families can and do overcome difficult circumstances through the force of their own wills, and this freedom must be respected in dealing with the problem.

Conversely, other persons fall into very advantageous circumstances of great wealth and privilege. (Incidentally, the distribution of wealth in the United States is more unequal than the distribution of income, though the former is probably improving more in recent years than the latter.)[12] Those who benefit from great inherited wealth are a prime example. They receive much without having worked for it, and often their fortunes grow in spite of themselves. What should be done about such undeserved wealth? There is little doubt that part of their wealth ought to be transferred by taxation so that the difference principle can be activated. Loopholes need to be closed, and the progressive nature of the income tax needs to be preserved and perhaps made steeper. But, as the difference principle stipulates, the wealthy ought to be taxed only to the point where further taxation would harm the prospects of the least advantaged. This recognizes that in many cases the rich are economically useful. Their savings and investments make important contributions to the economy. Therefore, public claim upon them should be measured and prudent, not confiscatory. Nevertheless, sharp taxation of undeserved wealth is morally convincing as a compensatory device for improving the condition of those in undeserved difficulty.

Other objections about the status of productive agents are less compelling. Rawls, among others, believes that the allocation of talents is arbitrary and should be compensated for by strategies of redress. I find his argument very unconvincing. Only those who are mentally retarded or handicapped fall under this kind of stipulation and they should be provided for by the difference principle. Others, from the two-talent to the five-talent, have enough native ability to secure sufficient remuneration, *if* they steward their talents responsibly and *if* their social circumstances are reasonably good. High native ability does not necessarily lead to high income; nor does modest ability lead to economic deprivation. In the absence of clearly demonstrated causative links between native ability and extreme deprivation or success, it is best to leave well enough alone. Choice, luck, ability, circumstance, and effort all interact in a highly complex way to reach goals somewhere between the poles of freedom and destiny. It is best that social intervention not attempt to disentangle such intricacies and, failing to do so, fall into policies that only muddy the waters further. Society should set its priorities on more serious problems.

In summary, then, we would argue that undeserved inequalities at both extremes need earnest social attention. But, for the great middle of American society, we should let the market deal out its rewards for contribution. This arrangement preserves both freedom and incentive. We should not fall into a kind of

229

economism that is alarmed at all measured differences in income and wealth. Those nonextreme differences are not the ones that matter the most, as most Americans apparently believe. If they believed differently, there would be much more hue and cry about inequality. And, regarding the taxation of the upper groups, it will be important to tax heavily those who *are* wealthy, not those who are *becoming* wealthy. The latter are important to the continued growth and efficiency of society. Meanwhile, the great middle should pay their share in tax money for the more effective activation of the difference principle. For it is the severely disadvantaged segments of the American population that really need attention.

The Severely Disadvantaged and the Difference Principle

The most serious challenge facing American society at present is the persistence of a severely disadvantaged underclass of perhaps 3 million families in which only one parent is present. These families are disadvantaged in many ways: lack of sufficient income, lack of education and marketable skills, disorganized and undisciplined family relations, poor health and nutrition, and poor and dangerous housing. Further, these conditions cause and in turn are caused by a pervading culture of poverty. Persons caught in it often adapt strategies of day-to-day survival entailing crime, escapism, and an improvident present-time orientation. In this culture the self-disciplined future orientation that is necessary for social mobility cannot develop or is quickly snuffed out by the pressures of survival. The economic and social cost levied on American society by the continued existence of this underclass is enormous. But the human waste is even more important. Millions of people are caught up in lives that are brutish, nasty, and short. Lives are drained of significance and possibility.

In the early 1960s, Michael Harrington, in his *The Other America,* called dramatic attention to the existence of this underclass. His book was the clarion call for a "war on poverty" that indeed penetrated the consciousness of America. Major efforts were mounted to grapple with the issue of poverty, but partly because of the stubbornness of the problem and partly because of political changes the poverty program never completely succeeded in "improving significantly the prospects of the most disadvantaged." The problem is still with us and is probably getting worse because of political neglect, economic recession, and despairing puzzlement about what can and should be done.

This challenge is the most serious problem facing us right now because it has such a clear moral claim. In the Rawlsian scheme of justice, it is precisely this underclass that is unjustly sentenced to deprivation. Persons born into it had no choice about their social entrance into those circumstances, and they have overwhelming odds stacked against overcoming them. Their prospects are arbitrarily and radically diminished by conditions beyond their control. From a Christian ethical point of view, these are the least and the lost that agape reaches out to reclaim for membership in the community. Therefore, this segment of humanity ought to be the prime object of the difference principle. The inequalities in the social system ought to be used to improve significantly the prospects of these, the most disadvantaged. The implicit social contract of American society demands that advances by the advantaged should at the same time contribute to enhanced possibilities for the disadvantaged. To do justice in contemporary American society is to work constructively on this challenge.

One of the serious obstacles to working constructively on this challenge is a misinterpretation of the dynamics of the problem. Simple moralism sometimes attributes the persistence of this underclass to "exploitation" or "oppression" by the majority, more well-off community. Most of that moralism is nonsense. Middle and working-class people want to distance themselves from the underclass in any way they can, not exploit it. Business enterprises of most sizes and types flee from the underclass because doing business with it is expensive, dangerous, and usually unprofitable. Middle and working-class families flee the chaos and crime of the underclass neighborhoods. No doubt there

231

is exploitation, but it is minuscule compared to the massive tendency to withdraw from the problem. The sin of the majority is that of omission rather than commission.

It is important to distinguish historical causes of the underclass from continuing causes. Historical causes are fairly clear. In the case of black Americans, the legacy of slavery, segregation, and discrimination took its toll. It is miraculous that so many black Americans have escaped or avoided deprivation in the face of the odds that were against them. But a significant portion of black Americans are part of that underclass. Native Americans were the object of the same kinds of oppression. The historical dynamics of the white underclass are less clear, but white presence in the culture of poverty is evident. The plight of Hispanics by and large was shaped by circumstances outside the United States. But whatever the historical causes, it is painfully obvious that significant portions of each of these groups are mired in the underclass.

And the underclass tends to reproduce itself; when this occurs, the continuing causes of its predicament are internally generated. Initiative, skills, and discipline tend to be low. The market responds weakly to weak contributions. Young people become discouraged and fall into patterns of survival. The broader society, realizing the difficulty of employment or coexistence in communities and schools with the underclass, begins stereotyping and withdrawing fair treatment of those in the underclass that are aspiring to get out. A vicious circle emerges which is difficult to break.

Thus, the challenge is a severe one. Options open to more authoritarian societies are closed to us. The state cannot intervene directly into the family patterns of the underclass. Choice must be respected. Civil liberties must be observed. Therefore, strategies to enact the difference principle in American society must operate within the limits and possibilities of the liberal society we have shaped.

What ought to be done that can be done? What measures will improve significantly the long-term prospects of this most disadvantaged group? One of the most important avenues is through the elementary and high school educational systems, which we propose to discuss later under the rubric of fair equality of opportunity. Bracketing that for the moment, let us focus on day care, job training, and employment, all of which involve the young people of the underclass.

In most of the following suggestions we rely as much as possible on the capabilities of the private sector, with public response as a back-up measure. By "private sector" we mean both for-profit business enterprises and the vast array of nonprofit voluntary organizations. This strategy coincides with our general argument that democratic capitalism, with its large, creative, and diverse private sector, has possibilities for grappling with its challenges that have not been fully explored and utilized. We have already mentioned in relation to ecological issues that certain kinds of intervention can reach desired outcomes without disrupting market mechanisms. We believe the same to be true in the area of social services. With Peter Berger and Richard Neuhaus in their provocative book, *To Empower People,* we believe that modern American society is characterized by two attitudes:

> Two seemingly contradictory tendencies are evident in current thinking about public policy in America. First, there is a continuing desire for the services provided by the modern welfare state. Partisan rhetoric aside, few people seriously envisage dismantling the welfare state. The serious debate is over how and to what extent it should be expanded. The second tendency is one of strong animus against government bureaucracy, and bigness as such. This animus is directed not only toward Washington but toward government at all levels. Although this essay is addressed to the American situation, it should be noted that a similar ambiguity about the modern welfare state exists in other democratic societies, notably in Western Europe.[13]

On the surface these two attitudes are in conflict, just as attitudes favoring governmental intervention on ecological concerns seem to conflict with those favoring market mechanisms. The irreconcilability of these attitudes can be overcome, how-

233

ever, when we explore afresh the various alternative modes of governmental intervention. Berger and Neuhaus make this point concerning the brokering of social services.

> The contradiction between wanting more government services and less government may be only apparent. More precisely, we suggest that the modern welfare state is here to stay, indeed that it ought to expand the benefits it provides—but that *alternative mechanisms* are possible to provide welfare-state services.[14]

They go on to suggest that those alternative mechanisms are what they call "mediating structures," those institutions standing between the individual's private life and the large institutions of public life.[15] These institutions—the family, neighborhood, church, voluntary association, ethnic group—are closer at hand to people than large public and private "megastructures," and therefore they resonate more closely to the values and decisions of ordinary people. They tend to be more efficient, less bureaucratic, and certainly more conducive to human community.

In the proposals about to be made, we include the profit-making enterprise in our private sector strategy, not because it has the characteristics of mediating structures (although if it is small it sometimes does), but because it tends to operate in economic affairs more realistically and efficiently than government units do. Its self-interest coincides with realism and efficiency and with economizing logic, which is not usually the case with government agencies.

Thus, the nub of our notion, which is certainly not startlingly original, is that goverment should not provide directly the services needed to enhance the prospects of the disadvantaged, but it should finance them through subsidy or a voucher to the person to be served. That person then has the freedom to shop around, while those providing the service must compete for the person's or family's "vote." Most of that competition would go on in the private sphere, but governmental units could add their offerings to the mix. And public agencies would always be needed to act as back-up responses, if the private sector cannot be induced to act. Once the power of choice resides in the recipient of the service, the power of large bureaucracies—

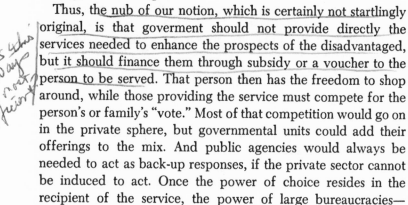

234

business, union, or government—tends to wane. Competition for the "vote" makes competitors more responsive to the needs and wishes of the voter, more lean and efficient and less capable of undue control over the process.

To return to the difficult problem of impoverished, one-parent families, attention should be directed at interrupting the vicious circle by which the culture of poverty is pushed forward into the future. One key element is the provision of day-care centers for preschool children. We should not be too eager to pressure the mother into full-time work, however. It seems that a crucial variable in mobility for poor young people is the presence of an aspiring, literate mother. Perhaps family assistance ought to be high enough so that mothers can be present at day-care centers for at least half the time. Together, the mother and her young children can work on basic skills, nutrition, family relations, and so on. The mother can receive counseling in financial affairs, family life, and planning for her children's future.

Three approaches to day-care policy are discernible. According to one approach, the government ought to stay out of the problem altogether. But this just continues a policy of neglect toward the severely disadvantaged. However, government should not provide support for day-care centers for the nondisadvantaged. Having children is a free choice. Nurturing them is the responsibility of families. There can be no convincing rationale for public responsibility for preschool care for children of nondisadvantaged families. A second approach advocates a federally funded, comprehensive child care system attached to the public schools. This seems a proper strategy when private sectors cannot be induced to respond. A third approach, which seems most promising to us and to Berger and Neuhaus, would be less closely linked to the public school system.

[This approach] was embodied in the Mondale-Brademas bill which President Ford vetoed in 1976. As in the Head Start program, this plan would work through prime sponsors. These sponsors could be private or public, voluntary associations, neighborhood groups, or simply parents getting together to run a day care center—the only condition being that sponsors be nonprofit in character.[16]

These centers would be financed through a voucher system.

> The voucher approach can be the more readily used in day care since there are not as yet in this area the powerful vested interests so firmly established in primary and secondary education. Vouchers would facilitate day care centers that are small, not professionalized, under the control of parents, therefore highly diversified. State intervention should be strictly limited to financial accountability and to safety and health standards (which, perhaps not incidentally, are absurdly unrealistic in many states). Considerable funds can be saved through this approach since it is virtually certain that economies of scale do not apply to day care centers. Imaginative proposals should be explored, such as the use of surrogate grandparents—which incidentally, would offer meaningful employment to the growing numbers of elderly persons in our society. . . . [17]

Even if youngsters have a better beginning in life, and they have more equal chances in schooling (which we will discuss presently), the enhanced promise achieved is a cruel hoax if there are not adequate opportunities for job training and employment. In these areas it would be wise to rely basically on the private for-profit sector. Business enterprises are more accurate in their judgment about what jobs will be useful in the future and are more disciplined and efficient in their training processes. Vouchers and subsidies would be available to young persons who seek training and jobs. At the same time, minimum wage laws could be rolled back for persons under twenty-one. This, in combination with subsidies for employing disadvantaged young people, would encourage enterprises both large and small to employ more of the young.

This approach would go a long way in providing more permanent jobs for persons coming from difficult social circumstances. In addition, antidiscrimination laws would have to be vigilantly applied. But these strategies would probably fall short of providing all necessary employment for the seriously disadvantaged. Therefore, there should be provision for the government being the employer of last resort. Such a program would have to be disciplined and realistic, based on a semimilitary model, for it would most likely have to provide for the most difficult cases.

Although the above efforts would focus on improving the prospects of the most severely disadvantaged, whom we have been calling the "underclass," they also could apply to the less disadvantaged—the marginal working poor who also have problems of child care and under- and unemployment. Vouchers and subsidies could be proportional to their income.

Both underclass and working poor are plagued by low income. The approaches suggested earlier would provide the "take-off" point for many to become independent providers for themselves and their own, but for others they would not. Additional economic maintenance would be necessary. There is a good deal of consensus among economists that a negative income tax system would help overcome the great economic inefficiency of the existing welfare programs and would significantly mitigate poverty and inequality. Liberals such as James Tobin of Yale and conservatives such as Milton Friedman of Chicago agree on the merits of this approach. The idea is really quite simple. If one defines the poverty level at $6000 for an urban family of four, then a family with an income under that would be judged incapable of paying any taxes. Indeed, we believe that family should be aided. Samuelson carries on from there:

> Yet how can these aids be given them so as not to deter their efforts and incentives? Here is where the negative income tax provides a great improvement over those welfare programs that deprive people of all assistance the moment they get even a poor job. (And, of course, those on assistance know this very well and are thus deterred from trying to improve their position.) Just as the positive income tax is geared between $12,000 and $13,000 to leave people with an incentive to better themselves, the formula for the negative income tax is gauged to leave the poor with more income after they have used their own efforts to raise their private earnings by a thousand dollars, or even a dollar.[18]

Samuelson provides a table for illustrating how the negative income tax might work.[19]

237

Private earnings	Tax (+ or -)	After-tax income
0	-$3000	$3000
$2000	-2000	4000
4000	-1000	5000
5000	-500	5500
6000	0	6000
7000	+500	6500

This system could be modified easily to apply to different sized families, and the formula could be changed to begin at a higher level. Other advantages are that it can replace much of present welfare assistance that destroys incentive, can help to equalize minimum levels of well-being regionally, is less demeaning to the poor, and can be simply administered by the Internal Revenue Service.[20]

Further, persons and families below the poverty level ought to be able to purchase food stamps that enable them to acquire food at reduced cost. And, in the case of health care, certain measures could be taken to enable them to purchase health insurance from private insurance companies. Again, vouchers would be appropriate. Such a system would not require recipients to use "green cards" or public hospitals, which in many areas are inferior. It would give them the ability to acquire health care equal to that accessible to the middle classes. The answer to health care for the poor is most emphatically not a national health care system. Such systems tend to be immensely expensive, bureaucratically nightmarish, and generally inferior. They distribute equally a gradually diminishing quality of health care. But they do provide for the poor and the not-so-well off. The American system can do this too, without creating state systems or blanket insurance plans. Medical care for the vast majority is excellent and well distributed. Access to the same system needs to be extended to the poor and the working poor in the way we have proposed.

Another type of severely disadvantaged people can be discussed briefly, though by no means is their claim less weighty than those of the underclass or working poor. In fact, many of these people come from those groups. We are speaking here of the mentally ill, the severely handicapped physically and mentally, the destitute elderly, and those with catastrophic physical maladies. Dealing with these cases is often beyond the means of middle class, let alone lower-class families. And, if a society can be judged by how it treats its most defenseless people, it must be said that we have significant room for improvement. Without belaboring our point, we would again argue that the private, non-profit sector does the best job of ministering compassionately to these unfortunates. Mechanisms can no doubt be found to transfer public support through affected persons or their families to these private agencies.

In summary, the preceding efforts would certainly apply the difference principle in such a way as to improve significantly the prospects of the least advantaged. The skills, talents, and creativity of the whole community would be shared. Those who prosper would be justly required to contribute to the advancement of the disadvantaged even while they themselves advanced. The whole corpus, of course, would have to be checked out for economic feasibility. Prudent decisions would have to be made as to how much the society can afford. But I am confident that we can afford as much as we are presently transferring, and possibly more, especially if programs are found to be effective. Further, the government would have a proper role in monitoring the private sector in terms of realistic standards and nondiscriminatory treatment. But government, with its tendency toward megastructures, would not have to be the major direct purveyor of human services. It could see that the difference principle is enacted yet make full use of the capacities of a diverse and innovative private sector.

Fair Equality of Opportunity

We have now responded to challenges to American society concerning several of our Rawlsian principles of justice: the principle of liberty and its "worth," and the difference principle.

239

We have suggested that not only is activation of programs toward these principles compatible with democratic capitalism, but the peculiar gifts and possibilities of that system can be harnessed to make the movement toward justice more effective. Our proposed strategies attempt to pursue justice in more efficient and decentralized ways. Our final consideration relates to striving toward a better approximation of equality of opportunity. With Rawls, we believe efforts toward ensuring equal liberty and fair equality of opportunity in the long run will strengthen the tendency toward equality more than the operation of the difference principle. The latter will provide a rising floor of primary goods which will improve the prospects of the least advantaged, but the rising floor will not necessarily unleash the latent talent and initiative among the least advantaged. But insistence on equal liberties, and especially on fair equality of opportunity, will more likely lead in that direction.

It is the latter principle to which we direct our attention here. As we indicated earlier, the principle can be broken into two parts: the assurance of open positions and the assurance of *fair* equality of opportunity for those open positions.

The principle of open positions is firmly grounded in American legal principle as well as in positive law. Our practice must be conformed to principle and law. And although we have pressed forward toward open positions, as we argued in Chapter 7, there is quite a distance to go in the face of persisting racial and sexual discrimination.

Our prime intention ought to be to achieve procedural fairness, that is, discrimination on the basis of relevant rather than irrelevant criteria. Our laws and practice in public institutions ought to make sure that those who can best do the job required are rewarded with those positions. We should not destroy the criteria of relevant discrimination as we are wont to do when we rely on notions of group rights or equality of results. Efforts enforcing those notions become enmeshed in governmental coercion that all too often destroys relevant criteria and leads to unfair practices toward majority or nondisadvantaged persons. Quotas or timetables applied to group membership ought to be used only in very rare instances where procedural fairness is impossible to achieve. Group rights and quotas pertaining to them tend to be destructive of the aspirations of both nondisadvantaged and disadvantaged. Our tradition has rightfully been aimed at *pro*scribing discrimination on irrelevant grounds—race, sex, and ethnic background—rather than *pre*scribing outcomes according to those categories.

However, there is a legitimate way that racial, sexual, religious, and even ethnic membership can be used in fair procedures. If it is true that fairness is rewarding those who can best do the job required with those positions, then there are instances in which the job requirement presses toward selecting members of particular groups who can do that job well.

For instance, black policemen, doctors, and lawyers can most likely relate to their particular communities better than those of other groups. Part of "doing the job required" may include relating to one's indigenous group. Thus, being a member of a particular group may be a relevant criterion. It can be charged, though, that positions so stipulated are not really "open." That is true, and it presents a sticky problem. For there are many whites who do more than a creditable job in the black community as policemen, doctors, and lawyers. Therefore, closure of positions cannot be done so easily and yet remain fair to all. It would seem best to allow group membership to be one factor among others in making a selection. But it should not be a weighty enough factor either to close positions or to skew the procedure decisively. This provides room for judgment on the basis of many relevant criteria. In extreme cases, such as urban police departments where unfair selection is an entrenched tradition, perhaps quotas are in order, but I believe that attention to fair procedure would be much better.

Open positions and fair procedures for selection of people for them are extremely important items in the future agenda of American democratic capitalism. But achieving that agenda would not silence those many critics who argue that open positions and fair procedures simply do not take into account the fact that many competitors for those positions do not start at the same position as others. They are disadvantaged by conditions beyond their control that make a mockery of the concept of equality of opportunity. Thus, Rawls introduces the notion of *fair* equality of opportunity, which involves using strategies of redress to move participants closer to the same starting line. Then a fairer race can be run, and we can be more satisfied with the outcome.

Rawls, however, argues that even differing talents dispersed in the natural lottery should be accounted for in strategies of redress. We disagree sharply with this notion. We doubt seriously whether there is any necessary connection between the extent of talent and success or failure. Rawls seems to disregard the human freedom to choose to what extent, and for what purpose, one wishes to exercise one's talents. Crucial differences that lead to success or failure, whatever those might mean, are more likely to flow from decisional and environmental factors than from genetic inheritance.

The Rawlsian insight into the role of unfavorable social circumstances, however, is right on course. We have already noted that a significant underclass is the most serious challenge to American aspirations toward justice. We have suggested programs under the difference principle that would significantly improve its prospects. But we believe that strategies of redress for past and present injustice are even more important in moving toward a more just society.

Regardless of the causes of extremely unfavorable social circumstances, and whether specific culpability can be affixed, there is little doubt of the existence of severely disadvantaged people. Urban centers and rural backwaters are crammed with them. For this group, open positions and fair procedures are mostly irrelevant since they do not have the acquired equipment to run the race. This is particularly true as we move toward a postindustrial society in which requirements for positions are constantly escalated.

The most effective strategy of redress would be aimed at education. It is ridiculous to say that the black child in a segregated, low-income community on Chicago's West Side has roughly the same chances of proper education as the white child

242

in the northern suburbs. Such glaring disparity is not so rife among the majority of American small-town, rural, and suburban people, but it is between the underclass and the rest of the population.

There are many reasons for the perpetuation of poor schooling for the underclass, and blame cannot be assigned easily. It is a reality, though, and one which affects the education of working- and middle-class children as poorer people migrate from one place to another. And it seems as though desegregation by busing schemes only exacerbates the situation in areas where racial and ethnic minorities are in fact the majority. (All this is not meant to suggest that there are not significant and heroic exceptions to the rule in educating the very poor.)

We believe that the most important move toward redressing severe deprivation in education would be the adoption of a specific kind of voucher system, particularly in urban centers. It is especially in those areas that we have the most severe problems. In urban centers we have the strange anomaly of a vast, dying private school system and large waiting lists of poor children hoping to get into that beleaguered system. The private system— especially the Catholic but also the smaller Lutheran and non-denominational components—provide education that is on a more human scale, more disciplined, more focused on basics of education, less bureaucratized, and staffed by teachers of generally high commitment and morale. (Again, important exceptions in both public and private systems should be kept in mind.) But the private system is in serious trouble because of the monopoly funding of the public schools. Private education must come out of the pockets of parents or be supported by hard-pressed nonprofit associations.

A voucher system would introduce much-needed competition into urban education. Naturally, it would have to be introduced in such a way that would not bring the collapse of the public system by traumatic change or by using it as a dumping ground for the most difficult cases. Such objections could be dealt with by the following arrangement: Families in the most disadvantaged cir-cumstances could be issued vouchers for each school-aged child

243

worth 150 percent of the cost of education, for use in either a public or private school. Both school systems would then find it attractive to set up educational approaches for the severely disadvantaged. Needless to say, these approaches would include vocational and trade schools as well as conventional types. Families in less disadvantaged circumstances—working and lower-middle classes—would receive 100 percent coverage if they sent their children to public schools and 75 percent for private education. The additional 25 percent could be provided by parents or school. Nondisadvantaged middle-income people would receive 100 and 50 percent for public or private educations respectively. Upper income families would receive 100 and 0 percent, respectively. This scheme would give significant advantage to the public system but would facilitate choice and competition. Further, it would provide significant alternatives for those coming from extremely unfavorable social conditions. It has redress built into it. It would stimulate other private, nonprofit groups to establish schools and enhance local participation in the process of education. There would no doubt be problems with both well-intentioned and not-so-well-intentioned incompetence among some private providers; therefore, the state would have a large role to play in seeing to it that minimal standards were maintained. But it is unlikely that parents could be duped for long by charlatans; the poor are more perceptive in assessing good basic education than their more affluent counterparts suppose.

This approach could not be expected to be a cure-all for improving the prospects of the urban poor. It would have to work in combination with programs working off the difference principle. But it would go an important distance in offering more equal chances for decent education for all. And it would redress some of the past injustice of discriminatory and segregated educational practices. It would move people closer to the same starting line.

There are, therefore, strategies toward more justice within the possibilities of democratic capitalism. The challenges are great, but the resources of creative response are just as great. We need not rely on ever-greater government provision of human services that make for more justice. Democratic polity can support those

244

services without encapsulating them in ever-larger and ineffective bureaucracies. Justice will certainly not be achieved without
political intervention on behalf of the whole people, and especially the disadvantaged, but the mode of that intervention is
crucial. We have suggested that the mode can be made consistent
with both justice and the gifts of a free, pluralist social order.
Justice can be pursued with more decentralization and efficiency.

NOTES

1. John Rawls, *A Theory of Justice* (Cambridge, Mass: Harvard
University Press, 1971), p. 204.
2. John Cort, "Why I Became a Socialist," *Commonwealth* (26 March
1976), p. 202.
3. Ibid., p. 205.
4. Peter Drucker, *The Unseen Revolution* (New York: Harper & Row,
1976), pp. 109ff.
5. Ibid., p. 1.
6. Milton Friedman, *Capitalism and Freedom* (Chicago: University of
Chicago Press, 1962), pp. 168-69.
7. Paul Samuelson, *Economics,* 10th ed. (Tokyo: McGraw-Hill Kogakusha, 1976), p. 85.
8. Ibid., p. 86.
9. Arthur Okun, *Equality and Efficiency: The Big Tradeoff* (Washington, D.C.: The Brookings Institution, 1975), p. 69.
10. Harry G. Johnson, *On Economics and Society* (Chicago: University of Chicago Press, 1975), pp. 214-15.
11. Okun, *Equality and Efficiency,* p. 41.
12. Samuelson, *Economics,* pp. 87-88.
13. Peter Berger and Richard Neuhaus, *To Empower People* (Washington, D.C.: American Enterprise Institute, 1977), p. 1.
14. Ibid.
15. Ibid., p. 2.
16. Ibid., p. 24.
17. Ibid., pp. 24-25.
18. Samuelson, *Economics,* p. 805.
19. Ibid.
20. Ibid., p. 806.

10

The Challenges
of Meaning and Value—
The Sociocultural Substratum

A final challenge to American democratic capitalism resides in the cultural sphere, the realm of symbolic meanings which give order, coherence, and moral direction to the whole society. The vast range of social institutions that are basically self-regulating carry those symbol systems. Family, church, ethnic group, neighborhood or locale, local school, and voluntary associations make up that essentially free layer of social reality. These agencies form individuals, giving them their "social self" which provides guidance for them throughout their lives and in many different contexts. This "social self" is obviously not static, but the basic formation of the self in early years makes a lasting imprint on the structure of the self throughout life. We have argued that this substratum of varied, free communal life is one of the great sources of both ordered continuity and dynamic creativity in American social, economic, and political life.

It is our contention in this final chapter that there are great challenges to the continued functional vitality of this sociocultural substratum. Therefore, because of the strength and seriousness of this long-term issue, we have chosen to discuss it in a separate chapter. In the shorter term, the moral claim of dealing with America's disadvantaged takes precedence. And, unfortunately, the nagging concern with immediate practical problems such as inflation, energy, and economic recession relegates even that intense moral claim to the back burner. But regardless of the moral and practical precedence of other issues, the cultural substance and quality of society is of paramount importance.

THE SIGNIFICANCE OF THE
SUBSTRATUM

The significance of this cultural substratum can scarcely be overestimated. In fact, it might be argued cogently that the cultural inheritance of a people or nation is far more important than either its economic system or its polity. Certainly the fact that the French are French, the British British and the Russians Russian—with all that means in their respective ethos—accounts for their differences in economic, social, and political life as much as the reverse. The deep-running ethos of a people is perhaps the decisive factor in shaping its destiny.

Although one cannot reduce American social reality to one ethos, its diversity should not be exaggerated. Its ethos has been decisively shaped by essentially European Judeo-Christian tradition. There are many variations in that tradition, and perhaps the Calvinist Protestant mentality has been dominant on American soil. But Catholic, Jewish, Lutheran, and sectarian variants have played an important part. These varieties of Judeo-Christian ethos were transmitted through a plurality of ethnic, racial, economic, and social groupings that has resulted in a colorful diversity of adaptations.

Nevertheless, these varieties succeeded in shaping a people who believed predominantly in an objective moral order that transcended them and that gave order and direction to their lives. There were rules to the game that led to a system of restraint, discipline, and integrity. This was coupled with an American adaptation of the Judeo-Christian exodus myth that promised a gracious future to those who shook free of the limits of their past through initiative and by following the rules. In addition to the obvious motivation this system of meaning provided, it bore a kind of *civitas*, "that spontaneous willingness to obey the law, to respect the rights of others, [and] to forgo the temptations of private enrichment at the expense of the public weal."[1]

248

From a sociological point of view, this American adaptation of Judeo-Christian myth, including its Enlightenment version, formed the worldview of Americans. They internalized an ethos that allowed for self-government in a primal sense; they acquired through their formative social agencies an internal moral gyroscope, a guidance system that allowed free social life to go on in an orderly fashion. Expectations had enough continuity so that self-regulating personal and communal life made sense. Likewise, the political order could count on this underlying substratum for gauging its own legitimacy and reflecting its impulses in the political life of the nation.

From a deeper religious and moral point of view, Judeo-Christian belief about the true "is" and "ought" of the world were communicated, though always partially and imperfectly, through family, church, and ethnic group. Commitment to objective moral order bestowed sanctity and permanence on promises involving friends, spouse, family, association, community, and even nation. Promises anchored in an objective and permanent moral order disciplined and guided the more chaotic impulses of the self for the benefit of communal wholes. In the face of personal and social unpredictability the promises held, or at least they were expected to. Thus, the law of love that undergirds the sustaining and claiming relations of mutuality was reflected in the human promises that held them together. Within those promises, humans could be protected from at least some of the vicissitudes of fallen existence and relations could be nurtured. But even more important, the principle of agape could be exhibited as the initiating, healing, and forgiving force that it can be. The summit of the Christian ordering of human values—agape—could be held out as that goal toward which all human selves should strive. The tension between the "is," with all its compromises and shortcomings, and the "ought" of agape could never be completely relaxed. Thus, there was always the moral summons, sometimes implicit but often explicit, to commitment to the good of others. Such a summons is indispensable to the political will toward justice, even though it must be given muscle by sufficient doses of self-interest. Put briefly, the Judeo-Christian views of mutual and agape love helped to sustain the fragile social, economic, and political relations of a fallen world.

All of this, of course, sounds terribly ideal, as if the Judeo-Christian system of meaning were fully incarnated in American life. That is certainly not the full truth. But, nevertheless, this system provided a normative perspective that transcended the brawling chaos of American practice. As such it could judge and guide from the outside, as it were. Even rebels and sinners knew they were such by referring to these norms.

THREATS TO THE GUIDANCE SYSTEM

We have been using the past tense in describing the predominant American cultural substratum. This is not meant to imply that it is completely dead but to dramatize the difference between the past consensus and the direction toward which we are moving. Indeed, we believe that the most significant threat faced by American democratic capitalism is not in the economic and political or ecological spheres but in the underlying cultural life of its people. This threat is intimately connected to the peculiar combination of liberal democracy and capitalism.

The confluence of three tendencies in American democratic capitalist culture make up this challenge or threat. These tendencies, stemming from a specific combination of capitalism and liberal democracy, have an ambiguous "neighborhood effect" on culture. Although they have brought many gains, which we have already celebrated in preceding pages, they also have a dark side. They threaten the guidance system of the society by eroding its moral substance.

Marketing Hedonism

The first of these three tendencies is provoked by capitalism itself. Free market arrangements have at least two negative effects on the sociocultural substratum in addition to the positive effects we examined earlier. First, the dynamism of free enterprise systems threatens the *form* of pluralist society. Capitalism is revolutionary in that, by constantly changing and improving the means of production, it also changes the social relations that accompany those means. The restless, driving enterprise economy changes cities, regions, towns, and neighborhoods. People move geographically as they move up and down the social ladder. This constant change and movement disrupts the continuity of social contexts out of which cultural generation and regeneration emerge. Intermediate structures lose their ability to form people, since they and their members are constantly beset by change. The "creative destruction" that we described earlier also has ambiguous effects on social as well as economic life. It spins off new groups and associations, but it also puts a good deal of pressure on those that are crucial in personal formation—family, church, and locale.

If capitalism revolutionizes the form of society, it also powerfully affects the *content*. Market systems seek out every manifest and latent desire of people and provide a good or service to meet them. They cater to the limitless desires of human nature. Further, since the health of firms is to a great extent dependent on growth, they must sell and sell more. Persuasive advertising is indispensable for this task. Everyone is encouraged to fulfill his or her limitless desires immediately. Buy now, pay later. In short, American capitalism markets hedonism. We indeed do have the freedom to resist the pitch, but nevertheless, its influence is pervasive.

These points are familiar criticisms, but they are telling despite their banality. The hedonism encouraged by our economy is akin to what Reinhold Niebuhr called "sensuality." Sensuality is an inordinate devotion to mutable goods: pleasures of food, play, sex, and drink. The American economy is remarkably adept at selling the goods and services pertaining to these and other pleasures. The character structure encouraged by sensuality is not marked by aggressive will-to-power. It is not so interested in dominating as in using others for its own gratification. Further, it uses job, income, and organizations as instruments of its own end—pleasurable negotiations with its environment. Sensuality is egoistic utilitarianism with a vengeance. Everything is negotiable except those expansions of pleasure. It is distinctly lax in relation to moral rules, discipline, and delayed gratification.

This kind of hedonism, or sensuality, may be endemic to societies characterized by affluence-in-freedom. At any rate, American capitalism creates that context. But there are certain effects of this ethos that undermine capitalism itself. Daniel Bell, for instance, believes that the hedonistic ethos undermines economic life.

> The result has been a disjunction within the social structure itself. In the organization of production and work, the system demands provident behavior, industriousness, self-control, dedication to a career and success. In the realm of consumption, it fosters the attitude of *carpe diem,* prodigality and display, and the compulsive search for play. But in both realms the system is completely mundane, for any transcendent ethic has vanished.[2]

So we have people, workers and managers alike, who are devoted to the pleasures of consumption. The capacity to work hard wanes in this atmosphere. The sense of moral responsibility among managers is displaced by the inclination to move toward the path of least resistance. But the economy needs more efficiency, energy, and discipline. How is productivity to be raised in this milieu? Capitalism suffers a threat to its motivational springs.

The pursuit of pleasure has no natural limits. An ever-escalating demand for new and unusual pleasures ensues, and we are caught in a never-ceasing search for satiation. Moral and aesthetic restraint is relaxed. Distance is collapsed. Private matters, dependent on protection from the light of publicity for their continued richness and potency, are splashed garishly before us, all for the sake of more pleasure and kicks.

Adversary Culture — Counter Culture

This marketing of hedonism combines with another tendency in liberal capitalist societies: the expansion of an "adversary society." The history of the adversary society is long and complex, having its roots in Dionysian subcultures of ancient societies. It has moved through history in various forms of romantic revolts against ordered existence and has reached our era through the modernist movement. We cannot go into a historical description of its meanderings, which Bell does in great detail.[3] We can, however, use his summary statements as a means of making our point.

> Whatever its political stripe, the modern movement has been united by a rage against the social order as the first cause. It is this trajectory which provides the permanent appeal. . . . Traditional modernism sought to substitute for religion or morality an aesthetic justification of life; to create a work of art, to be a work of art—this alone provided meaning in man's effort to transcend himself. . . . In the 1960's a powerful current of post-modernism developed which carried the logic of modernism to its farthest reaches. . . . Thus, against the aesthetic justification for life, post-modernism has completely substituted the instinctual. Impulse and pleasure alone are real and life-affirming; all else is neurosis. Moreover, traditional modernism, no matter how daring, played out its impulses in the imagination, within the constraints of art. . . . Post-modernism overflows the vessels of art. It tears down the boundaries and insists that *acting out* is the way to gain knowledge. . . . It provides the psychological spearhead for an onslaught on the values and motivational patterns of "ordinary" behavior, in the name of liberation, eroticism, freedom of impulse and the like.[4]

The postmodern temper is not confined to a small "serious" coterie of bohemians. Through the market mechanisms of capitalism it has penetrated a good deal of society. Its emphasis on immediacy, impact, sensation, and unfettered self-expression are evident in many facets of popular culture. Moreover, these emphases have found their way into various liberation and human potential movements. The underlying assumption in many of these movements is that the "felt-needs" of each self are trustworthy and good. If these needs can only be released from the constraints of conventional morality, full human potential will be realized. The harmlessness of natural impulse is posited as the underlying fact of human nature.

Thus, to the modernist temper, there is no given order that structures life in the world. In the realm of worldviews, a coherent universe is replaced by an absurd abyss. In aesthetics, dynamic energy overcomes form and beauty. In education, felt-needs supplant inherited wisdom and standards of excellence. In morality, the interaction of situation and desire rather than principle determine response. We have "values clarification" instead of moral education.

This ethos has always been represented in the intellectual community inside and outside academe. And it has been strengthened by several centuries of critical rationality in the social and historical sciences, where received tradition and morality have been radically relativized. What is left are self-validating impulses and desires, played out in the imagination and increasingly acted out in the street. What's more, liberal society does not know how to deal with the more bizarre eruptions of modernist sensibility. Its own libertarian principles prevent it from limiting them by legal means. It comes as a great relief when confused liberalism can finally find some aberrant behavior it can agree needs to be prohibited. Such an instance occurred recently when everyone, or close to everyone, agreed that exploitation of children for the manufacture of pornography was clearly out of bounds. Nevertheless, the liberties guaranteed by democratic capitalism inhibit a clear demarcation of what is acceptable. Abuses of freedom are hard to define and limit from above, as it were, and they are likewise less restrained by moral convention operating from below. Whatever is wanted, no matter how bizarre or ignoble, is produced and consumed.

Bell sums up the impact of these two eroding tendencies of hedonism and adversary culture:

> American capitalism, as I have tried to show, has lost its traditional legitimacy, which was based on a moral system of reward rooted in the Protestant sanctification of work. It has substituted a hedonism which promises material ease and luxury, yet shies away from all the historic implications of a "volupturary system," with all its social permissiveness and libertinism. The culture has been dominated (in the serious realm) by a principle of modernism that has been subversive of bourgeois life, and the middle-class life-styles by a hedonism that has undercut the Protestant ethic which provided the moral foundation for the society. The interplay of modernism as a mode developed by serious artists, the institutionalization of those played-out forms by the "cultural mass," and the hedonism as a way

of life promoted by the marketing system of business, constitutes the cultural contradiction of capitalism. . . . The social order lacks either a culture that is symbolic expression of any vitality or a moral impulse that is a motivational or binding force. What, then, can hold society together?[5]

Government Entitlements

A third tendency emerges from the democratic character of American society, rather than from its capitalist or liberal facets. As a more hedonist and "liberated" population makes its wishes known through the democratic polity, it expands its claims on the government. This is made possible by rising standards of living for the masses. In this ongoing trend, what were once luxuries become necessities. And what people regard as necessities soon enter the domain of "rights." We therefore have a gradual expansion of entitlements. We are not talking about entitlements for the disadvantaged, who have a just claim to effective strategies of redress, but for the large middle class. People ought to have work they like; therefore they are entitled to unemployment compensation if they quit work that was not to their liking. Women are unjustly—since it is an arbitrary fact of nature that they were born female—punished by loss of income during pregnancy; therefore they have a right to compensation for time lost. Families ought to be able to have both spouses working; therefore free day-care centers ought to be provided for their children. The list could be expanded with many other examples of claims that are already extant or soon will be. What this means is an increasing demand for human, professional, and technical services in the society.

The response to these increasing claims is not long in coming from social critics and government agencies. (The legislation for entitlements is slower since the Protestant Ethic is still filtered through elected representatives.) But as we argued in the introductory chapter, democratic capitalist societies are characterized by the rise of a New Class, a major part of which derives its livelihood from public-sector employment. This group has a vested interest in the expansion of entitlements since its employment, income, and status are dependent upon that expansion. It sniffs out the dynamic of luxuries becoming necessities becoming rights, and appeals for government intervention on behalf of these "rights." Most of the time this entails portraying American society in negative terms: the "injustice" involved in denying these "rights" is lamented and the more comprehensive welfare arrangements of the Scandinavian countries are pointed to approvingly.

The upshot of this is a growing dependency on the state. We shirk accountability for decisions about having children and choosing jobs. The state should pick up the tab for those decisions. We withdraw from the nurture of children. The state, through day-care centers and schools, should take care of that. We become clients of the state in crucial areas that ought to be our own responsibility.

Objective facts reflect this trend. In the last decade, health and education, along with government employment, have been the fastest growing sectors in the United States. Indeed, a recent study pointed out that in the state of California, on any given day, about 7.2 million of the state's 19.5 million people were under some institutional care, in day-care centers, schools (not colleges), hospitals, prisons, old age homes, and so on. That total was nearly as large as the state's labor force at that time.[6] Obviously, many of the entitlements indicated in this picture issue from the just claims of disadvantaged people, but others represent the inflated claims presently filtering through our democratic polity.

These three tendencies—a growing hedonism, a powerful adversary influence, and an increasing dependency on the state— are the peculiar products of late twentieth-century democratic capitalism. For Schumpeter, Bell, Habermas, and others they constitute the cultural crisis of capitalism. They undercut the motivational vitality of American society.

The social self being shaped by these tendencies is not the aggressive "I" that is intent on imposing its will on a resisting world, the favorite characterization of the capitalist by his critics. Rather, the self being formed is more closely akin to the narcissist analyzed by Christopher Lasch in his *Culture of Narcissism* or to the "psychological man" sketched some years earlier by Philip

Rieff. These portraits emphasize the emerging self as one of limited commitments. Commitments to spouse, family, community, and state are all relativized by a first commitment to the self. But the self's goals are not heroically aggrandizing. They are characterized by a subtle kind of pride that is devoted to the self's pleasure, the pride of sensuality.

This "new selfishness" is unguided by serious moral scruples. It lives according to a "hang-loose ethic." An objective moral order is unavailable to its consciousness. Principle is simply oppressive legalism. This orientation often leads to crisis in personal relations because it cannot summon enough long-term commitment to others to allow mutuality to develop and mature. It provides no guidance for responsible business or political life since there is no basis for disciplined fidelity. It provides little energy for productive work since this demands delayed gratification.

Incidentally, the "new selfishness" is usually opposed to competition in any of its forms. Competition demands too much discipline and self-reliance, and it judges performance on the basis of standards of excellence that are too objective for its taste. Its aversion to competition is another reason for demanding increased public intervention.

A CALL TO RESPONSE

What response can be made to such a challenge to the basic guidance system of our society? Are we victims of a deep, melancholy truth that people cannot be trusted with freedom and affluence at the same time? Will democratic capitalism have to give up the experiment that has brought about those elements in profusion? Will it have to depend on authoritarian solutions to discipline the chaotic hedonism that subverts its people's capacity for self-government, work, and sustained human community?

Our first response must be a qualification of the interpretation of American culture that we have just given. The Bell thesis is overdrawn. Perhaps the inclination to perceive growing decadence in the younger generation is endemic to the arrival of middle age. Or, more likely, too much sustained exposure to academe leads to an exaggeration of the impact of adversary culture and an underestimation of the basic health of common Americans. Too much contact with the former and too little with the latter can easily lead to bouts of Spenglerian pessimism.

Although the reality of the trends we have described cannot be questioned, their extent and depth of penetration can be. There are major segments of American society that are resistant to those trends. Small towns and rural areas of America are still imbued with some of the healthier aspects of the Protestant Ethic and the American Dream. It is surprising how many of the products of those social milieus provide the human energy for running the country's academic, business, professional, and especially technical life. Major religious groups—Southern Baptists, Mormons, many evangelical denominations—are intentionally opposed to the trends and seem to achieve major recruitment successes. Persisting ethnic identity among working and lower-middle classes exhibit elements of social cohesion and traditional morality that are not easily wiped out. Further, the children of these groups are anything but resigned to the status of their parents or to the allures of the counterculture. On the whole, they aspire to social mobility, enough to prompt Peter Berger to predict the "blueing of America" rather than its "greening."

Indeed, great Middle America is maligned by critics precisely because it is "repressed," "up-tight," boringly conventional, and trivial. This is probably a good sign of resilient health. Church membership and attendance seem again to be on the upswing. A great deal of attention is being paid to the renewal of marital and family life. There is a demand for schools to get back to teaching basic educational skills. Resistance grows to media efforts to promulgate adversary attitudes in Middle American communities. Not all this is unambiguously positive. Renewed bigotry can and does accompany Middle America's reaffirmation of its identity. But the evidence of Middle America's insistence on maintaining its own traditions—and the recognition by the courts that it has that right—does not indicate a wholesale collapse into hedonism, modernism, or dependency on the state.

Moreover, close encounters with recession reveal how superficial the "new consciousness" really is. As money and jobs
become scarcer, it is amazing how quickly disciplined hard work
returns to popularity among the children of the middle classes.
Thus, it is probable that there is much more traditional substance
left in American society than the interpretations of Bell or
Habermas indicate. The impact of traditional religion and morality continues to be filtered through the basic institutions of family,
church, and school. Further, the changes that take place from
generation to generation are more evolutionary than revolutionary. Tradition tends to be modified rather than jettisoned
completely.

But this is not to say that the cultural challenge is a trivial one.
American society experiences too many of the signs of cultural
deterioration to be complacent. One of the important strategies in
the sphere of public policy ought to be directed toward maintaining the health of mediating structures or social unions, which
bear forward the moral substance of the culture. Policy toward
this end will have to be very imaginative, however. Democratic
capitalism is a two-edged sword with regard to the sociocultural
substratum. Democracy can protect and extend the functions of
private associational life, but it can also swallow up its functions
by an inordinate expansion of the state. Market arrangements can
generate the wealth for discretionary support of mediating structures, but it can also sell a hedonism that subverts them. So,
several imperatives follow. Public intervention for the common
good—pollution control, macroeconomic health, medical care,
land use, and so on—should respect and preserve market arrangements as much as possible. Efforts to extend justice to the
disadvantaged and to provide needed social services ought to use
the private sector as much as is feasible. Moving in these
directions will allow for an important intentional role of the state
without making it omnicompetent, and at the same time it will
protect and extend the functions of the mediating structures
which transmit the cultural meaning systems of the people.

These strategies, however successful, do not reach the deeper level of religious and moral renewal. Authentic regeneration in those areas is unavailable to economic or political manipulation. The Spirit blows when and where it wills, and it is just as likely to burst forth in the religious communities of Russia, Latin America, or Africa as in those of Western Europe or the United States. The symbol systems that carry the needed religious and moral impulses of human culture cannot be *made* to function. They wax and wane, and sometimes even disappear, in mysterious fashion. It could be that Judeo-Christian tradition in the West is in irreversible decline. Or it could reemerge with power in the near or distant future.

There is not much that we can do to *ensure* its reemergence. But there is a good deal we can do to open ourselves to its coming, should the Spirit move. For one thing, we can begin to discern that the wellsprings of cultural health reside in religious faith and life. Technical reason can improve the external conditions of life; critical reason can chasten the pretentions that religious life and morality themselves promote; practical reason (in the Kantian sense) can illuminate formal principles of morality that inhere in us as images of God; but the nourishment of the spirit that energizes human life and culture is beyond, though not antithetical to, rationality. The symbol systems through which the Ground of Being grasps the human spirit are more fundamental to human purposiveness than our secularized reason admits. Religion finally is the substance of culture; culture is the form of religion.

This discernment of the importance of religious renewal appears refreshingly in the recent work of Daniel Bell:

> What, then, are the guides to human conduct? They cannot be in nature, for nature is only a set of physical constraints at one extreme and existential questions at the other, between which man threads his way without any maps. It cannot be history, for history has no *telos* but is only instrumental, the expansion of man's powers over nature. There is, then the unfashionable, traditional answer: religion, not as a social "projection" of man into an external emblem, but as a transcendental conception that is outside man, yet relates man to something beyond himself.[7]

And further:

> Despite the shambles of modern culture, some religious answer will
> be forthcoming. . . . [Religion] is a constitutive part of man's
> consciousness; the cognitive search for the pattern of the "general
> order" of existence; the affective need to establish rituals and to
> make such conceptions sacred; the primordial need for relatedness
> to some others, or to a set of meanings which will establish a
> transcendent response to the self; and the existential need to
> confront the finalities of suffering and death.[8]

Religious institutions should not let affirmations like those—
and the opportunities they represent—pass unnoticed. They
represent an opening in a struggling culture to which a word, or
the Word, might be addressed. The shape of the Word for this
epoch will not be easily discerned or communicated. Its proper
announcement entails a good deal more spiritual and intellectual
vitality than the churches show at present. But there are signs that
the thirst for such vitality is growing. Perhaps the Divine response
is near.

The challenges of and to American democratic capitalism are
many and real. As history moves on, the contours of both
democracy and capitalism will change. One of the strengths of
this peculiar social system is its ability to adapt. We ought to have
no ultimate commitment to its present form; but we should have a
more abiding commitment to the principles of justice it partially
embodies and insist that whatever replaces it will offer at least as
many gifts and possibilities. And if the preceding argument has
any credibility, its gifts and possibilities are considerable.

NOTES

1. Daniel Bell, *The Cultural Contradictions of Capitalism* (New York:
Basic Books, 1976), p. 245.
2. Daniel Bell, *The Coming of Post-Industrial Society* (New York:
Basic Books, 1973), pp. 477-78.

3. Bell, *Cultural Contradictions*, pp. 46ff.
4. Ibid., pp. 51-52.
5. Ibid., p. 74.
6. Ibid., pp. 233-34.
7. Ibid., p. 166.
8. Ibid., p. 169.

Bibliography

Adelman, M. A. "The Two Faces of Economic Concentration." In *Capitalism Today*. Edited by Daniel Bell and Irving Kristol. New York: Menton, 1971.

Bannock, Graham; Baxter, Ron E.; and Rees, Ray. *Penguin Dictionary of Economics*. Harmondsworth, Eng.: Penguin Books, 1978.

Bell, Daniel. *The Coming of Post-Industrial Society*. New York: Basic Books, 1973.

————. *The Cultural Contradictions of Capitalism*. New York: Basic Books, 1976.

————, and Kristol, Irving, eds. *Capitalism Today*. New York: Menton, 1971.

Benne, Robert, and Hefner, Philip. *Defining America: A Christian Critique of the American Dream*. Philadelphia: Fortress Press, 1974.

Bennett, John. *The Radical Imperative: From Theology to Social Ethics*. Philadelphia: Westminster Press, 1975.

Berger, Peter. "Ethics and the Present Class Struggle." *Worldview* 21, no. 4 (April 1978).

————. *Facing Up to Modernity: Excursions in Society, Politics, Religion*. New York: Basic Books, 1979.

————, and Neuhaus, Richard. *To Empower People: The Role of Mediating Structures in Public Policy*. Washington, D.C.: American Enterprise Institute, 1977.

Bergsten, A. F. C., and Krause, L. B., eds. *World Politics and International Economics*. Washington, D.C.: The Brookings Institution, 1975.

Birch, David L., "The Job Generating Process." *The Observer*, 22 April 1979.

Boulding, Kenneth. *The Organizational Revolution*. New York: Harper & Row, 1953.

Brandt, Richard. *Social Justice*. Englewood Cliffs, N.J.: Prentice-Hall, 1962.

Brogen, Yale. "The Ethical Consequences of Alternative Incentive Systems." In *Can the Market Sustain an Ethic?* Chicago: University of Chicago Press, 1978.

Chamberlain, E. H. *The Theory of Monopolistic Competition*. Cambridge, Mass.: Harvard University Press, 1962.

Cort, John. "Why I Became a Socialist." *Commonwealth*, 26 March 1976.

Dalton, George. *Economic Systems and Society*. Middlesex, Eng.: Penguin Books, 1974.

De George, Richard, and Pichler, Joseph. *Ethics, Free Enterprise, and Public Policy*. New York: Oxford University Press, 1978.

Dorfman, Robert. *The Price System*. New York, Prentice-Hall, 1964.

Drucker, Peter. "The New Markets and the New Capitalism." In *Capitalism Today*. Edited by Daniel Bell and Irving Kristol. New York: Menton, 1971.

———. *The Unseen Revolution*. New York: Harper & Row, 1976.

Edwards, R. C. *The Capitalist System: A Radical Analysis of American Society*. Englewood Cliffs, N.J.: Prentice-Hall, 1972.

Eltis, Walter. "The Union Veto on Economic Growth." *The Sunday Times* (17 September 1978).

Friedman, Milton. *Capitalism and Freedom*. Chicago: University of Chicago Press, 1962.

Galbraith, John Kenneth. *American Capitalism*. Boston: Houghton Mifflin Co., 1956.

———. *The New Industrial State*. Boston: Houghton Mifflin Co., 1967.

Gewirth, Alan. "Political Justice." In *Social Justice*. Edited by Richard Brandt. Englewood Cliffs, N.J.: Prentice-Hall, 1963.

Gilpin, Robert. "Three Models of the Future." In *World Politics and International Economics*. Edited by C. F. Bergsten and L. B. Krause. Washington, D.C.: The Brookings Institution, 1975.

Grønbjerg, Kirsten. *Mass Society and the Extension of Welfare, 1960–1970*. Chicago: University of Chicago Press, 1977.

Habermas, Jürgen. *Legitimation Crisis*. Trans. by Thomas McCarthy. London: Heineman, 1977.

Hampshire, Stuart, ed. *Public and Private Morality*. Cambridge: Cambridge University Press, 1978.

Harrington, Michael. "Corporate Collectivism: A System of Social Injustice." In *Ethics, Free Enterprise, and Public Policy*. New York: Oxford University Press, 1978.

Hay, Donald. *A Christian Critique of Capitalism*. Bramcote, Notts., Eng.: Grove Books, 1977.

Hayek, Friedrich. *The Road to Serfdom*. Chicago: University of Chicago Press (Phoenix), 1961.

Heilbroner, Robert. *An Inquiry into the Human Prospect*. New York: W.W. Norton, 1974.

Heyne, Paul. "Economics and Ethics, the Problem of Dialogue." In *Belief and Ethics*. Edited by W. W. Schroeder and G. Winter. Chicago: CSSR Press, 1978.

————. *Private Keepers of the Public Interest*. New York: McGraw-Hill, 1968.

————. *The World of Economics*. St. Louis: Concordia Publishing House, 1965.

Hook, Sidney, ed. *Human Values and Economic Policies*. New York: New York University Press, 1967.

Johnson, Harry. *On Economics and Society*. Chicago: University of Chicago Press, 1975.

Kelman, Steven. "Regulation That Works." *The New Republic* 179, no. 22, issue 3333 (25 November 1978).

Keynes, John M. *General Theory of Employment, Interest and Money*. London: Macmillan, 1936.

Kotz, Nick. "Feeding the Hungry." *The New Republic* 179, no. 22, issue 3333 (25 November 1978).

Kristol, Irving. "A Capitalist Conception of Justice." In *Ethics, Free Enterprise, and Public Policy*. New York: Oxford University Press, 1978.

————, and Bell, Daniel, eds. *Capitalism Today*. New York: Menton, 1971.

Lange, Oskar. *Problems of the Political Economy of Socialism*. New Delhi: People's Publishing House, 1965.

Lasch, Christopher. *The Culture of Narcissism: American Life in an Age of Diminishing Expectations*. New York: W. W. Norton, 1979.

Lewis, W. Arthur. *The Evolution of the International Economic Order*. Princeton, N.J.: Princeton University Press, 1973.

Lindbeck, Assar. *Can Pluralism Survive?* Ann Arbor: University of Michigan Press, 1977.

Lindblom, Charles E. *Politics and Markets: The World's Political-Economic Systems*. New York: Harper & Row, 1978.

Lubitz, Raymond. "Monopoly Capitalism and Neo-Marxism." In *Capitalism Today*. Edited by Daniel Bell and Irving Kristol. New York: Menton, 1971.

Mansfield, Edwin, ed. *Monopoly Power and Economic Performance*. New York: W. W. Norton, 1964.

Mason, Edward S., ed. *The Corporation in Modern Society*. Cambridge, Mass.: Harvard University Press, 1959.

Neuhaus, Richard, and Berger, Peter. *To Empower People*. Washington, D.C.: American Enterprise Institute, 1977.

Niebuhr, Reinhold. *An Interpretation of Christian Ethics*. New York: Harper & Row, 1935.

———. *The Irony of American History*. New York: Charles Scribner's Sons, 1952.

——— *Moral Man and Immoral Society*. New York: Charles Scribner's Sons, 1932.

———. *The Nature and Destiny of Man*. New York: Charles Scribner's Sons, 1949.

———. *Reinhold Niebuhr on Politics*. Edited by H. R. Davis and R. C. Good. New York: Charles Scribner's Sons, 1960.

Nutter, G. Warren, and Einhorn, Henry. *Enterprise Monopoly in the United States, 1899-1958*. New York: Columbia University Press, 1969.

Okun, Arthur. *Equality and Efficiency: The Big Tradeoff*. Washington, D.C.: The Brookings Institution, 1975.

Outka, Gene. *Agape: An Ethical Analysis*. New Haven, Conn.: Yale University Press, 1972.

Pannenberg, Wolfhart. "Faith and Disorder in Bangalore." *Worldview* 22, no. 3 (March 1979).

Phelps, E. S., ed. *Economic Justice*. Harmondsworth, Eng.: Penguin Books, 1973.

Pigou, A. C. *Economics of Welfare*. New York: Macmillan, 1932.

Rawls, John. "Distributive Justice." In *Economic Justice*. Edited by E. S. Phelps. Harmondsworth, Eng.: Penguin Books, 1973.

———. "A Kantian Conception of Equality." *Cambridge Review*, March 1975.

———. *A Theory of Justice*. Cambridge, Mass.: Harvard University Press, 1971.

Robinson, Joan. *Economic Philosophy.* Harmondsworth, Eng.: Penguin Books, 1978.
————. *The Economics of Imperfect Competition.* London: Macmillan, 1933.

Samuelson, Paul. *Economics,* 10th ed. Tokyo: McGraw-Hill Kogakusha, 1976.
Schultze, Charles L. "The Public Use of Private Interest." *Harper's* 254, no. 1524 (May 1977).
Schumacher, E. F. *Small Is Beautiful.* New York: Harper & Row, 1973.
Schumpeter, Joseph. *Capitalism, Socialism and Democracy.* New York, Harper & Row, 1940 (1975).
Shonfield, Andrew. *Modern Capitalism.* New York: Oxford University Press, 1969.
Silk, Leonard, and Vogel, David. *Ethics and Profits.* New York: Simon and Schuster, 1978.
Solow, Robert. "Economics of Resources and the Resources of Economics." *American Economic Review* 64, no. 2 (May 1974).
Stigler, George, and Kindahl, James K. *The Behavior of Industrial Prices.* New York: National Bureau of Economic Research, 1970.
Sweezy, Paul. *Modern Capitalism and Other Essays.* New York: Monthly Review Press, 1972.

Thurow, Lester. "The Myth of the American Economy." *Newsweek,* 14 February 1977.
Tillich, Paul. *Religious Socialism.* Trans. by Franklin Sherman. New York: Harper & Row, 1978.
————. *The World Situation.* Philadelphia: Fortress Press, 1965.
Tweeten, Luther. "The Hard (and Sometimes Hopeful) Facts About This Hungry World." *Worldview* 21, no. 12 (December 1978).

Vree, Dale. "A Fascism in Our Future?" *Worldview* 20, no. 11 (November 1977).

Weber, Max. *The Protestant Ethic and the Spirit of Capitalism.* New York: Charles Scribner's Sons, 1958.
Wogaman, Philip. *The Great Economic Debate.* Philadelphia: Westminster Press, 1977.
Wolff, Robert Paul. *Understanding Rawls.* Princeton, N.J.: Princeton University Press, 1977.

Zashin, Elliot. "The Progress of Black Americans in Civil Rights: The Past Two Decades Assessed." *Daedalus,* 107, no. 1 (Winter 1978).